Gift of

The John W. Bowman Family
in memory of
TIMOTHY DILLON BOWMAN

Gender in Play on the Shakespearean Stage

Gender in Play on the Shakespearean Stage

Boy Heroines and Female Pages

Michael Shapiro

Ann Arbor

THE UNIVERSITY OF MICHIGAN PRESS

Published in the United States of America by
The University of Michigan Press
Manufactured in the United States of America
⊗ Printed on acid-free paper
1997   1996   1995   4   3   2

A CIP catalogue record for this book is available from the British Library.

Library of Congress Cataloging-in-Publication Data

Shapiro, Michael, 1938–
    Gender in play on the Shakespearean stage : boy heroines and
female pages / Michael Shapiro.
        p.   cm.
    Includes bibliographical references and index.
    ISBN 0-472-10567-1
    1. Shakespeare, William, 1564–1616—Stage history—To 1625.
2. Shakespeare, William, 1564–1616—Dramatic production.
3. Shakespeare, William, 1564–1616—Characters—Women. 4. Theater—
England—Casting—History—16th century. 5. Theater—England—
Casting—History—17th century. 6. Children as actors—England—
History. 7. Gender identity in literature. 8. Sex role in
literature. 9. Disguise in literature. 10. Women in literature.
I. Title.
PR3095.S524   1994
822.3'3—dc20   94-34462
                                                               CIP

For Carolyn, Jonathan, Daniel, and Naomi
and
For Elizabeth, again

Acknowledgments

I began thinking seriously about cross-dressed heroines the year I was a Summer Fellow at the Newberry Library. After a sojourn there, what had seemed like the outline of a chapter in a book on self-referentiality in Renaissance drama grew into a plan for a book on one especially rich and exotic species of reflexivity. As most of the work on this project was done at the University of Illinois at Urbana, I wish to record my gratitude to its librarians (especially to Bill Brockman and the staff of the English Library), to the secretarial staff of the Department of English (especially Carol Severins), and to the Department of English and the Research Board of the Graduate College for released time from classroom teaching and for other timely subventions. I also want to thank the staff of the Newberry Library and Sarah Cobbold, librarian of Jesus College, Oxford. I have benefited from the labors of several research assistants: Debbie Hansen and Ananda Lal made important contributions, and Nely Keinanen, who worked the longest on this project, not only found much of the material surveyed in appendix A, but offered an endless supply of acute critical and theoretical insights.

I was fortunate to be able to test some of my ideas by presenting them to colleagues at meetings of our Renaissance discussion group. I also read papers at Knox College, the Central Renaissance Conference, the conference on New Evidence of Renaissance Theatres at the University of Georgia, the Sixteenth-Century Studies Conference, the International Congress on Medieval Studies, and at annual meetings of the Modern Language Association and the Shakespeare Association of America. Sections of the book, in different form, appeared in *Medieval and Renaissance Drama in England* and *Shakespeare Yearbook*.

Many friends and colleagues read and commented on parts of the book at various stages, but I wish to thank David Kay, Nely Keinanen, Carol Neely, G. B. Shand, and Michael Mooney for their careful readings of entire drafts, and James Shapiro for offering shrewd and generous counsel at a crucial stage. Mark Benbow, Henk Gras, Bruce Smith, Katherine Kelly, Iris Chang, and Stephen Orgel sent me unpublished work, as did fellow panelists on two sessions organized by Reginald Rampone for the 1993 Sixteenth-Century Studies Conference: Dana Aspinall, Alan Nelson, Heather McPhee, and Nicholas Radel. Donald H. Shapiro and Laurie Shapiro also lent their assistance. Elizabeth Klein Shapiro heard, read, and responded to virtually everything in this book many times over, to say nothing of sharing the life that lies behind it.

At the University of Michigan Press, I want to thank LeAnn Fields for her confidence in this project and for skillfully guiding it to its destination. The two readers of the original manuscript offered encouraging comments and keen advice. I also appreciate the careful work of the copy editor and the cheerful efficiency of Ms. Fields's assistant, Eve Trager.

If, in spite of all of this assistance, any factual or mechanical errors still remain in this book, I alone am responsible.

More profound obligations—intangible and unpayable—can be inferred from the dedication.

Contents

Introduction

Because of our own fascination with sexual identity and gender roles, contemporary scholarship has devoted considerable attention to various forms of cross-dressing in other historical periods. The period of the Shakespearean stage, roughly from 1576 to 1642, has received the lion's share of this attention. This book traces cross-dressing as a dramaturgical motif, a theatrical practice, and a social phenomenon in early modern England. For the modern reader or spectator, the heroine in male attire involves cross-gender disguise primarily within the world of the play, where she is usually a female page. In Shakespeare's day, a cross-dressed heroine, like any female character, also involved a gender switch in the world of the playhouse, for women's roles were normally assigned to young male apprentices called play-boys. For many spectators, women in male disguise as pages, squires, and the like bore some relationship to women who dressed or passed as boys or men in the audience and in the larger world beyond the playhouse.

Modern scholars continue to discover that relationships between mimetic illusion, theatrical practice, and cultural trends are multifarious, subtle, and intricate. Defining the dialectic between theater and society generates lively debate, while recent studies have demonstrated the social and intellectual diversity of playhouse audiences, depicting London theatergoers as a more heterogeneous sampling of the population than previously seemed plausible.[1] In addition, as many performance-oriented critics have noticed, even printed texts indicate moments of scripted metatheatrical or metadramatic disruption, some of them involving the play-boy's multiple layers of identity. In *As You Like It,* for example, we can almost hear him speak now as the female character, now as the assumed male persona, and occasionally in what might have passed as his own voice. The task at hand is to interpret this formalistic complexity in the light of our equally complex sense of early modern attitudes toward gender and sexuality.

Much of our current theorizing about cross-dressing both on and off the stage has been based on a few well-known historical, literary, and dramatic examples, specifically on the *Hic Mulier* controversy and on the same handful of plays. I attempt to enlarge the body of extratextual evidence and to consider a wider sampling of texts. I have also tried to adopt a broader and more supple approach to the various forms of cross-dressing, considering them in isolation and in combination, as inscribed in the dramatic texts of the period, in the practices of all-male theater troupes, and in social reality.

In approaching the topic of this book, I have learned much from and by reacting to other scholars, and I have indicated my debts and disagreements throughout the book, I fear without complete success. Three scholars whose work on the topic I have found especially helpful and challenging are Stephen Orgel, Jean Howard, and Marjorie Garber, for the insights they offer into early modern forms of cross-dressing not only draw power from efforts to redefine gender and sexuality in our own time but are grounded for the most part in historical detail.

In what promises to be the overture to a larger study, Orgel argues that England preserved its all-male acting companies as a way of containing female sexuality, a force felt to be more threatening than male homosexuality.[2] Women were therefore kept off the stage, he suggests, so that images of women could be mediated by male performers. But as I shall argue at greater length in chapter 2, England may have been late rather than recalcitrant in introducing actresses into commercial companies. Fear of female sexuality, moreover, was common throughout Western Europe, even in countries quicker to permit the innovative practice of allotting female roles to women. Overstressing the maleness of the female impersonator has led other scholars, notably Lisa Jardine, to extrapolate the homoerotic allure of such performances into a more general audience attitude, thus narrowing the range of erotic responses even for men and making no allowance for female spectators.[3]

If spectators of the Shakespearean stage were like most other theater audiences we know, they probably maintained a dual consciousness of both actors and characters and hence perceived both female characters and female impersonators. What they made of that duality is far from clear, but I would imagine a range of opinions on such questions as whether heroines who donned male disguise were thereby empowered to behave more assertively or whether they were confined all the more tightly in a masculine vision of the world. Such a diversity of opinion, I further suggest, would have permitted, possibly even encouraged, dramatists to experiment freely with the disguised-heroine motif.

In a recent essay, Jean Howard seems to be assuming just such diversity as she delineates the different ways Shakespeare used cross-dressed heroines to explore power relations between the sexes: *Twelfth Night* strips "female crossdressing . . . of nearly all of its subversive resonances, present in the culture at large"; Portia remains "an exception that continues to provoke uneasiness"; and *As You Like It* "reveals the constructed nature of patriarchy's representations of the feminine and shows a woman manipulating those representations in her own interest."[4] Howard reconstructs the range of gender politics of Shakespeare's day and permits herself the critical flexibility to register variations of tone and attitude as texts play off and against the social context.

Howard's differentiation among plays seems to me more useful than the generalizing tendencies of other critics, especially those who view the boy heroine/female page as an emblem of idealized androgyny. Phyllis Rackin sees such figures as Portia, Rosalind, and Viola as Shakespeare's celebration in fantasy of a transcendent union of opposed genders.[5] Others regard the androgyny of the female page, whether or not the male actor is revealed at the end of the play or in the epilogue (as in *As You Like It*), as the invocation of an unattainable ideal that "counterbalances the play's discovery of the polarity of the sexes."[6] Attributing wistful longing for idealized androgyny either to playwrights or to characters strikes me as an anachronistic reading of the play-boy/female page, for it derives more from a modern vision of complementary gender traits than from any historically plausible theatrical symbol. As William Slights has pointed out, although the androgyne could be a poetic or philosophical emblem of "unity, concord, and perpetuity" in Renaissance literature, on stage (especially when the female page was a play-boy) it tended to appear "as a mere grotesque, stripped of positive symbolic value." Instead of abstract symbols of androgyny, the stage offered images of physical bisexuality, or hermaphroditism, which was generally regarded as monstrous.[7] Jonathan Dollimore differentiates the woman who cross-dresses from the androgyne: "the transvestite represents subversive reinscription within, rather than a transcendence of, an existing order."[8] On the stage, the female page was neither a grotesque hybrid nor a static icon of androgyny, but a figure of unfused, discretely layered gender identities—play-boy, female character, male persona. Any one of them could be highlighted at a given moment because all of them were simultaneously present at some level in the spectators' minds.

For Marjorie Garber, among others, this very fluidity of gender boundaries implied by the use of cross-gender disguise and cross-gender casting exposed the social constructedness of gender roles in the world beyond the playhouse. In her book on transvestism, *Vested Interests: Cross-Dressing and Cultural Anxiety,* Garber argues that transvestism in general has this disruptive power, so that for her the cross-dressed heroine played by a boy actor was neither a layering nor a fusion of opposing genders, but a new category of its own in defiance of conventional categorization, and even in defiance of the very principle of binary opposition.[9] Garber's argument may have important implications for epistemology but seems to me to be too abstract in its use of historical material. She makes no distinction between theatrical and social forms of cross-dressing in the period, nor does it matter to her which direction the cross-dressing takes, as crucial a difference for early modern England as for our own day.

Like Garber's book, the work of several poststructuralists suggests that the "subversive reinscription," or parodic effect of theatrical transvestism on conventional gender roles, undermined the stability of those roles. For Catherine Belsey, cross-dressed boy heroines italicize gender roles and so "disrupt... the system of differences on which sexual stereotyping depends," presumably in order to expose the arbitrariness and limitations of that system.[10] Depending on a host of variables, different spectators would probably have held very different attitudes toward such disruption, ranging from hearty endorsement to guilt-edged delight to visceral horror. But Belsey's approach disrupts not only gender distinctions but all indicators of individual identity and hence any sense that dramatic characters represent coherent illusions of individuals. Dramatic scripts thus melt into a single master play about the brittleness of all identities based on gender and status.

In contrast to Garber's and Belsey's view of the disruptive power of cross-gender play, Linda Woodbridge argues that the subversive potentialities of disguised-heroine plays were confined to the theater, contained there by a massive extratheatrical discourse comprising sermons, conduct manuals, moral treatises, pamphlets, and the like, all promulgating conventional understandings of the role and status of women.

Woodbridge concludes that "transvestite disguise in Shakespeare does not blur the distinction between the sexes but heightens it," presumably to reaffirm it and so to confine women in subordinate positions.[11] She acknowledges that many female spectators would have challenged such orthodoxy and that plays often treated assertive women, whether or not in male disguise, with sympathy. But such treatment, she continues, represented a reaction against a dominant belief in distinct and essentialized gender roles. Whether or not these plays are direct expressions of what a patriarchal society feared and tried to suppress, Woodbridge assumes a difference between theatrical scripts and other forms of discourse. What Woodbridge and Belsey share is a sense that the dramatic heroine in male attire could stir up considerable anxiety, raise troubling questions about sexual identity and gender roles, and thus evoke lively engagement and divergent responses on the part of playgoers. But cross-dressed–heroine plays rarely provided any clear-cut answers, although the drive toward aesthetic closure, which demands undisguising and celebrates heterosexual union, often creates an impression of intellectual resolution even if little or none has been achieved.

To a certain extent play texts are a subclass of historical documents, but they also have special properties as particular kinds of material objects. They were often created by collaborating teams of writers, who derived them mainly from prose narratives and occasionally from Italian plays, a body of material that I survey in appendix A. As scripts, owned by the acting companies who paid the playwrights for them, they provided the raw material out of which the players created a theatrical production intended to provide pleasure for customers and employment for workers in a commercially oriented, mass entertainment industry. Like all such scripts, they were intended to be fleshed out in rehearsal and performance, but evidence of such realization is scanty, as is evidence of how scripts changed during long runs or after revival.

Some scripts may have taken clear-cut positions on topical matters, usually those involving controversial issues, persons, and factions under discussion outside the theater. But as recent scholarship has reminded us, politically committed plays are expressions of partisanship involving issues, persons, and factions important at the time, rather than concerns that are high on our own agendas and therefore projected back into the early modern period.[12] Plays taking sides in topical controversies had the advantage of attracting like-minded spectators but must also have risked the possible loss of spectators holding different opinions. Other scripts contain ambiguities and contradictions that may or may not have been ironed out in production, for popular mass entertainment is frequently more ideologically unstable than authentic popular culture or true coterie art. It frequently raises controversial topics in order to touch on live nerves, attract customers, provide excitement, and present itself to knowing patrons as equally au courant, but it may finally dodge or straddle the issues it raises, rather than articulate a position on them.

Although some dramatic texts were clearly polemical, the disguised-heroine plays, like most plays of the period in my view, usually acted as fields of play, that is, as arenas in which spectators could test or try on imaginary roles or respond to hypothetical situations without having to bear responsibility for their choices. It is worth remembering that such playfulness occurs in texts called plays, performed by men and boys called players in structures or spaces called playhouses, which were licensed for commercial entertainment. Located within liberties or suburbs beyond or exempt from municipal jurisdiction, the theaters of London in turn provided their own privileged minizones of licensed misrule. The boy heroine in male disguise was one of many counters used in these highly charged forms of play, in which all social roles could be exposed as inherently theatrical, nightmares and fantasies could be witnessed with impunity, and potentially disruptive energies could be safely agitated.[13] At the same time, choices made within fields of play could rehearse or help formulate attitudes to be used later in real situations, in a process Victor Turner calls the "human seriousness of play."[14]

If, as many scholars argue, ideas about sexual identity and gender roles were both highly unstable and hotly contested in early modern England, theatrical play with such figures as the cross-dressed heroine could evoke enormous anxiety and might be understood through the model of subversion and containment developed by Stephen Greenblatt.[15] One of the most important tactics for containing the power of the cross-dressed heroine to excite and disturb involved self-referentiality, reminding the spectators that this female character who was assuming a false male identity was being played by a male performer. In all theatrical situations, especially on the English Renaissance stage, where nonillusionistic plays were peppered with reflexive moments, spectators' consciousness is in flux rather than static. At any given moment, a performance of a disguised-heroine play could have emphasized any one of the three elements in the boy/girl/boy configuration without necessarily obliterating awareness of the other two. Because all coexisted within the spectators' consciousness, any one could have been played or merely flashed on the stage at a given moment.

Responses of actual spectators to these emphases must have involved highly subjective reactions, for, as our common film- and theatergoing experience tells us, different spectators respond differently to identical verbal and nonverbal cues. Nonetheless, I believe that virtually all spectators responded in some way to the layerings of gender identity, to the skillful and precise oscillations between them, and to the awareness, residual or activated, of the actor's own identity, so that the playboy, or rather the boy actor/female character/male disguise, conveyed an impression of depth. I call this effect *theatrical vibrancy*. I do not believe it is restricted to boy heroines donning male attire, but I maintain that it was encouraged by the combination of cross-gender disguise and cross-gender casting and that it served to contain, by means of aestheticization, some of the potentially disruptive power of the cross-dressed heroine. In short, the strategy here was to use self-referentiality to create a sense of detachment, to use Maynard Mack's terms, as a way of counterbalancing excessive engagement with the cross-dressed heroine.[16]

What Mack's model omits is that shifting one's focus from the mimetic to the metatheatrical level can itself be profoundly or intensely engaging. As Robert Weimann has argued, the interplay between representational and presentational elements was itself the source of considerable theatrical vitality.[17] When audiences suddenly recalled or were reminded that the female character was played by a male performer, any aesthetic detachment was undermined by another potentially disruptive concern—that the dramatic heroine herself was being played by a cross-dressed male performer, the topic of anxious concern in antitheatrical writings of the period.

In the three chapters that constitute part 1, I explore the extradramatic sources of the theatrical excitement surrounding the disguised heroine. In chapter 1, I examine female cross-dressing in early modern England from legal, social, and literary points of view in order to understand what associations, assumptions, and attitudes theater audiences might have brought with them when they came to see a play in which a female character adopted male clothing and identity. New documentary evidence of actual cases of cross-dressing (reprinted in appendix C) reveal that women in male apparel were severely punished by London magistrates, probably because the freedom of movement afforded by cross-gender disguise allowed women to violate patriarchal norms of female behavior. In chapter 2, I investigate the phenomenon of male cross-dressing, with special emphasis on the theatrical practice of cross-gender casting. This practice was evidently acceptable to playgoers even though surrounded by controversy, for Puritans regarded it as an example of the biblically forbidden practice of transvestism, while others alleged pederasty between adult male actors and their young apprentices. In chapter 3, I look at cross-gender disguise and cross-gender casting in combination, a combination embodied in the figure of the play-boy portraying a female character who adopts male disguise. An awareness of this effect can enrich our reading of these plays, as in Middleton's *More Dissemblers Besides Women,* the only play of the period to feature a pregnant female page. In this work, the heroine's male persona kindles homoerotic desire in a buffoonish adult male character, even as her power as a cross-dressed woman is undercut by a farcical treatment of her pregnancy and the onset of labor.

Even if we accept plays like *More Dissemblers* as arenas for serious play, rules for particular games differed from theater to theater and changed over time. Plays featuring heroines in male disguise occur in eighty-one plays (listed in appendix B) performed during the seven decades in which commercial theater flourished in London. Playwrights and audiences could not help but respond to changing social and cultural forces over so long a time, changes that include debates over women and the triumph of smaller, indoor "private" theaters over the larger, open-roofed "public" theaters. Commercial rivalry within the theater industry surely encouraged artistic competition, so that plays by different dramatists and companies may have been competing for spectators and hence responding to each other's work in ways intended to be noticed by cognescenti in the audiences.[18] This interplay of sophisticated spectators with a tradition of theatrical reflexivity demands a more complex model of play-going experience than has previously been deployed in studies of disguised-heroine plays.

In part 2, I move from the social resonances of cross-dressed heroines and from metatheatrical responses to play-boys to focus on the dramaturgical treatment of the female page. The very popularity of the motif is evidence of the power of boy heroines and female pages to generate theatrical excitement. To keep such power under control, dramatists made their audiences complicit in another game—a game depending on spectators' ability to savor artistic innovation within a well-established tradition.

These chapters make no attempt to map the overall chronological development of this convention from the 1580s to the closing of the theaters, because the eighty-one plays by nearly forty dramatists refuse, at least at my bidding, to fall neatly into temporal patterns. Dates of performance of many plays are uncertain because some plays remained in repertory or were revived long after their original productions. It may not be clear whether a printed text reflects the original script or a revised version, as is the case with the *Wars of Cyrus,* probably acted between 1576 and 1580, but not published until 1594, with Heywood's *The Wise Woman of Hogsden,* first acted around 1604 but not published until 1638, and with several plays by Middleton. Even when smaller gaps exist between performance and publication of plays, questions of priority and influence remain clouded. For example, was *Cymbeline,* which did not appear in print until the publication of the Folio in 1623, performed before or after *Philaster* around 1608 or 1609? In short, uncertainties of exact performance dates preclude confident assertions about the precise evolution of the motif of the boy heroine in male disguise.

Evolutionary theories also founder because the tradition of the cross-dressed heroine is itself multiple rather than unitary and because its various strands developed in spiral rather than linear fashion. This pattern results from Shakespeare's influence: in each of his five plays involving a cross-dressed heroine, he tried something different. He varied or complicated the motif with increasing ingenuity, and each of those experiments in turn spawned a series of imitations and extensions. Each chapter of part 2 is therefore an analysis of one of Shakespeare's five disguised-heroine plays. I sometimes contrast the play with its sources, testing the patience of readers already familiar with those texts, in order to focus with some precision on Shakespeare's innovative handling of the cross-dressed female characters. I also frame each of Shakespeare's plays with a discussion of similar plays he might have known and of plays by other dramatists that complicate or develop his variations.

In chapter 4, I look at Shakespeare's use of the cheeky page of Lylian comedy as a male persona for Julia in *The Two Gentlemen of Verona,* his solution to the problem of adapting narrative sources to available theatrical models. In chapter 5, I focus on the multiplication of cross-dressed heroines in *The Merchant of Venice,* while in chapter 6, I study the addition of another layer of cross-gender identity, if not full disguise, when "Ganymed" pretends to be "Rosalind" in *As You Like It.* In chapter 7, I discuss *Twelfth Night* as an experiment with intimate duet scenes between the female page and the man "she" loves, as well as between the female page and the woman who loves "him." (And from here on I will dispense with the quotation marks around names and pronouns, trusting the reader to follow rapid shifts of gender identity as keenly as Shakespearean spectators did). These duet scenes, innovative and subsequently imitated, enabled Shakespeare to evoke and control the audience's anxieties over the presentation or suggestion of heterosexual intimacy by an all-male troupe. Finally, in chapter 8, I turn to *Cymbeline,* which Shakespeare probably wrote at least seven years after *Twelfth Night.* A radical departure from his previous work, *Cymbeline* is derived more directly from the genre of romance, where the heroine in male disguise is usually not so much a cheeky page as a frail and helpless waif.

Although I discuss Shakespeare's five plays in the generally accepted order of composition, I try to place each of them in a chronological framework of similar plays written earlier and later. Invariably, there are precursors for each one of Shakespeare's experiments, but I think it will become clear that he developed those ideas with even greater artistry. Similarly, most of the other dramatists I discuss were in fact elaborating or varying dramaturgical ideas that had originated or crystallized earlier in one of his plays. My purpose is not so much to argue for Shakespeare's originality or uniqueness, but rather to accentuate his ability to follow leads suggested by other playwrights and to do so in ways that stimulated fellow dramatists. Some of these playwrights, such as Chapman and Middleton, display considerable skill and ingenuity in developing Shakespeare's ideas, and I have no wish to sacrifice the best of their work on the altar of bardolatry.

By organizing part 2 around dramaturgical technique rather than strict chronology, I hope to clarify these intertextual links and to demonstrate how English Renaissance dramatists, like writers in many periods, rang changes on ideas they borrowed from fellow craftsmen. Each playwright doubtless took into account the company and theater he wrote for, and while I indicate the troupe that performed each play (when known), as well as its (approximate) date, it is beyond the scope of this study to compare and contrast the treatment of cross-dressed heroines in different repertories.

I hope the reader will understand and indulge two kinds of rhetorical shorthand I sometimes employ: (1) I use the language of authorial intent from time to time because I believe that demonstrable effects and probable responses were usually intended, especially by experienced commercial playwrights closely connected with professional acting companies; (2) if I also seem to ascribe full human psyches to roles that are constructed out of words, it is the result of a conviction based on modest but valued experience that the medium of theater is not words but actors. Having read those words and pondered them, the actors then use them, as well as silence and movement, to convey illusions (however stylized) of human beings, some of whom may even be "actors" attempting to create plays-within-plays or even subtler illusions within the world of the play. At the same time, the actors were physically present in the world of the playhouse and that presence was, then as now, a part of the audience's consciousness. This interplay between the actor as character (in or out of disguise) and the actor as actor, sometimes taking place on the stage and sometimes in the spectators' minds, seems to me a crucial if elusive dimension of English Renaissance drama.[19]

In offering imaginative reconstructions of the playboys' performances and of audience responses to those performances, I claim no certainty but hope rather to offer plausible models of how things might have been in the past, when theatrical practices and cultural attitudes were different from what they are today. I invite readers to modify those models as they see fit in accordance with their own understandings of the theatrical history and dramatic literature of early modern England.

Part 1

Cross-Dressing in
Early Modern England

Chapter 1

A Brief Social History of Female Cross-Dressing

On June 3, 1611, Arabella Stuart escaped from "house arrest" to run off to the continent with William Seymour, the man she had secretly married against King James's wishes nearly a year before. To evade detection she donned male attire, "disguising her selfe by drawing a pair of great French-fashioned Hose over her Petticotes, putting on a Man's Doublet, a man-lyke Perruque with long Locks over her Hair, a blacke Hat, black Cloake, russet Bootes with red Tops, and a Rapier by her Syde."[1] She was able to get aboard a French ship and was halfway across the Channel before she was overtaken by a pursuing English vessel. She was recaptured and lodged in the Tower of London.

But Arabella Stuart was not apprehended for cross-dressing. As a descendant of Henry VII's older sister Margaret, as was James, she too had a claim to the English throne. Her husband, William Seymour, was another rival claimant, tracing his lineage to Mary, the younger sister of Henry VII. James wanted Arabella confined and under his control, fearful she might make a marriage that could enhance her claim or allow it to be taken up by domestic or foreign enemies. Arabella seems not to have pressed her claim and accepted her status as a dependent on her royal cousin, although others may have hoped to use her and Seymour or both together to challenge James's title. She probably married Seymour, twelve years her junior, out of love and hoped to make a life with him on the continent. In donning male apparel to be with her fiancé, she was imitating countless heroines of the epics, romances, novelle, and plays surveyed in appendix A. Because of the romantic or literary quality of her cross-dressing, as well as her high social position, she differed from most of the women who donned male apparel in early modern England.

Pragmatic Cross-Dressing, or Disguise

At the other end of the social scale, lower-class women were accused of cross-dressing, rightly or not, in order to conceal their identities while they conducted illicit sexual liaisons. The extant Repertories of the Court of Aldermen and Minute Books for the Court at Bridewell Hospital record a dozen such cases, none previously published, but now reprinted in appendix C. In three cases, the accused are clearly identified as being of low social status, that is, a porter's wife (case no. 3), a female servant (no. 4), and a fruitmonger married to a cobbler (no. 5).

Sexual behavior fell within the jurisdiction of these two courts and included cases running the gamut "from occasional fornication to the habitual fornication of professional vice," making no distinction between prostitution, adultery, and extramarital sex.[2] Cross-dressing in and of itself was evidently considered a sexual misdemeanor, or evidence of such. These officials drew on the sanction against transvestism in Deuteronomy 22:5 in lieu of any statutory prohibition and construed female cross-dressing as a sign of involvement in punishable sexual offenses.

The policing of sexual behavior in London became more intense after about the middle of the sixteenth century. In medieval London, as elsewhere in Europe, prostitution had been a legal and hence regulated activity. Ethical and religious objections were often raised, and the social status of prostitutes was low. Specific items or styles of female apparel were often mandated for prostitutes, and a London ordinance of 1351 "forbade them to wear clothing of honest and noble women."[3] Stow claims that the brothels of Southwark were "put down by the king's commandment" in 1546, but much evidence indicates their existence during Elizabeth's reign, outside the juridiction of the municipal authorities, as well as the presence of streetwalkers in London throughout the early modern period.[4] After the Reformation, and the alarming spread of venereal disease, London magistrates evidently prosecuted prostitutes with particular rigor, poor freelance streetwalkers more often than women who worked in the well-established brothels beyond municipal jurisdiction. How many of the former dressed as men or boys we cannot say, but from discussions of prostitution in early modern London, one would conclude that female cross-dressing was not a common practice.

Conversely, whether or not most prostitutes cross-dressed, most women in male attire were accused or suspected of prostitution or fornication. As the first case in appendix C indicates, male attire—"a mans cape and cloke" and "a peare of mens hose and a dublett"—was standard garb for some prostitutes, here supplied by a pimp, John Mordreyte, the man convicted of having "procured and intysed a certayne damesell to horedome and incontine[n]te lyf." Two other women found wearing male apparel, Dorothy Clayton and Hellen Balsen, were charged, respectively, with "incontynancy of Lyfe" (no. 6) and with being "a notorious whore" (no. 11). Jane Ludloe, who "came in a manes gowne and a hatt and laye one night with [Oratio Plafaryne]," was evidently one of the "harlottes" whom Plafaryne regularly asked his servant to procure for him (no. 9).

In other cases, the link between male attire and illicit sex was merely assumed, as in the case of Margaret Wakeley, who was punished after she "confessed that she hath had a bastard and that she went in mans apparrell" (no. 10), or in the case of Eliz[abeth] Griffyn, who was found wearing men's clothing and punished simply "upon suspicon of ill and lewd liefe [sic]" (no. 12). Two other women, Alice Yonge (no. 7) and Elizabeth Mason (no. 13) were punished for nothing more than cross-dressing, while Jane Trosse was cited for wearing "unsemely apparrell more manlyke then women lyke," as well as for going from "taverne to taverne" (no. 8). The magistrates' attitude toward these women is illustrated by such phrases as "devyllishe and wycked purpose" (no. 1), and the formulaic expressions "contrary to all honestye of womanhood" (nos. 4, 6) and "incontynancy of Lyfe" (nos. 6, 1). The court records use similar puritanical diction for sexual infractions: for example, Margaret Madwell was punished for "detestible whoredome . . . not mete to be recyted of," while a farrier's apprentice named Stephen Hall was punished for intercourse with a widow in his master's house as well as for "other sodomitical synne not mete to be written."[5]

Two or three women were tried for cross-dressing with no clear link to prostitution. With her husband's help, Johan Godman disguised herself as a soldier and lackey, that is, a military servant (no. 3). No illicit sex was alleged, but both husband and wife were punished, evidently for the offense of a woman going abroad "in a souldiers garments with weapons accordinglie." One wonders whether Johan Godman was accompanying her husband on military service as his "squire," perhaps modeling herself after heroines of the romances, novelle, and ballads surveyed in appendix A.

Mawdlin Gawen, who disguised herself as a man or boy in order to keep a rendezvous with her lover (no. 4), might have been the heroine of a novella or romantic comedy. When her lover failed to appear for a meeting at Paul's Wharf at four in the morning, she asked a waterman for passage westward. He told her it was too early, became suspicious when she asked him to "powle" her (i.e., cut her hair), and sent for a constable. Unlike the good-hearted watermen in Middleton's *A Chaste Maid in Cheapside,* who were entirely sympathetic with young lovers on the run, and more like the aldermen and the Bridewell magistrates, he feared that a woman in male apparel on the docks before dawn could be up to no good.

The immediate purpose of male apparel in these cases was temporary concealment of identity, that is, total disguise. Prostitutes seeking customers, maidservants slipping off to meet lovers, women delivering love letters, and others who wished to remain unrecognized for whatever purposes dressed as men in order to move about the city without being detected. Mawdlin Gawen agreed to meet her lover but "wolde not come in hir owne apparell." Even Margaret Bolton and her daughter "went a broade in mans apparell" (no. 5) apparently to conceal their identities while they delivered messages from John Gallawaie to one Mrs. Luddington, a married woman whom he was attempting to seduce. Whatever the women's reasons for cross-dressing, the courts treated them as sexual offenders and meted out punishments accordingly. Sentences included "correction," that is, whipping, and confinement to Bridewell Hospital for a time, where inmates were forced to wear special blue gowns and set to hard labor.[6]

The London magistrates' linkage of cross-dressing and illicit sex was not totally unfounded. In the first case, John Mordreyte supplied male apparel for a woman he enticed into whoredom, but very few contemporary allusions to or discussions of prostitution in London make any mention of cross-dressing. I conclude that most London prostitutes did not cross-dress but that women found cross-dressing were readily, and often imprecisely, labeled as prostitutes for a different kind of sexual transgression—the misuse of sartorial gender markers to accomplish their own private ends.

This bias, embodied in the records of the London alderman and magistrates, is illuminated by a recent study by Rudolf Dekker and Lotte van de Pol of roughly contemporaneous Dutch legal records.[7] Whereas the English records make no mention of the women's motivation, or simply assume that cross-dressing is a function of sexual misbehavior, the Dutch documents admit a wider variety of motives: some women passed as men in order to find work and so escape from poverty, some engaged in criminal activity, some wanted to be with men they loved, some wished to serve their country on land or at sea or to satisfy a desire for adventure, and some sought to conceal sexual relations with other women. Some of them lived as men for long periods of time, concealing their true identities from everyone, while others passed as men only briefly, say, long enough to collect earnest money from military recruiters, and were often known to be women by close friends and relatives. Dekker and van de Pol also refer to a tradition of short-term ritualistic or carnivalesque cross-dressing by women on specific festal occasions, occasions on which women sometimes rioted to articulate social and economic grievances (7), but festal cross-dressing by men is far more common.[8]

Dekker and van de Pol note instances of Dutch prostitutes adopting male attire as a kind of "erotic masquerade" and record a few isolated cases of cross-dressed prostitutes, but they maintain that women who escaped poverty by cross-dressing took up male apparel as an alternative to prostitution. When Maria van Antwerpen lost her job as a servant, "She did not want to be a prostitute, so becoming a man was the only way to stay a pure and chaste virgin," as Dekker and van de Pol put it, paraphrasing van Antwerpen's own account and perhaps not discounting enough for disingenuousness (26). Their general conclusion about the connection between Dutch cross-dressed women and prostitution is totally at odds with the extant official accounts of the London cases that Benbow has collected: "Finally, the relationship—or better said, the virtual absence of a relationship—between cross-dressing and prostitution is striking" (38–39).

Unlike the London aldermen or the magistrates at Bridewell, the various Dutch municipal courts whose records were studied did not assume a connection between male attire and illicit sexual behavior and therefore did not punish the women for prostitution or fornication. In the absence of any statutory prohibition against cross-dressing, they punished some women who dressed as men for such offenses as fraud, desertion, theft, burglary, bigamy, drunkenness, rowdiness, or lesbianism (76– 80). The evidence from the Dutch legal records is more extensive than what has thus far emerged from the London courts charged with policing sexual misdemeanors, but the contrast suggests that English authorities and some witnesses routinely or automatically associated female cross-dressing with prostitution and fornication. Thus far,

English records outside of London have not yielded examples parallel to those found in Holland, in which women cross-dressed for a variety of economic, patriotic, and romantic motives. Perhaps cross-dressed women in the provinces went undetected or were ignored, whereas in London a puritanical municipal government tried to regulate sexual morality and curtail women's independence in accordance with traditional religious and ethical norms. In doing so, the aldermen and the Bridewell magistrates deliberately blurred the boundaries between prostitution, adultery, and fornication.

Like commercial sex, commercial theater also evoked the opposition of Puritan-influenced city governments. The two enterprises even shared physical space. Like the stews of Southwark, playhouses were on the Bankside, as in the northern suburbs, beyond the reach of municipal authority. Within playhouses, as many allusions testify, prostitutes were regularly to be seen, but nowhere are they described as cross-dressing.

If we can isolate the social phenomenon of cross-dressing from the moralistic terms used in policing conduct, we note that one of its distinctive features seems to be its pragmatism. The London courts regarded female cross-dressing as a manifestation of women's illicit sexual behavior, but the Dutch evidence demonstrates that women who cross-dressed were not usually prostitutes but adopted male apparel in order to go unrecognized as women for very specific purposes of their own. To curtail such independence, the London courts labeled all female cross-dressers as whores, itself a form of punishment, and sentenced them as they did those truly guilty of sexual misdemeanors. As Sandra Clark puts it, "The staple charge against women who transgress male-defined codes of propriety in whatever way is always that of sexual looseness."[9]

Symbolic Cross-Dressing, or Confrontation

In view of such labeling, it is not surprising that another group of women, economically more secure than those who appeared before the courts, would adopt sartorial markers of gender expressly to challenge conventional attitudes toward women. Sometime shortly after the accession of James, a number of women began wearing selected articles of male attire, such as feathered hats and doublets and real or ornamental swords. Unlike the women in Dutch or London court cases, these Jacobean women made no effort to pass as men or boys. This phenomenon was a manifestation of a controversy over gender roles between 1610 and 1620, although there are some earlier allusions to the practice, a controversy often referred to by the title of one of the pamphlets it evoked, *Hic Mulier* (1620). An unorganized protest rather than a coherent movement, the issues involved the moral and spiritual equality of women and aspects of social freedom.[10]

Allowing for satiric exaggeration, we can form an idea of this style of dress from a passage in *Hic Mulier*, which bemoans the "cloudy Ruffianly broad-brimmed Hat and wanton Feather; . . . the loose, lascivious civil embracement of a French doublet, being all unbuttoned to entice, all of one shape to hide deformity, and extreme short waisted to give a most easy way to every luxurious action; . . . the short, weak, thin, loose, and every hand-entertaining short bases" [or plaited, knee-length, open skirts].[11] In a letter dated January 25, 1620, John Chamberlain also cites "broad-brimmed hats" and adds such items as "pointed doublets, . . . hair cut short or shorn, . . . stilettos or poignards, and other such other trinkets of like moment." He also reports that James instructed the clergy to preach against "the insolency of our women" who dressed in this manner.[12]

The fashion illustrated on the title page, as well as on that of the 1611 edition of *The Roaring Girl* by Dekker and Middleton, is a far cry from any kind of realistic male attire, that is, from the men's cloaks and boys' doublet and hose allegedly worn by women punished for cross-dressing by London magistrates. Indeed the *Hic Mulier* style of dress combined attributes of both masculinity and femininity—the hats and swords of male gallantry contrasted with the exposed breasts advertising female sexual identity. This mingling of codes produced a special kind of androgyny that combined male aggressiveness and female sexuality. Critics of the style therefore stigmatized it as monstrous and hermaphroditic. Its purpose was not the pragmatic concealment of disguise, but the overt confrontation of symbolic transgression.

Like the London aldermen and magistrates, the author of *Hic Mulier* regularly associates female cross-dressing with sexual wantonness. So did William Harrison, who complained, a quarter of a century earlier, that women wearing "doublets with pendant codpieces on the breast" caused a total confusion of gender: "I have met with some of these trulls in London so disguised that it hath passed my skill to discern whether

they were men or women."[13] Harrison seems to be using "trull" figuratively and exaggerating his confusion hyperbolically, but he makes the
connection between cross-dressing and illicit sex.

Although the women attacked in *Hic Mulier* were not charged with
prostitution, they were often accused of more generalized forms of sexual depravity, in particular, of flaunting sexuality in an assertive and
therefore masculine manner and of usurping visual signs of maleness,
thus blurring gender boundaries. The author of *Hic Mulier* warns his
female readers in particular that such contemporary cross-dressing
should not be confused with or justified by examples of women warriors
in epic and romance, who respected gender hierarchy even as they cross-
dressed:

> and do not become the idle Sisters of foolish Don Quixote, to
> believe every vain Fable which you read or to think you may be
> attired like Bradamant, who was often taken for Ricardetto, her
> brother; that you may fight like Marfiza and win husbands with
> conquest; or ride astride like Claridiana and make Giants fall at your
> stirrups. (270–71)[14]

Heroines like Bradamante and her Spenserian counterpart Britomart
never actually intended to pass as men, and they, like other viragos and
women warriors of epic and romance, often defied male villains of various kinds yet usually supported legitimate patriarchal authority.

Whereas the women who had been punished at Bridewell seem to
have been from the lower classes of London society, the *Hic Mulier*
phenomenon involved women of all classes, from Mary Frith, the model
for Moll Cutpurse, the heroine of *The Roaring Girl,* to city wives and
women of the gentry. The author of *Hic Mulier* complained that this
"infection . . . throws itself amongst women of all degrees, all deserts,
and all ages" (269) and so rebuked the fashion for blurring class distinctions, since all cross-dressed women dressed alike.

Woodbridge finds little evidence of female cross-dressing in the
1590s or early 1600s, when Shakespeare wrote his first four disguised-
heroine plays, but argues that the topic became controversial early in
James's reign, when conventional gender roles were modified by intellectual and social trends that gave women greater social freedom than
they had previously enjoyed. These changes, Woodbridge argues, include the shift from martial to peacetime values, the increasing urbaniza-

tion of London, and the greater participation by middle-class women in the economy, although it has been suggested that women were in fact being pushed out of economic niches they had previously occupied. It also seems likely that the large number of plays featuring cross-dressed heroines encouraged some women to use male clothing symbolically, to challenge sartorial markers of gender boundaries in order to challenge moral and spiritual inequalities, as well as to secure greater social liberties. Resistance to the movement indicates that it was indeed seen as challenging traditional gender roles, for it is husbands and fathers whom the author of *Hic Mulier* urges to control their unruly wives and daughters. Whereas women were earlier accused of dressing as men to conceal illicit sexual relations with men, the women castigated in *Hic Mulier* were accused of using male attire to usurp male prerogatives, including but not exclusively sexual ones.[15] If covert cross-gender disguise undermined the moral basis of society, overt cross-dressing disrupted its stable hierarchical form.

Along with freelance prostitutes, none of whom are described as wearing male apparel, theatergoers probably saw cross-dressed *Hic Mulier* women at playhouses, especially at the more expensive and fashionable so-called private theaters, as the author of *Hic Mulier* charges (273). Henry Fitzgeffrey, in *Notes from Blacke-Fryers* (1617), claimed that he felt or feigned horror to see "a *Woman* of the *masculine Gender*" enter the playhouse and sit among the gallants. John Williams in *A Sermon of Apparell* (1619) reprimanded cross-dressed women coming to church for daring "to enter Gods house, as if it were a Play-house."[16] Despite possible differences between onstage and offstage masculine garb worn by fashionable women, partially cross-dressed women in the audience might have had interesting reactions to plays featuring women disguised as pages or attired in other versions of male dress, and their presence probably evoked diverse reactions from male spectators as well as from other women in the audience.

Theatrical and Literary Refractions of Female Cross-Dressing

If the fashion attacked in *Hic Mulier* fell well short of cross-gender disguise as represented in court cases, so did it differ from theatrical representations of women in male apparel. The doublet and hose usually worn by disguised heroines in plays represented male attire pragmatically as a way of preventing recognition while women sought to forge or resume liaisons with men. But most of the plays that use the motif offer a romantic revision of the view held by the London magistrates who castigated and punished cross-dressed women for sexual misdemeanors.

Indeed, most of the plays involving heroines in male disguise take a positively sympathetic view of cross-dressing. They usually present it as a stratagem used by wives and girlfriends to follow or rejoin the men they love. In many such plays, the link between cross-dressing and illicit sexuality is usually articulated by curmudgeonly parents or their surrogates, who fail to see the heroine's male disguise as a sign of devotion and fidelity. In other plays illicit sexuality is ascribed to men, as when heroines put on male apparel during travel as protection against predatory male sexual desire, what Julia refers to as "the loose encounters of lascivious men."[17] Even the link between prostitution and female cross-dressing, assumed by the London magistrates, is suppressed on the stage: of the many plays including characters who are prostitutes, I know of only a handful in which such women wear male apparel.[18]

In two works, cross-dressed whores occur in contexts of generic anticourt satire. In Jonson's *Cynthia's Revels* (Chapel, 1600), Anaides's "punquetto" Gelaia dresses as a boy but is not in disguise. In Middleton's *Your Five Gallants* (Chapel?, 1604– 7), several prostitutes disguise themselves as pages in order to accompany their lovers to court as shield bearers in a masque. In the tradition of anticourt satire, both of these plays satirize decadent and corrupt aristocracies whose squires or pages are not well-born young men or boys or even loyal wives or fiancées in disguise, but punks and courtesans.

In *The White Devil* (Queen Anne's, 1612), Webster evokes both condemnatory and romantic views of female cross-dressing when Flamineo proposes a plan of escape to his sister, Vittoria, who has been sentenced to confinement in the House of Convertites, a prison for penitent whores reminiscent of Bridewell. Having just helped to reconcile her to Bracciano, his employer and her former lover, Flamineo suggests that they take advantage of the commotion caused by the papal election to spirit her out of town:

The city in a great confusion;
We may attire her in a page's suit,

Lay her post-horse, take shipping, and amain
For Padua.[19]

Bracciano approves of the plan, and it apparently is carried out, although Vittoria never appears in male garb, nor do subsequent reports of her flight in the play mention cross-gender disguise. Webster's specification of male disguise seems to be his own addition to the sources he used.[20] Although Flamineo's plan is merely sketched, it produces complex effects, for it adds romantic and literary coloration, as well as a realistic and sordid note, to a relationship at once glamorous, scandalous, and adulterous. His suggestion might even be a shared joke among the three characters, along with the spectators, for by 1612 the female page had become a cliché on the English stage.

Dekker and Middleton's *The Honest Whore*, part 1 (Prince Henry's, 1604), also evokes both positive and negative views of female cross-dressing but inverts the usual association of male apparel with prostitution. When Bellafront, the title character, disguises as a page, she does so neither to conceal her movements about the city nor to provide her customers with exotic pleasures, but to gain access to the home of Hippolito, the man she has fallen in love with and for whom she proposes to give up her trade. Male disguise is intended as a romantic motif, a gesture signifying Bellafront's reformation and dedication to the man she loves. Whereas the London magistrates saw the wearing of male attire as evidence of a woman's involvement in sexual misdemeanors, Dekker and Middleton used it to establish the purity of her love for the cad who rejects her, not as the embodiment of illicit sexual pleasure in its urban, commodified form. Middleton and Dekker develop the characterization of Bellafront and her use of complete male disguise not from the viewpoint of the London courts, but from literary models and their theatrical adaptations well known to readers and playgoers. As in many narrative works and the plays derived from them, the concealment of gender beneath male apparel, typically that of a page, permits Bellafront greater self-assertiveness in pursuing Hippolito, but it also increases her vulnerability.

No such vulnerability is involved in plays featuring women of the *Hic Mulier* type, women who use male attire for confrontational statements rather than pragmatic concealment. Like the viragos or women warriors of romances and epics, heroines like Bess Bridges in Heywood's *Fair Maid of the West* take up arms and armor. Others do battle with their wits, like Portia, who disguises as a man to joust with men in a court of law, and of course many women become active and aggressive intriguers without cross-dressing. But whereas most plays present female pages and other completely disguised heroines in sympathetic terms, there is considerable division in the presentation of the woman warrior. For every Bess Bridges, whose aggressiveness is directed at bullies and heathens and who never challenges the authority of her true love, Spencer, there is a Joan La Pucelle, whose military prowess is characterized as Amazonian, monstrous, and diabolic. On the domestic front, women like the collegiate ladies, Mistress Otter, and Morose's "bride" of Jonson's *Epicoene* (Queen's Revels, 1609), women who adopt mannish behavior if not actual clothing, are satirized for their impudence in usurping male prerogatives and authority.

Dekker and Middleton draw on ambivalences toward cross-dressed viragos in *The Roaring Girl* (Prince Henry's, 1611).[21] The title character, Moll Cutpurse, is a woman who dresses and acts as a man but who makes no sustained effort to deceive anyone in the world of the play as to her real gender. Her first entrance "in a frieze jerkin and a black safeguard" identifies her as sartorially, at least, hermaphroditic.[22] Later in the play, she is measured by a tailor "for your new breeches" (II.ii.75), and when she subsequently enters "like a man" (III.i.37) she is briefly mistaken for "some young barrister" (l. 49), first by Laxton and then by Trapdoor.

The character of Moll Cutpurse was based on a real person named Mary Frith, who could be seen on the streets of London. She had even appeared that same year on the stage of the Fortune, where the play itself was performed. In the eyes of the London magistrates, Mary Frith was a thoroughly disreputable figure. The Consistory of London Correction Book for 1611 notes her presence at "all or most of the disorderly & licentious places in this Cittie as namely she hath usually in the habite of a man resorted to alehowses[,] Tavernes[,] Tobacco shops & also to play howses there to see plaies & pryses & namely being at a playe about 3 quarters of a yeare since at the ffortune in mans apparell & in her bootes & with a sword at her syde."[23] The play exploits the notoriety and sensational exploits of the real-life model, but throughout, and explicitly in the epilogue, it distinguishes her criminality from the more benign idiosyncracy of the play's heroine.

Like Long Meg of Westminster, Bradamante, Britomart, and Bess

Bridges, Moll of the play is the woman warrior of legend and earlier literature reborn and recast as a good-natured contemporary eccentric. Whereas Portia does figurative battle with men in the ritualized lists of a Venetian law court, Moll fights them literally in the streets, fields, shops, and theaters of Jacobean London. A defender of marital chastity, she punishes men like Laxton who prey on "Distressed needlewomen and trade-fallen wives" (III.i.92). She herself refuses to marry: "I love to lie o' both sides o' th' bed myself, and agin o' th' other side; a wife you know ought to be obedient, but I fear me I am too headstrong to obey, therefore I'll ne'er go about it" (II.ii.35ff.). Nevertheless, one of her main functions in the plot is, like the tricky slave of New Comedy, to help a pair of young lovers overcome a father's greed and snobbery. Despite her deviancy, she supports conventional marriages for others, just as she uses her underworld connections to protect her bourgeois and aristocratic friends.[24] Partially sentimentalized into a sponsor of true lovers and the defender of the chastity of citizens' wives, Moll is just as truly at home in the penultimate canting scene, where she rejoices in celibate independence with her fellow roarers, who constitute the play's alternative society, and in the final scene, where she supports law and order by exposing the real criminality of rogues like Trapdoor.[25]

As the title character of the play and its most powerful dramatic figure, Moll dwarfs the play's romantic heroine, another "Mary," who also assumes male attire for one scene. A London magistrate might perceive her as doing so in order to have an illicit encounter with a man. That is indeed the way villains like Laxton and Sir Alexander Wengrave perceive Moll, despite her asexuality and refusal ever "to prostitute myself to a man" (III.i.111). The play also dissociates Mary from this juridical perspective by informing us in the opening scene that she and Sebastian Wengrave have been betrothed, consider themselves bound "by th' hands of heaven" (I.i.74), and would be married but for old Wengrave's desire for a wealthier daughter-in-law. Dressed "like a page" (IV.i.38), Mary Fitzallard meets her beloved, Sebastian Wengrave, in his father's house, protected by romantic idealization and chaperoned by Moll.

This scene, as Theodore Leinwand points out, highlights the differences between the docile romantic heroine in cross-gender disguise derived from literary sources and the aggressive and confrontational cross-dressed woman of the current urban scene.[26] Like Shakespeare's disguised heroines, Mary Fitzallard adopts male disguise, as Mary Beth Rose emphasizes, as a *temporary* expedient for achieving a traditional union.[27] Moll is a colorful virago drawn both from the contemporary Jacobean underworld and the *Hic Mulier* movement, a robust lower-class version of *Hic Mulier* whose confrontations with men are channeled toward bullies, adulterers, and curmudgeonly fathers.

With play-boys in both roles, the play's juxtaposition of contrasting cross-dressed heroines would probably have generated a striking moment of reflexive allusiveness. Alone with his beloved, Sebastian welcomes her with a kiss, while Moll comments in mock consternation: "How strange this shows, one man to kiss another" (l. 45). Moll's comment must have engendered nervous laughter: even spectators who regularly accepted heterosexual love scenes played by all-male companies were doubtless aware of allegations of homoerotic use of apprentices who played female roles. Just as Laxton is attracted by Moll's mannish demeanor, Sebastian explains the piquant effects of kissing a woman dressed as a man:

> Methinks a woman's lip tastes well in a doublet.
> . . . As some have a conceit their drink tastes better
> In an outlandish cup than in our own,
> So methinks every kiss she gives me now
> In this strange form is worth a pair of two.
> (ll. 47–56)

Sebastian's lines refer not simply to a real woman in male attire, but to a play-boy whose own identity is highlighted when his female character adopts male disguise. Mary herself hardly speaks during the scene, or during any other for that matter, and she and Sebastian listen to Moll sing and accompany herself on the viol, amid much bawdy joking about this "un*man*nerly instrument for a woman" (l. 96; emphasis added). I suggest that the frequency of double entendre in this episode raised the audience's awareness of the gender of the performers, just as the presence of two heroines in male attire brought the theatrical reality of the boy actors close to the spectators' consciousness.[28] The scene would thus have sharpened the contrast between the two roles, italicized both as theatrical constructs, and in so doing re-presented them as benign versions of women who cross-dressed, whether covertly or overtly, to challenge moral and social norms instituted and enforced by patriarchal authority in the name of romantic love.

Chapter 2

Male Cross-Dressing in Playhouses
and Plays

There is far less evidence of male cross-dressing in the early modern period than there is of women wearing male apparel, either in literature or in life. Dekker and van de Pol "encountered only a few cases" in Dutch legal records and conclude that it "occurred far less frequently . . . than it does today" (54). Some English literary works allude to male cross-dressing. The fifth satire of Middleton's *Microcynicon* (1599) features Ingling Pyander, a male transvestite posing as a female prostitute, while the answer to the riddle posed by Thomas Randolph's poem of the 1630s, "On a maide of honour seene by a schollar in Sommerset Garden," is that the maid is a boy.[1] Perhaps such literary figures were modeled on actual male transvestites, but I know of no corroborating nonliterary evidence.

The only case of male cross-dressing Benbow discovered in the London court records involves a kind of temporary masquerade rather than a regular practice: on July 23, 1556, Robert Chetwyn was accused of "going abrode in the City yesterday in a womans apparell"; he was ordered to find a master or leave London and was pardoned of his "folye" (no. 1). Chetwyn's offense was treated not as a sexual misdemeanor or as evidence of depravity, but as a single instance of youthful high spirits erupting on a particular day, in part a function of idleness. It was classified not as vice but as folly. He was not sent to Bridewell Hospital for penance and rehabilitation but instead was ordered to find a place in society where he would be kept busy and under surveillance. Whether or not the magistrates were correct in their classification of Chetwyn's cross-dressing, they treated him more leniently than they did the women cited for cross-dressing. As they saw the case, and as the official account implies, Chetwyn seems not to have had the pragmatic motives of actual prostitutes nor the confrontational attitudes associated with the *Hic Mulier* movement. Male cross-dressing could be tolerated, permitted, or only mildly punished if licensed as festal rite, but as a habitual practice it was taboo, virtually unthinkable, even if covertly practiced. This mind-set is revealed in the comment on berdaches made by an English voyager to Africa: "They are beastly in their living for they have men in women's apparel, whom they keep among their wives."[2]

Festal Cross-Dressing

Other records of early modern England reveal a plenitude of examples of ritually authorized male cross-dressing—Maid Marian of the Robin Hood fragments, the Bessies or Betties of mummers' plays and alehouse entertainments, the Fool's Lady of the type of folk play known as the Wooing Ceremony, and the mock wives of charivaris and skimming-tons.[3] In these folkloric forms, more common in English villages than in cities or towns, boys or young men dressed as women on specific occasions sanctioned by local custom and often by local authorities. Their intentions were not to pass as women but to entertain both men and women, to engage in traditional rites, and to reinforce social norms, often by representing scolds, shrews, and adulteresses, the culture's most blatant female stereotypes. Where the artificial woman was not a negative stereotype, such occasions may also have permitted the expression of otherwise impermissible homoerotic impulses.[4]

Plays performed under academic auspices resemble such folkloric forms in that they were frequently associated with seasonal revelry or with entertainment provided for visiting dignitaries. Cross-dressing associated with such occasions was therefore limited in duration, framed by social custom, and approved by institutional authorities. The records of dramatic activity at Cambridge, for example, complete with inventories of female clothing for use as costumes, indicate a long tradition of young men temporarily dressing as women for such purposes.

The Cambridge records also mention a few men, who, mindful of the Deuteronomic prohibition against cross-dressing, were reluctant to play female roles or even to attend performances involving male cross-dressing. (1) At Queen's College, in preparation for James's visit in 1614, Samuel Fairclough, being "but little and of low stature," was asked to play the role of Surda, an old woman, which "required him to be cloathed in Womans Apparel." Despite the vice-chancellor's urging, Fairclough stuck to his position that "it was unlawful for a man to wear Womens Apparel, even in a Comedy." (2) The *Life of Doctor Preston* includes the story of a student named Morgan, who "was a comely modest gentleman, and was supposed would well become a woman's dress." Despite his protestations, his superiors prevailed upon him to play a woman's part, with appallingly dire consequences noted by the reporter: he "afterwards removed unto Oxford, & suffer'd to play what part he would, and so relapsed to Popery, which hath proved fatall to him and his." (3) In 1635–36, Simonds D'Ewes refused to attend a play at Trinity College "because of womens apparell worne in it, by boyes and youths."[5] Even in professional English companies, the casting of young male actors as female characters bears certain resemblances to the festal or folkloric practices of female impersonation. The play-boys took on female roles for a limited duration and did not attempt to pass as women but rather to represent them within mimetic illusions in playhouses used for commercial entertainment.

Theatrical Cross-Dressing

Although cross-gender casting was normative theatrical practice when Shakespeare wrote for the English stage, it was no longer so in most places on the continent. Nevertheless, the English were not as anomalous as some scholars have tried to maintain. Stephen Orgel has recently stressed the uniqueness of English theatrical companies in not using actresses, but the phenomenon may represent a lag behind changes taking place on the continent rather than an indication of English sexual attitudes. In the three centuries since the introduction of "real" actresses, audiences have come to accept the use of women in female roles as natural, when in fact it is merely conventional and at one time was considered innovative. Perhaps the appropriate question is not why the English theater resisted the use of actresses, but rather when, where, and why they came to replace male female impersonators in the first place.

Acting was an all-male activity in ancient Greece and Rome. The same was true in medieval Europe, when theatrical activity was far less organized, although there is some evidence of performances in nunneries and of limited participation by girls or young women in craft cycles.[6] In the early modern period, women did not act in plays performed by professional theater companies until Italian popular companies, the commedia dell'arte, introduced actresses in the 1560s, "the first record of which is the appearance in a troupe list of 1564 of a certain Lucrese Senese."[7] The innovation was not welcomed everywhere, as women were forbidden to act in public in the Papal States even into the eighteenth century. In Spain, an Italian troupe petitioned the authorities for permission to use actresses in 1587, and the practice was then adopted by competing Spanish companies, not without clerical opposition, and it was outlawed, at least in theory, between 1596 and 1600.[8]

Nevertheless, the use of actresses eventually spread, as Italian companies traveled in Western Europe. Although there are records of women performing in France as singers, dancers, and even in mystery plays, audiences in those countries did not see female actresses in professional companies until commedia dell'arte troupes introduced the practice. Italian companies played at court and publicly in Paris in the early 1570s, while the French troupe of Valeran LeComte introduced actresses in Bordeaux in 1598 and shortly thereafter in Paris. In Holland, actresses did not appear in commercial theaters until 1655.[9]

There are also records of occasional visits to England by Italian companies. While they seem to have been confined to court appearances, there is evidence of widespread familiarity with their work, although not always with their use of female performers. A French troupe employing actresses appeared at Blackfriars in 1629.[10] Given the infrequency of visits by continental troupes, all-male English companies may have felt no need to match their competition from abroad by introducing actresses, for they had no trained women on hand but were well-stocked with boys already working as apprentices. Still, one wonders why some enterprising English theatrical entrepreneur did not exploit this new Italianate practice and gain a commercial advantage over the competition long before 1660, when English playgoers responded avidly to the introduction of actresses.

Orgel explains this lag in terms of English sexual attitudes. He argues that pre-Restoration England tolerated foreign actresses but preferred that English companies remain all-male because of a generalized fear of female sexuality and a tolerance of male homoeroticism. These attitudes, however, were just as prevalent in Italy and France, countries that antedated England in permitting actresses. The one uniquely English cultural practice of relevance is the puritanical antitheatrical hysteria, but attacks from that quarter objected to both the theatrical image of erotic women and to the theatrical use of female impersonators. English Puritans, like religious authorities elsewhere in Europe, surely would have objected to the use of actresses. Orgel's rephrasing of the issue, "Why were women more upsetting than boys to the English?" predetermines his answer.[11] Sexual attitudes may have less to do with the late introduction of actresses to the English stage than the fact that the commedia dell'arte, for political, linguistic, and geographical reasons, exerted more influence on the continent. In the use of actresses, as in the adoption of other Italianate influences, England may have been slow to change rather than anomalous.

Although cross-gender casting was an accepted convention on the English stage, the practice may have been italicized in performance. One way of highlighting it was to assign female roles to recognized specialists in female impersonation. Half of the doubling schemes printed with English plays of the 1560s and 1570s indicate the use of such specialists, presumably boys or young men, for female roles.[12] Such specialization is suggested by a short exchange in *Sir Thomas More* between the title character and the leader of an itinerant troupe:

> *More.* How many are ye?
> *Player.* Four men and a boy, sir.
> *More.* But one boy? Then I see,
> There's but few women in the play.
> *Player.* Three my lord: Dame Science, Lady Vanity,
> And Wisdom, she herself.
> *More.* And one boy play them all? By'r Lady, he's loaden.[13]

More assumes correctly that all three female roles will be played by the same boy, whose doubling in these parts adds theatrical point to Wit's mistaking of Lady Vanity for Lady Wisdom. After the mid-1590s, when the more successful troupes found permanent venues in London, apprenticeships might have become readily available, more stable, and perhaps more attractive, with a concomitant rise in the quality of female impersonation.

Although Colley Cibber was later to disparage the "Boys, or young Men of the most effeminate Aspect" who played female parts as "ungain Hoydens," most pre-Restoration accounts suggest that play-boys were highly skilled. There was ample time and opportunity to develop whatever talent they had, for they were often apprenticed from the age of ten for seven or more years to individual members of adult companies, who were responsible for their training and maintenance.[14] Extant casting lists for seven plays acted by the King's Men between 1611 and 1632 indicate that performers like Richard Robinson, Robert Pallant, and Richard Sharpe changed from female to male roles at about the time their apprenticeships ended. Ezekiel Fenn evidently played his first adult male role at the age of nineteen. If puberty came several years later than it does now, as recent studies suggest, play-boys could have represented women even into late adolescence, perhaps with a seemingly precocious intellectual and emotional maturity proportionate to their chronological ages.[15]

Boy-Bride Plays

Within several plays of the period, a male character adopts a female disguise. In so doing, he not only reminded the audience of the metatheatrical fact that he and other female characters onstage were played by male actors, but he also invoked a social context that linked female impersonation (both in the world of the play and in the world of the playhouse) to ritualized forms of cross-dressing licensed by tradition and limited in duration. When such male characters pretended to be women, cross-gender disguises on the mimetic level paralleled cross-gender casting on the theatrical: male characters in the world of the play impersonated women, just as male performers did in the world of the playhouse.

Victor Freeburg cites about twenty English plays with "boy brides," a term of convenience, for some are neither boys nor brides.[16] In cases when a mature adult male actor adopts female disguise, his beard, size, voice, or movement may turn the impersonation into broad farce, as in the film *Some Like It Hot* (1959) or in the Hasty Pudding type of musical comedy performed at formerly all-male American colleges, where the burliest, hairiest undergraduates (usually football players) played chorus girls in tutus and the like. Similarly, in *The Merry Wives of Windsor* (Lord Chamberlain's, c. 1597), Falstaff becomes just such a "Panto Dame" when he escapes by pretending to be the "fat woman of Brainford" (IV.ii.75), and the farcical or burlesque effect is echoed at the end of the play when Slender and Caius each discovers that his bride is "a great lubberly boy" (V.v.184). In a handful of plays derived from the episode in Sidney's *Arcadia* in which Pyrocles disguises himself as Zelmane, male characters disguise themselves as Amazons. Most boy-bride plays, however, reinscribe male cross-dressing within the world of the play by having young male characters impersonate more conventional romantic heroines.

Boy brides are outnumbered by female pages on the English Renaissance stage by about four to one. In part, the greater prevalence of female pages reflects the culture's belief that it is more shameful for men to impersonate women or to cross-dress than vice versa. Flute in *A Midsummer Night's Dream* (Lord Chamberlain's, c. 1595) resents having to play a woman, just as the "actor" playing Antonio in Marston's *Antonio and Mellida* (Paul's, 1599–1600) complains about having to play a male character disguised as an Amazon. As apprentices, play-boys were lower on the social scale than adult actors and for that reason too were therefore more likely to play women's roles.

Whenever young male characters adopt female disguise, playwrights generally let the audience in on the secret of the character's male identity. In the induction to *The Taming of the Shrew* (Queen's? c. 1591?), for example, only Sly believes that the lord's page is his wife. The spectators of Middleton's *A Mad World, My Masters* (Paul's, 1604–6) were not merely forewarned but could actually watch while Follywit disguised himself onstage as his grandfather's courtesan. *Epicoene* (Queen's Revels, 1609) is an exception, for Jonson achieves a coup de théâtre by concealing the true gender of the boy bride until the very end of the play.[17] Another type of variation, often found in plays performed by children's troupes, deliberately italicizes the boy bride by adding a female page, as in *The Wars of Cyrus* (Chapel? 1576–80?), where page and mistress change clothing, or as in Marston's *Antonio and Mellida*, where hero and heroine escape disguised, respectively, as an Amazon and a page. Both in their variety and their reflexive capabilities, these treatments of the boy bride suggest that dramatists invited their audiences to appreciate ingenious play with the convention. The problem for the modern critic is to decide, from the evidence of the text and a knowledge of performance practices of the period, when the enactment of a dramatic text was issuing such an invitation, what kinds of playfulness were involved, and precisely which social and sexual attitudes were in circulation.

Jonson's *The Devil Is an Ass* (King's, 1616) uses the boy bride with an amusing reflexive twist. A young man named Wittipol plays two different women. He first represents Mrs. Fitzdottrel by replying for her when she remains silent while he woos her, by prior arrangement, in her husband's presence. Later he comes onstage dressed as a Spanish lady, as he and his fellow conspirators have planned, in order to gain access to Mrs. Fitzdottrel. The conspirators had considered hiring a play-boy as their Spanish lady, and even considered using Dick Robinson, a well-known apprentice with the King's Men, but decided he was too old to play a woman. They turned instead to Wittipol, who, as Ann Barton suggests, was probably played by Robinson, then near or at the end of his career as a female impersonator.[18]

The play also raises the question of whether men and women in the world of the play, and by extension male and female spectators, responded differently to boy brides. One of the conspirators tells how Dick Robinson attended a "Gossips feast . . . Drest like a Lawyers wife, amongst 'hem all . . . [where he did] lay the law; and carve; and drinke unto 'hem" (II.viii.69–72). It is not clear whether the other women knew he was a boy and enjoyed the impersonation as a performance, or whether they were the victims of the joke, and in any case this anecdote is reported in a play. Characters in boy-bride plays who are taken in by the pretense rarely enjoy being gulled; Daw and La Foole are deservedly humiliated in *Epicoene,* as is Simplicius in Marston's *What You Will* (Paul's, 1601), who is also robbed of purse, hat, cloak, and rapier.

Similarly, people off the stage also resent being fooled by female impersonators. Rainoldes reports that at one Oxford production the audience resented the deception when boy actresses in minor roles, evidently costumed in contemporary attire, briefly passed as female spectators and so blurred the distinction between on- and offstage cross-dressing:

> Howe many did observe, and with mislike have mentioned, that *Penelopes* maides did not onely weare it (wemens raiment), but also sate in it among true wemen in deed, longer then *David* woare *Sauls* armour? neither were more knowne to them to bee men, then *Achilles* was at firste to Deidamia; untill they suspected it, seeing them entreated by the wooers to rise and danse upon the stage.[19]

Such "mislike" is less likely when the real gender of the offstage female impersonator is known, for he seems to evoke delight in his ability to represent women, as he does in the theater. Cibber describes how "the

Ladies of Quality prided themselves in taking . . . [Kynaston] with them in their Coaches to *Hyde-Park* in his Theatrical Habit, after the play."[20]

As in festal situations, male cross-dressing presented within plays is confined to specific situations limited in duration. Barthol'mew in *The Taming of the Shrew* takes a woman's part for the sake of a saturnalian joke, while the casting of Flute as Thisbe has ritualistic overtones, for he is a member of an amateur troupe invited to entertain their duke at his wedding.[21] By extension, even a professional boy actor in the commercial theater could be seen as donning his female costume for a limited period of time both in the play proper and in the jig that followed, where clowns and female impersonators may have provided something even closer to the communal revelry of folk drama than the preceding scripted text.[22] In boy-bride plays, female disguise in the world of the play, like cross-gender casting, drew on associations of male cross-dressing with traditional forms of revelry, as well as with practical joking and coney catching. Cross-dressing by theatrical heroines, by contrast, involved a more complex transaction, for it could be linked to illicit sexuality (whether actual or imagined) and to the mannishly dressed *Hic Mulier* movement, that is, to practices perceived to defy patriarchal norms, as well as to innumerable romanticized treatments in literary sources.

Cross-Gender Casting and the Disruption of Gender Roles

We may never know exactly how much distance play-boys put between themselves and their female characters: they may have merely indicated these roles rather than representing women more or less illusionistically. Considering our limited knowledge of performance practice, we are unlikely to know whether their performances were consistent with or different from the prevailing style(s) of acting in the period, itself a vexed question. However play-boys enacted female roles, the known physical presence of male performers must have registered at some level in the spectators' consciousness and thus raised questions about the stability of established gender roles, generally defined as male assertiveness and female submissiveness. The boy actor, apprenticed to an adult male, would himself become an adult male, but for the present had been trained to play women, that is, to offer theatrical constructions of the social constructions that constituted the culture's notions of femininity.

He therefore embodied a blurring of gender boundaries, a blurring that evoked considerable anxiety among those who felt the need for a clear and rigid separation of the sexes.

Fulminations against play-boys are therefore common and virulent in antitheatrical tracts by such writers as Stephen Gosson, Phillip Stubbes, and William Prynne and grow shriller and more voluminous over time. These works reflect the writers' acute discomfort over cross-gender casting and probably made theatergoers more conscious of the practice. Such writers also object to the presentation of what they regard as erotic material and to the kinds of women being represented on stage, attacking lascivious plots derived from pagan sources and warning against the power of male actors in female clothing to inflame spectators with undifferentiated sexual desires. They also cite the Deuteronomic injunction against transvestism, warning specifically against what Prynne was later to call "that unnaturall Sodomiticall sinne of uncleanesse."[23] Replying to such charges in his *An Apology for Actors* (1612), Thomas Heywood claimed that the audiences never forgot that they were watching boy actors temporarily impersonating women and were even aware of particular performers:

> To see our youths attired in the habit of women, who knowes not what their intents be? who cannot distinguish them by their names, assuredly, knowing they are but to represent such a Lady, at such a time appoynted?[24]

Heywood's argument would not have impressed such opponents of the stage as John Rainoldes, whose allusion to Sporus, Nero's homosexual lover, reveals his fear that some male spectators might be sexually attracted to the boy actor himself.[25] Prynne cites Stubbes's account of such occurrences and then adds his own embellishment:

> Yea, witnes . . . M. Stubs, his Anatomy of Abuses p. 105. where he affirmes, that Players and Play-haunters in their secret conclaves play the Sodomites: together with some moderne examples of such, who have beene desperately enamored with Players Boyes thus clad in womans apparell, so farre as to solicite them by words, by Letters, even actually to abuse them . . . . This I have heard credibly reported of a Scholler of Bayliol Colledge and I doubt not but it may be verified of divers others.[26]

There is, in fact, some evidence from other sources to indicate that antitheatrical polemicists were not alone in linking play-boys with homosexuality. Ben Jonson echoes the charge twice iñ *Poetaster* (Chapel, 1601). The elder Ovid fears that his son's determination to write plays for an acting company will lead to homoerotic debauchery: "What, shall I have my sonne a stager now? an enghle [ingle] for players?" (I.ii. 15–16). Later in the play, Tucca shows off the acting skills of his two "pyrgi" to a player named Histrio. He has them play various roles— King Darius, a soldier, a ghost, an avenger, and a Moor. When Histrio asks that "one of them doe a little of a ladie" (III.iv.259–60), Tucca agrees, promising or warning that "he will make thee eternally enamour'd of him" (ll. 261–62). Shortly after this sample of female impersonation, Histrio offers to buy or rent the boys, and Tucca, either out of a change of heart or to drive up their value, withdraws his offer to sell them: "No, you mangonizing slave, I will not part from 'hem: you'll sell 'hem for enghles you" (III.iv.275–76). Tucca's self-righteousness suggests that *he* may be peddling the boys as ingles, a term Florio uses to define *catamíto:* "one hired to sinne against nature, an ingle, a ganimade."[27]

In *Poetaster,* performed by the newly reactivated Children of the Chapel Royal at Blackfriars, Jonson seems to suggest that homosexual activities involving boys were prevalent in the adult troupes, where apprentices took on female roles. Thomas Middleton, in his satiric work *Father Hubburd's Tale,* also refers to the children's company at Blackfriars, where boys played all roles, as a "nest of boys able to ravish a man."[28] It is not as clear in these examples as it is in the antitheatrical tracts that the sexual appeal of the boys was enhanced by or resided in their ability to impersonate women. Aside from accusations in antitheatrical tracts and other evidence of homosexual practices among the actors, there is no evidence of a coterie of male spectators whose primary interest in the representation of women by play-boys was homoerotic. Lisa Jardine overstates the case, I believe, in arguing that homoerotic attraction was the primary source of the appeal of boy actresses, in or out of male disguise.[29] Nonetheless, the more skillful the female impersonator in offering a theatrical construction of a social construction of femininity, the more likely that the culture's essentialized notions of maleness were called into question.

Although it may seem clear from our vantage point how such notions were culturally constructed, the prevailing views of Shakespeare's contemporaries were essentialist with regard to gender identity, in spite of what Thomas Laquer calls a "one-sex model" of embryology. This theory, derived from Galen, maintained that male and female sexual organs were homologous, for all human fetuses were at first undifferentiated and went through a female stage; some were arrested and remained female, while others went on to achieve "perfect" male form.[30] A concomitant folk belief held that under extreme physical or emotional stress, girls or women could complete their development and become male, but such cases were extremely rare and for the vast majority of individuals sexual classification was permanent.

Laquer also warns against confusing the one-sex theory of anatomy with social parity of the two sexes. His remark on classical antiquity seems to me applicable to the Renaissance: "This 'one-flesh,' the construction of a single-sexed body with its different versions attributed to at least two genders, was framed in antiquity to valorize the extraordinary cultural assertion of patriarchy, of the father, in the face of the more sensorily evident claim of the mother" (20). Similarly, the dominant view in early modern England held that one's sexual identity was determined by anatomy and developed thereafter through the social practices we now understand as forming gender. The treatment and status of women was often based on or justified by such essentialist assumptions. All children, it seems, were dressed in long skirts until the age of seven, when boys were "breeched,"[31] but underlying sexual differences were thereafter powerfully reinforced by differentiating cultural practices. Many English boys (but no girls) were sent to grammar school, where they would be prepared to take their places as men in a patriarchal society with all rights and privileges thereto appertaining. Whatever its underlying doubts and anxieties, only a culture convinced that anatomy was destiny and confident of its ability to imprint gender differences at a later age would have dressed boys as women throughout their early childhood years.

The theatrical practice of cross-gender casting, along with cross-gender disguise, is often cited as evidence of constructivist attitudes. Woodbridge disagrees, describing theatrical female impersonation as a temporary form of inversion in which one sex mimics the other but in which there is no fundamental challenge to a binary gender system.[32] But such a system may have looked questionable to theatergoers as they watched young male actors playing women, for such representation clearly involved a theatrical construction of femininity. Whether femininity in the social world was an essential or constructed phenomenon, its representation on stage was obviously the result of theatrical artifice and was therefore to some degree or at certain times transparent. If boys or young men could successfully create illusions of female gender identity, cross-gender casting disrupted the sense of difference undergirding the strict binary gender system, as Catherine Belsey and others have argued, just as theatrical impersonation in general, by suggesting the arbitrariness of all social roles, destabilized any sense of a hierarchical social structure.[33] Such destabilization was countered by its confinement to theatrical space, a licensed zone in which such subversive views could not only be advanced or tested, but also satirized or contained.

Audience Reponses to Male Performers in Female Roles

Any current theory about the responses of English Renaissance theatergoers to female characters performed by play-boys runs the risk of being anachronistic. Nor can we assume a homogeneous collective response by audiences to play-boys, for in every theater audience there is a range of sophistication, alertness, and theatergoing experience, plus differences in gender, class, and other variables. The evidence suggests two opposing but compatible conclusions: on the one hand, the power of cross-gender casting to disrupt conventional gender roles implies a high level of awareness by audiences of the presence of play-boys in female roles; on the other hand, English theatergoers seem to have accepted boys in women's parts as the norm of theatrical representation.

Why did they do so? Gras argues that the English believed at some level that boys and women were interchangeable. Both shared a common temperament—irrational, emotional, mercurial; as Rosalind/ Ganymed puts it after explaining why a "moonish youth" could easily impersonate Orlando's mistress, "Boys and women are for the most part cattle of this color" (III.ii.414–15).[34] Despite Rosalind's witty remark, which may have received some support from psychological theories of the day, differences between boys and women would also have been obvious. As characters in plays of the period (Shakespearean sons and mothers, for example), boys and women hardly share a common temperament. As apprentices in adult acting companies, play-boys are thought by some scholars to have been as powerless as women, but the crucial difference (in addition to differences of social class) was that the play-boys' situation was temporary. In opposition to arguments derived from Renaissance theories of psychology, statements by witnesses closer to the theatrical experience enable us to outline a broader range of attitudes toward play-boys and the phenomenon of female impersonation.

One such witness, the English traveler Thomas Coryate, was stunned when he saw actresses for the first time while visiting Venice in 1608:

> Here I observed certaine things that I never saw before. For I saw women acte, a thing that I never saw before, *though I have heard that it hathe beene sometimes used in London,* and they performed it with as good a grace, action, gesture, and whatsoever convenient for a Player, as ever I saw any masculine Actor.[35]

Coryate's astonishment at the ability of women to perform female roles indicates just how rare those occasions in London he alludes to must have been. Chambers lists the recorded instances and concludes, "The exceptions are, I think, such as prove the rule,"[36] but for some spectators the exceptions may have underscored the arbitrariness of the rule without necessarily kindling a desire to change it. We have seen that continental troupes made occasional visits to England and usually appeared under court auspices rather than in the commercial playhouses of London. Englishmen abroad, including members of English acting companies, encountered Italian troupes using actresses on the continent.[37] The French troupe's brief appearance at Blackfriars in 1629 is unique. An indeterminate but influential segment of any audience would be likely to have seen amateur female performers play women in court masques or other private theatricals. These exceptions aside, typical English theatergoers, like Coryate, had never seen women onstage and would not do so until the Restoration.

In addition to reactions to continental actresses, we have a few responses to the English play-boys themselves. One group of responses, already considered, is found in puritanical attacks on transvestism in the theater and in Heywood's rejoinder to those attacks. Another type of response emerges from an account of a performance of *Othello* by the King's Men at Oxford in September 1610. Henry Jackson of Corpus Christi College wrote, in Latin, to commend the company as a whole for acting decorously and aptly (*decore, et apte agebant*) but singled out the boy who played Desdemona for the ability to evoke pathos in the murder scene:

> not only by their speech but by their deeds they drew tears. —But indeed Desdemona, killed by her husband, although she always acted the matter very well, in her death moved us still more greatly; when lying in bed she implored the pity of those watching with her countenance alone.[38]

Jackson was consciously responding to the character's emotional situation and paying tacit tribute to the actor's skill in presenting it. The two blend in his mind, as he uses the character's name and feminine grammatical forms and only indirectly praises the actor's ability to evoke pathos for Desdemona by referring to her facial expressions. Jackson is far more absorbed in the character of Desdemona than in the artistry of the male performer, but one wonders what his response would have been had Desdemona appeared in male apparel.

Another kind of response is suggested by two metaphoric allusions to boy heroines in *The Countess of Montgomery's Urania,* a long prose romance written by Lady Mary Wroth, the daughter of Robert Sidney of Penshurst and the niece of both Philip Sidney and the Countess of Pembroke. Unlike Henry Jackson's comment, neither of these passages is a direct response to specific dramatic productions, but they nonetheless reveal ways of looking at male representation of women that seem likely to have grown out of play-going experience. In these passages, the author compares a woman to a young male actor impersonating a woman on stage.

The first passage occurs in book I of the printed portion of *The Urania.* A queen, having pledged her love to a servant, has persuaded him to kill her husband, the king. When a delegation from a neighboring kingdom arrives at her court to offer official condolences, she falls passionately in love with one of the captains. The more he resists her wooing, the more ardently this "chastlesse Queene" pursues him. Her first lover and "companion in mischiefe" learns of her attempts to seduce this stranger and spies on them when they are alone in her "Cabinet":

> there hee [her first lover] saw her with all passionate ardency, seeke, and sue for the strangers love; yet he [the stranger] unmoveable,

was no further wrought, then if he had seene a delicate play-boy acte a loving womans part, and knowing him a Boy, lik'd onely his action.[39]

The passage also depicts the queen's first lover as an audience whose presence theatricalizes the scene and introduces the stranger, that is, the captain, whom the queen tries to seduce and who is explicitly compared to a spectator watching a boy actor impersonate a woman. His reaction is twofold: he resists her charms and her pleas for his love, but like an experienced theatergoer he admires *"onely* her action," that is, her technical expertise in pretending to be what she is not.

The second passage occurs in the unpublished continuation of *The Urania*. Here the author compares a deceitful woman to a boy actor but does so in the course of an extended character description in the narrative voice. Whereas in the previous passage the image of the boy actor is used to articulate the reaction of a man who is sexually unmoved by a woman's seductive wiles, the metaphor here is a direct attempt on the author's part to present in vivid detail a villainess's guileful duplicity:

A woeman dangerous in all kinde, flattering, and insinuating aboundantly, winning by matchless intising, and as soone cast of, but w[ith] hasard sufficient to the forsaken, or forsaker, her traines farr exceeding her love, and as full of faulshood as of vaine and endles expressions, being for her over acting fashion, more like a play boy dressed gaudely up to shew a fond loving woemans part, then a great Lady, soe busy, so full of taulke, and in such a sett formallity, w[ith] so many framed lookes, fained smiles, and nods, w[ith] a deceiptfull downe cast looke, instead of purest modesty, and bashfulness, too rich Juells for her rotten Cabbinett to containe, som times a little (and that while painfull) silence as wishing, and with gestures, as longing to be moved to speake againe, and seeming soe loath, as supplications must bee as itt were made to heare her toungue once more ring chimes of faulse beeguilings, and intrapping charmes, witt being overwourne by her farr nicer, and more strange, and soe much the more prised, inchanting inventions, soe as her charming phansies, and her aluring daliings makes true witt a foole in such a scoole, and bace faulenes, and luxury the Jalours of her house, and unfortunate prisoners.[40]

Here, the play-boy and the villainous woman are skilled at creating the illusion of a model of femininity, an illusion completely contrary to their true natures.

Although both passages use the simile of the boy actor to denigrate a woman, the image is employed without any condemnation of the player, his creation of a theatrical illusion, or his transvestism. Whereas the opponents of the stage regularly castigate actors for such transformations of social and sexual identity and are especially anxious about the kindling of erotic fantasies by the boy player or the female character or both, Wroth uses the image of the actor without moral bias against cross-gender casting. She uses the simile in the first passage to indicate that the stranger is *not* sexually excited by the queen's "passionate ardency." Wroth's use of the image of the play-boy bespeaks an aesthetic sophistication that is consistent with her experience as a participant in court masques and, one presumes, as a spectator at performances given by professional players at court and perhaps in their own playhouses.[41]

The second passage suggests a formal style of playing. Both the deceitful female character and the boy actor *"shew* a fond loving woemans part [rather] then a great Lady,"* that is, represent an overly demonstrative type of woman rather than one whose demeanor is marked by aristocratic reserve. The woman's emotions, moreover, are feigned. The excessiveness and falsity of her feelings are underscored by mention of her gaudy attire and "her over acting fashion," a phrase which suggests that both the woman and the boy player exaggerate their portrayal. The woman does so because she is deceitful, the boy because it is the way he plies his craft. The phrase "sett formality" also connotes a studied artificiality on the part of the woman and the play-boy, and the passage indeed catalogs what seem to be conventionalized theatrical codes (looks, smiles, nods, gestures) used by a woman who wants to entrap a man, as in Wroth's narrative, or by a boy actor depicting a foolish inamorata.[42]

The two passages from Lady Mary Wroth's *The Urania,* considered alongside other pieces of evidence, suggest that a range of responses toward the male actor/female character was possible. Such a range includes Henry Jackson's recording not only of his rapt engagement but of the "character's" facial expressions that evoked it, as well as responses by polemicists and Lady Mary Wroth, which despite their differences share an awareness of both play-boy and female character.

It was surely possible for a talented apprentice actor playing female roles to do so without reminding the audience of his male identity. Explicit verbal allusions in plays to cross-gender casting are rare, although any strong marker of gender, any verbal or nonverbal moment of reflexivity, might well have had such an effect. The only unambiguous verbal self-reference I know of to a play-boy occurs in a much-discussed passage near the end of *Antony and Cleopatra* (King's, c. 1606), when Cleopatra fears that, as Caesar's prisoner, she will suffer the humiliation of being forced to watch "the quick comedians" present satiric sketches of her and Antony's "Alexandrian revels." Worst of all, "I shall see / Some squeaking Cleopatra boy my greatness / I' th' posture of a whore" (V.ii.216–21).

Even what seems inescapably self-referential has been read differently by other critics, such as W. R. Davies, whose reading is guided by principles ostensibly derived from naturalistic theater:

> In the excitement of the moment they [the spectators] would hardly connect the reference to the boy actor with the figure whom, for the previous four Acts, they had accepted as Cleopatra, nor, as the speech takes no more than fifteen seconds in delivery, would they have much opportunity to do so.[43]

Davies is wrong to discount any theatrical effect on the basis of its brevity. Some spectators may have been so absorbed in the illusion of Cleopatra's femininity that they shared her horror at the prospect of its desecration. Most playgoers, however, are capable of the kind of dual consciousness described by Samuel Johnson: "the spectators are always in their senses, and know, from the first act to the last, that the stage is only a stage, and that the players are only players."[44] If Johnson is correct, spectators would not only have shared Cleopatra's fear, as Davies claims, but admired the performance of the play-boy who so engaged them in theatrical illusion, fusing admiration for the histrionic abilities of both actor and character.[45]

Given the widespread theatergoing of the day, few spectators could have retained the kind of naïveté Davies postulates, for when the text provided an invitation, however brief, to focus on the play-boy representing the heroine, most members of the audience probably did so. In this moment, Shakespeare invokes the metatheatrical context through verbal reflexivity, as he does a moment later by calling attention to the absence of actual breasts when Cleopatra nurses an asp or much earlier in having Cleopatra exchange bawdy jokes about penises with her female servants. Here, the play-boy is given the chance to blend his technical dexterity with the character's self-dramatization of her "infinite variety." It must have been a daring moment in the original production, depending upon the audience's willingness to admire a talented play-boy portraying a woman of legendary sexual power. Such readiness to applaud the play-boy's skill required not only an acceptance of cross-gender casting but also some metatheatrical awareness. Both attitudes were reinforced by the survival of older festal traditions in early modern England, by the frequent use of plays and dialogues within all-male academic institutions, and by widespread familiarity with the use of play-boys in professional troupes.

Chapter 3

Cross-Gender Disguise plus Cross-Gender Casting

If Cleopatra's reflexive allusion to the play-boy made explicit what audiences "always know," then it is possible that even without such self-referential reminders spectators' awareness of a boy actor's presence may have had some influence on the presentation and perception of a female character. The assertiveness of characters like Beatrice, Kate, Lady Macbeth, or Volumnia might well have been enhanced by a cheeky boy or pert young man, although actresses have been performing such roles for centuries with no diminution of aggressiveness. In a few other plays featuring viragos or women warriors, male attire may have heightened spectators' awareness of the male actor.

Male disguise was another powerful reminder of the presence of the male performer and remained in the audience's view longer than a single phrase, like the noun-as-verb *boy* in *Antony and Cleopatra,* could resound in their ears. Whereas such phrases could at most occasionally point reflexively to the presence of the actor, cross-gender disguise did so in more sustained fashion by creating a third layer of gender identity, the disguised male persona, often difficult to distinguish from the actor himself.

For the Elizabethan boy actor, this third layer presented a technical problem. To distinguish the female character from either her assumed male disguise or his own male identity, the play-boy had to establish the heroine's femininity with unmistakable clarity. However skilled he might be at female impersonation, his performance would probably have been perceived, and perhaps even applauded, as a relatively artificial and constructed version of femininity. How then did such a play-boy per-

49

forming a female role handle the characters' assumption of male disguise?

Victor Freeburg hypothesized that play-boys represented the disguised male persona by signaling their characters' femininity through male disguise.[1] This solution sounds more like the practice of Victorian actresses, who implied psychological distance between their character, or themselves, and the "breeches" part of the role, just as some modern actresses project a patently artificial theatrical caricature of male assertiveness through which one can easily glimpse the female identities of character and performer. A number of commentators have theorized a blending of disguised heroines' various layers of gender identity, and in recent years a few actresses have experimented with this "unisex" approach.

The play-boy's solution to the problem of the heroine's male disguise is illuminated by a passage in the induction to *Antonio and Mellida* (Paul's, 1599–1600). The actor playing Antonio announces that he will begin the play disguised as an Amazon named Florizel, or what he calls a "hermaphrodite, two parts in one," but he describes his male and female roles as utterly distinct: "Ay, but when use hath taught me action to hit the right point of a lady's part, I shall grow ignorant, when I must turn young prince again, how but to truss my hose."[2] The passage suggests that actors playing cross-dressed female characters clearly differentiated the character from her assumed male persona, rather than enacting the disguised identity as an androgynous blend. Antonio is a boy bride, but the principle also applies to female-page roles, where the disguised male identity could most simply be represented by a version of what might pass in real life for boyishness—pert audacity or winsome shyness. However contrived from the play-boy's point of view, either of these modes would have seemed less artificial to the audience than the more obviously constructed female character he was portraying.

Current theatrical practice, as I understand it, corroborates the Renaissance stylistic separation of genders. It is virtually impossible to present *simultaneously* two distinct layers of identity in a coherent fashion for more than a few moments. Actors generally project one layer at a time, relying on audiences to recall the layer not shown. Sometimes actors remind audiences of the other layers of identity by shifting rapidly between layers, a movement that can be as brief as a glance at another character "in the know" and as subtle as a facial expression seen only by the audience.[3]

For a play-boy of Shakespeare's day, however talented and experienced, to present a woman in the process of impersonating a man would have been extremely difficult and would probably have produced either a very broad farcical effect or a muddle. The simpler, more effective solution was a clear stylistic differentiation of the two genders, playing the female role in the usual style and making the male disguise seem like a version of himself, as if the performer were stepping out of character.

The version of himself that the boy actor used to portray the heroine's disguised male identity need not have been, and most likely was not, his "authentic" self, but was itself a fabricated persona, perhaps an enlargement or modification of some aspect of his personality, or more likely one of the two cultural norms for boyish behavior—audacity or shyness. If done as artfully as the play-boy portrayed women, an audience might have difficulty distinguishing the heroine's male disguise from the male performer. Elizabethan stage clowns like Tarlton and Kemp evidently displayed such crafted public versions of themselves when they seemed to step out of character. Whenever an actor breaks character and becomes "himself," what he usually reveals is itself an artistically constructed performance persona, although audiences accept it as being more real than his mimetic role. As Raymond Pentzell has explained:

Indeed, once an audience perceives the actor as a *persona* distinct from his scripted character, there appears a dimension in which the actor will inevitably be taken as greater than his role, no matter the role. . . . Once our willing pretense that the actor *is* the character is broken, empathy flows toward the necessarily more human *persona* of the actor as iron filings toward a magnet.[4]

This phenomenon exists even in the naturalistic theater and its cinematic offspring, but seems even more likely in the English Renaissance theater, with daylight playhouses, repertory companies, and presentational conventions. Under such conditions, the self-referential practices of the English Renaissance theater would probably have encouraged spectators to see the heroine's assumption of male disguise as the play-boy's resumption of his own identity.[5]

This calculated ambiguity of heroine's male disguise and play-boy's "real" personality was probably stronger in adult troupes than in boy companies. Female pages occur in a dozen plays acted by children's troupes, roughly the same proportion as in the repertories of adult companies. Given the greater prevalence of imitation, parody, and self-conscious theatricality in the plays of the boy troupes, one would have expected their playwrights to make even greater use of the motif.[6] They did not, I suspect, out of fear that a female character disguised as a boy would be hard to distinguish from any other male character, their companies consisting entirely of boys or young men. In fact, two disguised-heroine plays acted by boy companies, *The Wars of Cyrus* and *Antonio and Mellida,* exploited precisely this kind of confusion by pairing boy brides with female pages.

In contrast to disguised heroine plays performed by boy companies, such plays acted by adult troupes would have made the boy/girl/boy stand out from all other characters. Adult plays almost never juxtapose female pages with male pages but instead contrast female pages with their masters/lovers played by adult male actors (e.g., Proteus, Orlando, and Orsino). The effects of that contrast are difficult to measure. Juliet Dusinberre suggests that "a real man on the stage throws into relief the boy actor's femininity," even when he is playing a heroine disguised as a boy.[7] But it is also true that in many plays acted by adults, the female page is juxtaposed to one or more boy heroines *not* in male disguise (as Julia is with Silvia, Rosalind is with Celia, and Viola is with Olivia), which probably heightened any self-referential effect and for the moment countered the enhancement of femininity Dusinberre describes. The resumption of male identity by the actor playing the cross-dressed heroine may even have activated the audience's residual awareness that *both* women were played by male performers.

In adult companies, the assumed male identity of the boy heroine in cross-gender disguise existed in the world of the play, but the resumed male identity of the performer belonged to the world of the playhouse and was no less real to spectators. This phenomenological reality, combined with the illusion of depth created by his/her/his multiple identities and with the virtuosity required to maneuver rapidly among them, enabled this figure to achieve an effect I term *theatrical vibrancy.*

The Example of Middleton's Pregnant Page

Middleton's *More Dissemblers Besides Women* (King's Men? 1619?)[8] illustrates the interplay of social attitudes, theatrical practices, and literary and dramatic traditions surrounding heroines in male disguise. Writing for the same troupe that had performed Shakespeare's disguised-heroine plays about a generation earlier, Middleton here produced a novel variation on the well-established tradition of such works and their narrative analogues. He also drew on contemporary views of female and male cross-dressing explored in previous chapters. Finally, the play provides a vivid example of how ingenious variations on the tradition not only displayed the playwrights' dramaturgical inventiveness and sophisticated social awareness but also encouraged play-boys to demonstrate *their* virtuosity.

By the time he wrote this play, Middleton could assume that his audience was familiar with the motif of the female page. He could therefore feel free to elaborate it, even to extend elaborations previously developed by Shakespeare. Like *The Merchant of Venice, More Dissemblers* multiplies cross-dressed heroines. Two of the women are more or less betrothed to the same man. The first is foil for the second: just as Jessica's conventional disguise as a torchbearer sets off Portia's more audacious and innovative appearance as a lawyer, Aurelia's brief appearance as a young gentleman is the foil for the novel phenomenon of a pregnant page, an invention that extends the range of tonalities beyond earlier treatments of heroines in male disguise.

By 1619 or so, Middleton could expect a London audience not only to appreciate such innovations but also to pick up the barest of hints. For example, the audience never actually hears Lactantio tell Aurelia to don male apparel, but that is undoubtedly what spectators must imagine he whispers to "Thine ear" in the opening scene (l. 63). He alluded to it earlier in coded language decipherable to those familiar with the motif of the female page:

> I've provided
> A shape, that at first sight will start thy modesty
> And make thee blush perhaps, but 'twill away
> After a qualm or two. Virginity
> Has been put often to those shifts before thee
> Upon extremities.
>
> (ll. 40–45)

"You make me blush, sir" (l. 64), she says to Lactantio after he whispers his plan to her, just as he had predicted.

She arrives disguised not as a mere page but as "a gentleman / That lately came from Rome" (I.ii.137–38), complete with "weapon" (l. 173) and "hangars and all" (l. 175). These accessories might well have had considerable impact in 1619, at the height of the *Hic Mulier* controversy, but she is not quite the virago or woman warrior her disguise suggests, or perhaps does not sustain that aspect of her disguise after the cardinal leaves her alone with her lover. Lactantio "arrest[s] thee / In Cupid's name" (ll. 172–73), takes her "prisoner" (l. 177) in his embrace, and finally makes her swear she loves him.

In the first two scenes, Middleton used dramaturgical shorthand to set up a conventional romantic comedy featuring a cross-dressed heroine but deviated from the Shakespearean prototype by creating a world allowing greater sexual freedom. Aurelia is not only resourceful, assertive, and energetic, just as Portia and Rosalind were, but instead of pursuing the man she has just married or just fallen in love with, she is involved in what seems to be a torrid, long-standing, and clandestine liaison. The London aldermen and magistrates would have classified the relationship as a sexual misdemeanor and punished her, as they did Mawdlin Gawen (no. 4), for going abroad in male apparel in order to keep a rendezvous with a lover.

Her father takes a similar view of her behavior when he barges into the cardinal's house, where he and the old governor he has chosen as prospective son-in-law have followed Aurelia. Mocking Aurelia's and Lactantio's use of a mock foreign language, he addresses his daughter as "Strumpettikin, bold harlottum, queaninisma, whoremongeria" and chastises her for adopting this "shape for reputation / And modesty to masque in" (ll. 202–6). His attitude is extreme, for he is the typically tyrannical father of New Comedy, but Aurelia, despite her blushes and claim to virginity, is not the typical heroine, but rather an extremely headstrong, audacious, and sexually independent nineteen-year-old woman. She not only protests against physical confinement, but is one of the few romantic heroines to complain "'Tis prisonment . . . to be a maid" (II.iii.409).

If her donning male apparel was Lactantio's somewhat hackneyed idea, Aurelia's subsequent stratagems exhibit greater resourcefulness. To rejoin Lactantio, she escapes from confinement by means of another disguise, as a gypsy, this time in a plan devised by Andrugio, her former lover, whom she misleads into thinking that the two of them will run off together. Her intent from the outset is to exploit Andrugio's love for her so she can rejoin Lactantio. She finds the role of gypsy "doxy" entirely congenial, for even though Lactantio fails to find her, she can flirt with other gypsies and with Lactantio's servant Dondolo. Taking courage from the fact that her blackened face will not show blushes, she uses her disguise to ridicule her father with impunity and to mock the governor by telling his fortune: to be jilted by one "so wild, you could never rule her" (IV.i.289). She is just what her father calls the gypsy woman she pretends to be: "a bold daring baggage!" (IV.i.259). At the end of the play, she makes one last desperate bid for Lactantio, but when he rejects her, she gives herself to the ever-faithful Andrugio, for she is desperate to fulfill her vow to "have a child by twenty, if not twain" (V.ii.157). Andrugio hesitates to be made "your property" but is won over when, like other sexually experienced brides in Middleton's city comedies, she swears henceforth to be "as true for ever to your bed / As she in thought or deed that never err'd" (ll. 166–67).

The conventionality of Aurelia's male disguise is undercut not only by her volatile character but also by Lactantio's duplicity. His cryptic proposal that she now don "a shape, that . . . will start thy modesty" is initially offered "for thy further safety" (I.i.40), but as the speech unfolds, his concern modulates first to "our safeties" (l. 47) and finally to "my fortune's sake" (l. 58). He wishes to remain in favor with his uncle, the cardinal, in whose house he resides and who insists that his nephew live as celibate a life as he does. Lactantio's motive for concealing the affair is not solicitude for Aurelia's reputation but his own desire to inherit his uncle's wealth, "for I am like to be his only heir" (l. 59).

In the next scene, just before Aurelia arrives in the shape Lactantio has provided for her, the audience discovers additional dimensions to his hypocrisy, for it turns out he is involved with another woman, this one also in male attire. A page, later called Antonio, announces the arrival of "a gentleman / That lately came from Rome." The audience might suspect the page to be Aurelia, but Lactantio makes it clear that the gentleman is Aurelia in disguise. But before Aurelia can enter, Middleton drops a large bomb when he has the page announce, in an aside to Lactantio's question about the cause of her sickly pallor, "I fear, sir, I'm with child" (I.ii.145). With that disclosure, the familiar plot lines derived from New Comedy begin to tangle.[9]

This page is the only female page in all of English Renaissance drama to be with child, a startling variation on the motif that undercuts its conventional romantic treatment by adding real-life details. These details not only include such clinical concerns as morning sickness and, later on, labor pains but allude to the reluctance of employers, parishes, and municipalities to support illegitimate babies and unwed mothers. Had the page been brought before the London magistrates, bearing a bastard and wearing male apparel would have been more than enough evidence of her moral depravity, as it was in the case of Margaret Wakeley (no. 10).

Lactantio himself adopts this moralistic tone, blaming the page for becoming pregnant. He calls her "a piece of touchwood" (III.i.4) and praises those "That never sham'd their master" (l. 6), presumably women who did not inconvenience their lovers by conceiving. Her account of their relationship differs:

> When I left all my friends in Mantua,
> For your love's sake alone, then, with strange oaths
> You promis'd present marriage.
>
> (ll. 13–15)

Lactantio confesses that he has "sworn the same things / I'm sure forty times over" (ll. 17–18) and admits ruefully, or perhaps boasts, that marrying them all "'Twould make one vicar hoarse" (l. 22). He cynically belittles her vision of marriage as "a toy till death" (l. 20), hopes to conceal her condition by finding other garments besides "those masculine hose" (l. 24), and considers packing her off to his own nurse, "A good sure old wench" (26). His callousness not only clashes with the page's shame, disillusionment, and physical discomfort, but with the other characters' responses to this complex figure of a play-boy impersonating a pregnant woman disguised as a boy.

To the cardinal, for example, the page resembles Imogen in *Cymbeline* or Bellario in Fletcher's *Philaster*,[10] for what he sees is a frail and melancholy youth afflicted with mysterious sorrows and needing the protection of a stronger adult male. Within ten lines of the revelation of the page's pregnancy, which he does not hear, the cardinal describes the departing youth as "The prettiest servant / That ever man was bless'd with! 'tis so meek, / So good and gentle" (I.ii.151–53). He goes on to describe the boy's grief and what he believes to be its cause:

> I've oft took him
> Weeping alone, poor boy, at the remembrance
> Of his lost friends, which, as he says, the sea

Swallow'd, with all their substance.

(ll. 154–57)

The grief is authentic if its cause is not, but the portrait that the cardinal paints here, and later when he accuses his nephew of maltreating this sensitive boy and sends the page to serve the duchess, is an intensified version of winsome shyness, a stylized image of the female page as melancholy, lachrymose castaway.

To Dondolo, Lactantio's comic other servant, the page is a stimulus to homoerotic fantasy and an object of sexual desire. The play allows us to see his vision of the page as the antithesis of the cardinal's or as its unsublimated alter ego. In their first scene, Dondolo notes the page's feminine demeanor—"thou wouldst have made a pretty foolish waiting-woman but for one thing" (I.iv.60–61)—and praises the page's singing in terms that call attention both to the female character and to the alleged use of young male servants and play-boys as "ingles"—"Well, go thy ways for as sweet a breasted page as ever lay at his master's feet in a truckle-bed" (ll. 100–102). In their next scene, Dondolo reveals his own sexual desire for the page. He resents the servant for "not suffer[ing] me to come to bed to him" (III.i.84) and for not swimming in the nude with him like other pages, most especially because "I could never get that little monkey yet to / Put off his breeches" (ll. 95–96). On one level, the joke is on Dondolo for failing to understand that the page is a woman, but on another level his crude homoeroticism illuminates what was widely perceived as the common treatment of apprentices in all-male theatrical troupes.

In contrast to the cardinal's frail waif and Dondolo's homosexual playmate, the duchess has come to see the page at the end of the play as a "gentlewoman," and presents her, as the stage direction puts it, "in a female dress" (V.ii.213). According to the duchess, the birth of the child makes Lactantio as good as married to the page (she is also called simply "Page" and later "Antonio," but her real name is never given), "the match . . . made / Near forty weeks ago" (ll. 214–15).

The page's diverse layers of gender identity are all heightened in the final act, when the play-boy, enacting a pregnant woman disguised as a boy taking a dancing lesson, must also represent a woman experiencing the onset of labor. The scene is set up in IV.ii, when the duchess tells her servant Celia to have this "pretty boy" (l. 60) to dance as well as sing.

Celia observes that "He is well made for dancing: thick i' th' chest, madam; / He will turn long and strongly" (ll. 83–84).

In V.i, Celia oversees the page's lessons with two masters, Crotchet and Sinquapace, the joke (such as it is) being that these exertions have brought the child she is carrying to term. Unlike any other heroine in male disguise, the page reveals her identity not by doffing a hat or losing a helmet, nor by a playful or triumphant undisguising, but by going into labor. As the page becomes increasingly uncomfortable and distraught, the play-boy must have indicated the woman's condition and her vain effort to conceal it in the guise of a boy learning to dance. The play-boy understandably sent conflicting gender signals. The dancing master, who like Dondolo also seems sexually attracted by the boy, is appalled to see that "he makes a curtsy like a chambermaid" (l. 181), while a musician chastises him: "did you ever see a boy begin a dance and make curtsy like a wench before?" (l. 183) Coming closer to the moment of delivery, the page tries to dance with her legs held close together, while the dancing master's rising exasperation seems to reflect the play-boy's frenzied oscillations between layers of gender identity:

> Open thy knees; wider, wider, wider, wider: did you ever see a boy dance clenched up? he needs a pick-lock: out upon thee for an arrant ass! an arrant ass! I shall lose my credit by thee; a pestilence on thee! . . . a pox, his knees are soldered together, they're sewed together: canst not stride? O, I could eat thee up, I could eat thee up, and begin upon thy hinder quarter, thy hinder quarter! I shall never teach this boy without a screw; his knees must be opened with a vice, or there's no good to be done upon him. (ll. 190–204)

Finally, as the musician observes, "the boy swoons" (l. 221), as the page, unable to continue the deception, calls for "A midwife!" (l. 223) and is led away to give birth. Unable to interpret what has happened, the dancing master calls it a "miracle": "The boy's with child . . . . Some woman is the father."

Labeling the dance as "grotesquely comic" and "intensely disturbing," George Rowe makes it emblematic of the play:

> Middleton places before us a powerful example of the rebirth celebrated by all comedy, but usually from a comfortably symbolic

distance. Forces which in conventional comedy are figuratively inti-
mated . . . are here concretely depicted onstage.[11]

The jarring combination of farce and pathos accords with the play's
complex attitudes toward love embodied throughout; characters who
seem to be released from bondage into the freedom to gratify their
passions discover themselves to be restricted in unforeseen ways. All of
the lovers must settle for less or other than what they initially wanted.

But the moment has important theatrical ramifications as well. The
dancing master's perspective and the character's plight provide powerful
and opposed gender markers—on the one hand, a homoerotic interest
in the male body of the page (here evocative of and inseparable from the
actual male body of the performer); on the other hand, a representation
by that same male actor of the nonexistent pregnant female body of the
character experiencing uterine contractions. On the stage and in the
minds of the audience, the quicksilver shifts and fusions of layers of
gender identity created a splendid opportunity for the play-boy to display his virtuosity and to produce the effect I have called theatrical
vibrancy—a layering of gender identity and the rapid oscillation between
layers.

Such heightened awareness of the play-boy playing the page, an
important ingredient in the effect just described, probably also influenced
spectators' responses to the play-boy performing in the other major
female role, that of the duchess of Milan, the heroine of the main plot.
At her husband's deathbed seven years earlier, the duchess had vowed
to her dying spouse not to remarry but to live in chaste fidelity to his
memory. The cardinal has made her resolution the basis of his own
successful career. He has invested heavily in her as an emblem of celibate
widowhood, having "writ volumes of your victories and virtues"
(II.i.110), "books that I have publish'd in her praise" (III.i.263). Even
though he persuades her to test her vows by receiving Andrugio, he is
very uneasy when she shows interest in remarrying, so she dissembles
by telling him that the object of her affections is not the returning general
but the cardinal's own nephew, Lactantio. Like Aurelia, she contrives a
witty intrigue to win Andrugio's hand in marriage but abandons her
claim when she finds his heart belongs to Aurelia. At the end of the play,
she therefore renews her commitment to remain celibate, not because
the cardinal or other men require a model of chaste widowhood but

evidently because in losing Andrugio to Aurelia she has suffered "a just cross led in by a temptation" (V.ii.131).

Her rededication to widowed chastity is far more authentic than the cardinal's lavish praise of it, praise that echoes conservative conduct books by writers like Vives. The cardinal actually reverses his position when he realizes that she has fallen in love with his nephew, and in a soliloquy of dexterous casuistry, "set[s] his holy anger by awhile" to rationalize the mysterious ways in which "the hand of heaven . . . pick'd him out / To reward virtue" (II.ii.15–16). Given the duchess's wealth and power, "reward" has a strong materialistic coloration. Addressing his entourage of lords, he revises his previous views and now echoes more liberal conduct books, which redefine a woman's second marriage as a higher proof of chastity than mere celibacy and dismissing the duchess's vows as "but a thing enforc'd" (III.i.293).[12] The cardinal believes he must also overcome the celibate vows of Lactantio, who has not only kept his philandering a secret from his uncle but established a reputation for harboring "that bashful maiden virtue . . . / That never held familiar league with woman" (ll. 192–93).[13]

But duplicity runs deep in this family. Lactantio allows himself to be persuaded to exchange his "present barrenness" for "a fruitful life" (153, 156), and despite his commitment to Aurelia, to say nothing of his proposing to and impregnating the page, he agrees to marry the duchess. Invoking the play's title in its final line, she observes that "There's more dissemblers than of womankind" but leaves the audience to notice the gendered difference between modes of dissembling: that is, between the unsuccessful amorous intrigues of Aurelia, the page, and the duchess, and the avarice, faithlessness, and hypocrisy of Lactantio and the cardinal.

One might imagine that the duchess, like Valeria in Middleton and Fletcher's *The Widow* (King's, 1616), was meant or understood both as a theatrically energized embodiment of idealized widowhood as described in more liberal conduct books and as a corrective to the stereotypes of greedy and lustful widows like Lady Goldenfleece in Middleton's *No Wit, No Help Like a Woman's* (Lady Elizabeth's? c. 1611).[14] Linda Woodbridge agrees but regards such characters as meretricious pandering to female theatergoers, the Jacobean equivalent of soap opera.[15] It seems plausible to me, if unprovable, that the reflexive awareness of the male actors behind the two cross-dressed heroines also heightened the spectators' awareness of the play-boy in the role of the duchess. Thus loosened from its mimetic moorings, the constructedness of the role both as a theatrical role and as a token in a cultural debate on widowhood would enable different spectators to interpret that role in radically different ways. To some, the duchess might indeed have seemed a corrective to negative stereotypes, while others could dismiss the same interpretation as a flattering concession to growing numbers of female spectators. To still others, she could be read as a satiric caricature of contemporary dowagers or as a parody of female stereotypes held by men.

Given the heterogeneous nature of theater audiences of the period, all we can be sure of is that cross-gender casting, perhaps in conjunction with cross-gender disguise, focused attention on the theatrical representation of anxieties and current conflicts over gender roles. The playhouses, which were essentially private businesses engaged in purveying mass entertainment, provided an atmosphere in which various and often conflicting views on such controversial topics could be evoked as a kind of highly charged play. Whether such play was basically a release of dissident energy, a containment of such energy, a utopian vision, or a rehearsal for cultural change surely also varied from work to work and from spectator to spectator. The combining of cross-dressed heroines with the practice of cross-gender casting created conditions and opportunities that dramatists could exploit to add excitement to material that even at the textual level was testing conventional gender boundaries.

Much recent scholarship in this field has explored the disruption or destabilization of gender roles that resulted from this theatrical testing. In part I of this book, I have drawn on much of this work, but in fact I am working in the opposite direction. I am not asking what the various theatrical treatments of gender reveal about the larger culture because I think these theatrical treatments need more detailed study as works of theatrical art before they can be made to yield insights into attitudes toward sexuality and gender in early modern England. Instead, I wish to note that given social and intellectual pressures we can only partially articulate, spectators and playwrights sharing a common but complex and diversified culture agreed on forms of collective fantasy, one of which featured heroines in male disguise. I then wish to ask how rather than why they found aesthetic satisfaction in the ingenious and seemingly infinite reformulations of familiar components. In deploying an old approach, one that might now be termed something like "historically sensitized formalism," I have tried to use what we know of early modern

English culture and society to understand how plays involving cross-dressed heroines played by male actors might have worked in their own day.

To summarize part 1 of this book, then, I have been arguing for the importance of reflexive effects produced by a layering of gender identities, when cross-gender disguise was superimposed on cross-gender casting, that is, when a dramatist could make self-referential use of a play-boy portraying a woman who adopted male disguise. The boy heroine in male disguise was a figure of considerable theatrical potency, for as the performer shifted from one layer of gender identity to another, sometimes quite rapidly, and as spectators shifted their focus from one layer to another with equal rapidity, what emerged even when the character lacked psychological complexity was a figure of mysterious depths and shadows, of fluid yet multiple layers of identity, of enormous power. That power, theatrical vibrancy, had at least two sources. One was disguise per se, but here heightened significantly by oscillation between genders, often with quicksilver dexterity and speed. The other source of power was the capacity of cross-gender disguise to underscore the actor's presence: rather than simply disengaging the audience from the mimetic illusion, this stress on the actual identity of a real male performer engaged the audience more deeply in playful complicity in games of illusion-making.

That complicity also included the spectators' knowledge of a long tradition of literary treatments of the heroine in male disguise, as well as their social experience with cultural forms involving male and female cross-dressing. The combination of these literary and social resonances with theatrical vibrancy generated a dense network of possible responses, creating a rich field of possibilities for play. In the five chapters of part 2, I want to explore the dramaturgical aspects of such play, that is, to examine some of the ways in which Shakespeare and his fellow playwrights consciously developed and varied the motif of the cross-dressed heroines, often bandying it back and forth with skilled artistry and renewed expressiveness.

Dramaturgical Variations on Variations

Chapter 4

Bringing the Page Onstage:
The Two Gentlemen of Verona

Although heroines in male disguise are a common feature of medieval and Renaissance narratives, Shakespeare's *The Two Gentlemen of Verona* (c. 1593) is one of the earliest English plays to bring the motif onstage.[1] It is also the first in which a heroine disguised as a page pretends to be a "saucy lackey," the kind of precociously witty boy servant who had already become a stock character on the Elizabethan stage, probably because of the close fit between these cheeky pages and the assumed personalities of boy actors. As a theatricalized page, Julia, the cross-dressed heroine of *The Two Gentlemen of Verona*, displays an audacity not found in the play's primary narrative source. Not only does Shakespeare himself redeploy the cheeky page as a persona for disguised heroines, but other writers, such as Fletcher and Massinger, adapt the saucy lackey in inventive and effective ways.

The Theatricalized Page

The heroine in male disguise has a long history in medieval and Renaissance literature, a history surveyed in appendix A. In these earlier narrative treatments of the motif, the author's use of cross-gender disguise gave the heroine a secret to share with readers and so engaged them emotionally in her predicament. Adoption of disguise also implied the inevitability of undisguising, and with it the assurance that even the most assertive heroine, if she were to survive, would eventually resume her female identity and her place within a patriarchal society.

Each literary usage of cross-gender disguise was undoubtedly a function of the sexual politics of its own time and place. In female transvestite saints' lives, originally intended for monastic audiences who regarded female sexuality as the greatest threat to asceticism, the cross-dressed, asexually chaste protagonist was a martyr to the ideal of celibacy, the direct opposite of the pregnant woman who accused the saint of fathering her child. In romances, epics, and pastoral narratives, cross-dressed women demonstrated fidelity to their lovers, fiancés, and husbands, donning male disguise to follow them unrecognized as their pages or squires, and frequently dying as martyrs not to celibate chastity, as transvestite saints did, but rather to loyalty, unrequited love, or romantic ardor. In novelle, clever wenches occasionally donned male apparel to outwit the male world of fathers, authority figures, and unacceptable suitors, and to arrange their own marriages. In so doing, these women embodied female intelligence and audacity, readily acknowledged by increasing numbers of bourgeois readers of prose fiction, many of them women.

When dramatic adaptations of narrative treatments of heroines in cross-gender disguise were performed, cross-gender casting added another, entirely new, layer of gender identity—the play-boy himself. The presence of that layer was highlighted, as I have argued, by the very presence of the motif of male disguise. The performer's gender gave the disguised boy heroine another "secret" to share with the audience: beneath her male disguise she might be a woman within the world of the play, but she was a boy within the world of the playhouse.

By the mid-sixteenth century, the theatrical—as opposed to the literary model for pages, squires, and other male servants—was the brash and witty "jack" or "crack." Groups of such cheeky servants, usually male but sometimes including boy actors playing maidservants, appear in brief episodes or subplots in plays written by Richard Edwards, John Lyly, and others for children's troupes performing at court as well as at Paul's and Blackfriars. These characters were in part derived from the wily slaves of Roman comedy, but their function was not so much to generate intrigue as it was to provide tonal contrast. Usually played by the smaller, younger boys in the company, the theatrical pages typically offer cynical commentaries or ironic perspectives on the main action by parodying their masters and discomfiting figures of authority through asides, parody, punning, choplogic, and song. Satiric episodes involving such impudent servants appeared in plays written for children's troupes by such writers as Marston, Chapman, and Middleton as late as the early 1600s.[2] The plays of adult companies, by contrast, usually use a single

cheeky page rather than a group, probably because they lacked the numbers of smaller and younger boys more readily available in chorister or
schoolboy troupes. The result, as G. K. Hunter has observed, is a much
sharper confrontation, especially in Shakespeare's work, where characters drawn from different social levels frequently jostle each other in the
same scenes, unlike the children's plays, where small groups of servants
appear in low-comic scenes, usually interacting with each other rather
than with their social superiors from the main plot.[3] Despite this difference between adult's and children's plays, Shakespeare imitated the impudent Lylian page in some early plays and seems to be the first English
playwright to use this character type as the male identity for a female
character who adopts cross-gender disguise.

Three earlier extant English plays have heroines in male disguise,
but all of them are closer to the narrative tradition of female squires and
the like than to the stage tradition of the cheeky page. Neronis, the
heroine of *Clyomon and Clamydes* (1570–83), escapes from imprisonment
in "painfull Pages show," which in fact is a detail not found in the source,
but the play gives her no opportunity to be a smart-aleck page, and she
remains a forlorn maiden.[4] Gallathea and Phillida, the disguised heroines
of Lyly's *Gallathea* (Paul's, c. 1585), never become servants and are
uncomfortably shy in male attire. Phillida speaks for both when she
chides herself for not being aggressive enough in addressing Gallathea:
"Why stande I still? Boyes shoulde be bolde."[5] Similarly, Dorothea, the
heroine of Greene's *James the Fourth* (Queen's? c. 1590), disguises herself
as a squire but lacks the satiric, mocking wit of the theatricalized servant
boy.[6] In all three plays, characters other than the female pages serve as
agents of irony and ridicule.

Early in *The Two Gentlemen of Verona*, Shakespeare introduces two
pert Lylian servants, Lucetta and Speed, as if to establish models for Julia
when she disguises herself as a page. Unlike Launce, who derives from
the popular rustic clown adapted by Tarlton and Kemp for the public
theater, Lucetta and Speed evoke and direct the audience's mockery
toward the play's protagonists. Appearing in two scenes early in the
play, Lucetta mocks Julia's suitors, teases her mistress over her infatuation with Proteus, and—in a remark that seems to be directed to the
audience—pokes fun at Julia's assumed reluctance to read his letter: "She
makes it strange, but she would be best pleas'd / To be so ang'red with
another letter" (ll. 99–100). Lucetta is somewhat muted in her second
scene, II.vii, where Julia takes the initiative in planning to follow Proteus

in disguise, and disappears entirely from the play once Julia appears on stage as the page Sebastian.

Like Lucetta, the page Speed is a kind of satiric choric commentator. Robert Weimann contrasts him with a traditional clown like Launce: whereas Launce's monologues allow the actor to "share the audience's bemusement over the scene so enacted," Speed's asides involve "some contact not simply between the audience and the character Speed, but between the audience and the actor of Speed's part who, as comic chorus, enjoys a level of awareness that is not strictly limited by the play world."[7]

Although Shakespeare brings both clown and page onstage in several scenes, he also gives Speed several duet scenes of mocking repartee with his master. In II.i, when Valentine tries to sing his mistress's praises, Speed deflates the attempt by a rapid-fire stream of riddles, jests, puns, and wisecracks:

> *Val.* I have lov'd her ever since I saw her, and still
> I see her beautiful.
> *Spe.* If you love her, you cannot see her.
> *Val.* Why?
> *Spe.* Because Love is blind.
>
>   (ll. 66–70)

When Silvia enters and Valentine prepares to greet her and give her the letter he wrote at her dictation, Speed comments directly to the audience in one of several speeches first indicated as asides by Capell and Rowe: "O excellent motion! O exceeding puppet! Now will he interpret to her" (ll. 94–95). When Silvia leaves, Speed offers the audience his most extended commentary:

> O jest unseen, inscrutable; invisible,
> As a nose on a man's face, or a weathercock on a steeple!
> My master sues to her; and she hath taught her suitor,
> He being her pupil, to become her tutor.
> O excellent device, was there ever heard a better,
> That my master being scribe, to himself should write the letter?
>
>   (ll. 135–40)

The scene ends with another duet between page and master, in which Speed tries to explain to the slower-witted Valentine why Silvia has returned the letter, his exasperation finally culminating in a couplet of feminine fourteeners:

Or fearing else some messenger, that might her mind discover,
Herself hath taught her love himself to write unto her lover.
(ll. 167–68)

A moment later, he feels the pangs of hunger, as Lylian pages frequently do: "'tis dinner-time" (l. 170).

Once the play shifts to Mantua, Speed's relationship with Valentine is curtailed. Speed accompanies his master in IV.i when they are accosted by the outlaws but has only two short speeches—one an exclamation of fear and the other an appeal to his master to accept the outlaws' invitation to join them in what he calls "an honorable kind of thievery" (l. 39). The page's terror and willingness to survive at all costs, though briefly sketched, comically counterpoints his master's high-minded heroics. But at the opening of the play's final scene, V.iv, when we next see Valentine in the woods as outlaw chieftain, he is no longer accompanied by his Lylian page, Speed, who has been gradually supplanted in the play's dramaturgic economy by Julia, disguised as a page named Sebastian.

Julia as Cheeky Page

When Julia first appears in disguise in IV.ii, she comes onstage with the host, listens to Proteus's musicians serenading Silvia, and masks her own sadness by complaining about the music. Although she is not yet the Lylian page, her tone becomes sharper in three asides uttered while Proteus and Silvia speak. She sounds far more like the Lylian page in V.ii., when Sebastian makes a half dozen barbed jests at Thurio's expense during a dialogue between Proteus and Thurio.[8] The opening exchange, in which Sebastian mocks Thurio in asides, is typical of the impudent Lylian servant:

Thu. Sir Proteus, what says Silvia to my suit?
Pro. O, sir, I find her milder than she was,
And yet she takes exceptions at your person.
Thu. What? that my leg is too long?
Pro. No, that it is too little.

Thu. I'll wear a boot, to make it somewhat rounder.
Jul. But love will not be spurr'd to what it loathes.

(ll. 1–7)

To whom does Julia/Sebastian address this remark? As Proteus gives no indication that he hears Sebastian's jests, eighteenth-century editors are probably correct in labeling this line and subsequent jests as asides. As asides, these lines resemble the familiar mockery of the cheeky page and invite the spectators to ridicule the inept and foolish Thurio, just as Speed had earlier invited them to join in mocking Proteus and Valentine.

Shakespeare found only the slightest hint of a Lylian page in Montemayor's *Diana,* his principal source.[9] There, when Felismena enters the service of Don Felix as a page named Valerius, she displays neither the mocking wit nor the bold sauciness of the Lylian page. These characteristics are lightly sketched in the other young male servant in the narrative, Don Felix's page Fabius. As Valerius, Felismena never plays the cheeky page, and neither she nor Fabius ever confront Don Felix with wit, irony, parody, or ridicule. In adapting Montemayor's narrative for the stage, Shakespeare eliminated Fabius, expanded the role of audacious servant, and assigned it to Julia.

As Sebastian, a theatrically constructed Lylian page, Julia utters the usual wisecracks and asides and so becomes what Weimann called a "comic chorus," with whom spectators felt a special rapport. Modern spectators might understand these asides as a kind of ventriloquism, whereby Julia is now free to be witty in ways not permitted by her earlier feminine identity, free to express her contempt of a foolish male suitor. For Elizabethan spectators, the pert audacity that Julia seems to discover in her disguised identity as Sebastian also underscored the boy actor's resumption of his own identity (or whatever version of that identity he used to play a cheeky page). At the same time, this complex of boy actor and Lylian page inhabited the same body known as Julia in the world of the play, permitting if not encouraging a lively interplay between the various identities of play-boy, female character, and male disguise. This interplay, I suggest, generated sufficient vibrancy to enliven and deepen the multilayered figure of actor/Julia/Sebastian and thus to endow the character with an illusion of depth, an effect quite different from the more direct representation of Julia's growth often achieved by actresses.

However achieved, an illusion of Julia's depth or growth is desirable, for the Julia we first meet seems incapable of the resolute action assigned to her in reclaiming Proteus at the end of the play. In I.ii, her scene with Lucetta, she is herself the object rather than the agent of ridicule. As in *Diana,* she denies her eagerness to read Proteus's letter, even tears it up, but then fondles and kisses the pieces, all the time protesting to Lucetta, her maid, mostly in formulaic exchanges of one line or less, that she has absolutely no interest in men, Proteus, or love letters, protests that she twice rescinds in soliloquies when Lucetta is offstage. The comedy is achieved *at* Julia's expense by mocking her childish refusal to admit her affection for Proteus. In her farewell scene with Proteus in the first eighteen lines of II.ii., she has three very short speeches, exchanges rings and embraces with him, and dutifully obeys his command to "answer not" by leaving the stage in silence.

Julia begins to change in her next scene, II.vii, as soon as the idea of male disguise is broached. By reflexively alluding to the play-boy, the prospect of male disguise added a dimension of boldness and vivacity to the characterization, enabling Julia to take control of the conversation with her maid. She asks Lucetta for advice about "How with my honor I may undertake / A journey to my loving Proteus" (ll. 6–7) but rejects her servant's lukewarm response to the project, so that Lucetta is reduced to asking questions while Julia counsels herself:

> *Luc.* But in what habit will you go along?
> *Jul.* Not like a woman, for I would prevent
> The loose encounters of lascivious men:
> Gentle Lucetta, fit me with such weeds
> As may beseem some well-reputed page.
>
> (ll. 39–43)

The discussion of male disguise in II.vii has no counterpart in *Diana,* for Montemayor has Felismena simply announce her determination "to adventure that, which I think never any woman imagined; which was to apparell my selfe in the habit of a man."[10] Considering how many narratives had used the motif, Montemayor is being playfully ironic in making Felismena proud of the originality of her plan, but the irony is at her expense and the mention of disguise does not embolden her as it does Julia.

Like the discussion of male clothing, the discussion of Julia's hair alludes to the presence of all three layers of gender identity:

Luc. Why, then your ladyship must cut your hair.
Jul. No, girl, I'll knit it up in silken strings,
With twenty odd-conceited true-love knots:
To be fantastic may become a youth
Of greater time than I shall show to be.

(ll. 44–48)

Although there is some evidence that long hair was sometimes worn by
men in the period,[11] Lucetta assumes that a woman disguising herself as
a page must wear short hair. The discussion of hairstyle probably called
attention to the several planes of illusion involved in the theatrical convention by reminding Elizabethan spectators that a boy actor, presumably with relatively short hair, was wearing a wig in order to represent
a woman's longer hair. The hair or the wig was then pinned or tied up
(rather than cut) to look like a fantastic youth's coiffure and possibly
concealed under a hat. The discussion also foreshadows the possibility
of staging the undisguising through the falling or sudden release of Julia's
hair, as in narratives by Ariosto, Tasso, and Spenser, although neither
the dialogue nor the stage directions in the folio text explicitly require it.
The dialogue continues to underscore the presence of the boy actor by
referring to such details of male attire as the codpiece that will go with
Julia's breeches. Any stress Julia places on the first syllable of "mannerly"
would have had a particular resonance on the Elizabethan stage, where
both girls were played by boy actors. This passage is the first of those
moments when the boy actor emerges from the mimetic surface of the
play—even before Julia dons her disguise—and it begins, indirectly, to
add an illusion of depth to Julia's character. In modern productions,
actresses find more direct ways to deepen Julia's character, suggesting
greater psychological complexity than the text itself indicates.

    As in Montemayor, Shakespeare has Julia reflect not only on the
immodesty of donning male garb, but also on the propriety of pursuing
a man: "But tell me, wench, how will the world repute me / For under-
taking so unstaid a journey?" (ll. 59–60). This shift at the end of the scene
away from discussion of male attire (and hence away from reflexive
allusiveness to the male actor) may well have intensified the pathos of
Julia's plight. Julia's risk might have been reinforced by the association
of female cross-dressing with prostitution in the world outside the play,
a world in which "lascivious men" also figured prominently. The pathos
underscored by her risk and its social resonance was deepened by the

audience's knowledge that she was risking her reputation to follow a man who has already announced his decision to be unfaithful. Julia's vulnerability to Proteus's duplicity is further accented by Lucetta's ominous wish, "Pray heav'n he prove so [far from fraud] when you come to him!" (l. 79).

When Julia reappears in IV.ii, she wears the male attire she described in II.vii, but she must somehow signal to the audience that she is Julia when she first comes onstage with the host or at some point early in their dialogue. A modern actress can use some of her feminine "Julia" mannerisms and then switch to playing the page with exaggerated and patently artificial boyishness, as many do. But a boy actor would probably have done the reverse, signaling that he is Julia through whatever feminine mannerisms he devised to establish himself in a female role, and then switching abruptly to the equally constructed but seemingly more "natural" persona of a pert and witty boy. Although everything actors do on stage is artificial, audiences are inclined to accept as "natural"— that is, unconstructed, spontaneous—behavior that accords with their notions of the performer's authentic personality. In our own day, the entertainment industry devotes enormous expense and effort to devising and publicizing such offstage personas. In Shakespeare's day, as I argue, the reflexive use of male disguise called attention to the presence of the male performer, to his performance persona, and to his virtuosity in negotiating the separate layers of gender identity.

Theatrical Vibrancy vs. Narrative Reflexivity

Shakespeare's theatrical tactics achieve sharper focus if we contrast them with Montemayor's narrative techniques. The tale of Felix and Felismena is embedded in the main story of *Diana* and merges with the narrative frame: in the course of their travels, three young women meet a mysterious and nameless Amazonian shepherdess; as she entertains them with a story told in the third person, she suddenly reveals that she herself is the heroine of her own tale, "the wofull woman that tels you her mishaps" (1:230). Whereas Montemayor makes his cross-dressed heroine oscillate between inserted tale and overall narrative frame, Shakespeare creates opportunities for the performer to move in and out of various layers of gender identity.

For example, in the scene where a concealed Julia sees and hears Proteus serenading Silvia, Julia assumes the role of onstage commentator, a position of enormous theatrical power. She cryptically alludes to her real identity in speeches to the host, as well as in three asides during Proteus's wooing, two of them commenting on her alleged "death." Julia's presence, theatrically amplified, now ironically undercuts Proteus's pursuit of Silvia, for he is unaware that the girl he left behind and now plans to betray is onstage, disguised, and watching him. He seems likely to fall victim to her intrigue, but not immediately, for it is too early for her to claim the victory she is now poised to achieve. The scene ends by temporarily restraining her theatrical power, that is, by stressing the pathetic aspect of the character's plight. Instead of emphasizing the male actor/Lylian page, Shakespeare evokes the docile, confused, and forlorn girl we saw earlier, for whom the revelations of Proteus's deceitfulness have created "the longest night / That e'er I watch'd, and the most heaviest" (IV.ii.139–40).

In IV.iv, Shakespeare heightens the theatrical vibrancy by encouraging the performer to shift between layers of gender identity, rather than remain confined in the role of the female character. Still disguised as the page Sebastian, Julia briefly discusses with Proteus the terms of the page's employment, a conversation absent from *Diana*. Proteus turns to Launce and becomes the butt of a sixteen-line comic turn about the lost dog, before the clown leaves the stage. He then speaks to Sebastian, as if trying to return the play to its mimetic surface.

At this moment in *Diana*, there is no inserted popular clowning and perhaps greater emotional complexity than in the play, as Don Felix begins to confide in his new page, Valerius, much as Orsino does with Cesario in *Twelfth Night*. In *Two Gentlemen*, Proteus is more brusque: within a few lines he instructs his page to deliver a letter and a ring, and to bring back Silvia's portrait. But Shakespeare makes Julia complicate the scene dramatically and theatrically when instead of simply obeying her master's orders she expresses pity for his first love, none other than Julia herself:

> *Jul.* It seems you lov'd not her, [to] leave her token:
> She is dead, belike?
> *Pro.*   Not so; I think she lives.
> *Jul.* Alas!
> *Pro.* Why dost thou cry "alas"?
> *Jul.*   I cannot choose
> But pity her.

Pro.   Wherefore shouldst thou pity her?
Jul. Because methinks that she lov'd you as well
As you do love your lady Silvia:
She dreams on him that has forgot her love;
You dote on her that cares not for your love.
'Tis pity love should be so contrary;
And thinking on it makes me cry "alas."

                                                    (IV.iv.74–84)

In *Diana,* Valerius also reminds Don Felix of his previous love (Felismena herself) and also speaks an aside to her to the same effect, but in
Two Gentlemen the play of voices and gender identities is more rapid.
The involuntary "alas!" greatly amplified through discussion and repetition, represents the pathos of Julia but is denied, more or less unsuccess-
fully, by Julia's attempt to conceal her identity, so that traces of Julia,
perhaps only in the spectators' minds, are heard even in the voice of
Sebastian, in quicksilver shifts of tone that a skilled performer would
have made with precision.[12]

The scene continues to alternate between stressing the pathos of the
character's situation and underscoring the performer's virtuosity. The
character's plight rather than the performer's presence is accentuated by
the long self-pitying soliloquy midway through IV.iv, in which she
articulates her confusion, but multiple identities of heroine and page (and
performer) come into play once again when Silvia comes onstage. It is
Sebastian who offers the letter and the ring to Silvia and asks for the
promised portrait, just as it is Sebastian who expresses Julia's gratitude
to Silvia for refusing: "She thanks you" (l. 138), which cannot be a full
aside to the audience because of Silvia's next line, "What say'st thou?"
(l. 139). Shakespeare then proceeds to juggle Julia's various identities in
a series of questions and answers. Silvia asks the page if he knows Julia
and receives the reply, "Almost as well as I do know myself" (l. 143).
In answer to a question about Julia's complexion, Sebastian replies that
Julia "did neglect her looking-glass, / . . . threw her sun-expelling mask
away," lost her usual red-and-white coloring, and "now . . . is become
as black as I" (ll. 152–56). The last question, "How tall was she?" (l.
157) evokes still more self-referentiality. Julia's first three words—
"About my stature"—supply the factual information requested, but
Shakespeare elaborates the reply with a mass of theatrically reflexive
detail, including an inserted miniaturized sketch of the play-boy:

for at Pentecost,
When all our pageants of delight were play'd,
Our youth got me to play the woman's part,
And I was trimm'd in Madam Julia's gown,
Which served me as fit, by all men's judgments,
As if the garment had been made for me;
Therefore I know she is about my height.

(ll. 158–64)

Here the speech might easily have ended, but Shakespeare goes on to add still other dimensions of theatrical reflexivity:

And at that time I made her weep agood,
For I did play a lamentable part.
Madam, 'twas Ariadne passioning
For Theseus' perjury and unjust flight;
Which I so lively acted with my tears
That my poor mistress, moved therewithal,
Wept bitterly; and would I might be dead
If I in thought felt not her very sorrow.[13]

(ll. 165–72)

Once the boy heroine/female page recalls playing a woman, the jilted Ariadne, the speech can no longer be confined to the world of the play. The recollected performance of an imaginary boy playing a mythical victim of male duplicity fuses with Julia's performance as Sebastian and with the boy actress's as Julia. It was so moving it brought tears to the eyes both of the fictive actor, the page Sebastian, and the imagined spectator, a fictive Julia. But the real Julia is also present and, having been forsaken by Proteus as Ariadne was by Theseus, may now be in or on the verge of tears, as so may the boy actor—all in answer to a simple question about a girl's height.

By examining the comparable moment in *Diana*, we can see how Shakespeare's focus on multiple identities enhances theatrical vibrancy. In *Diana*, when Celia asks Valerius if he knows Felismena, he says yes, adds a bitter parenthetical aside—"although not so well as it was needfull for me to have prevented so many mishaps" (1:243)—and then explains to Celia that they were neighbors. Montemayor makes Celia ask about

Don Felix's former love twice more, but he keeps focus on Celia's passion for Valerius, a passion that eventually leads to her death.

Shakespeare keeps the spotlight on Sebastian. He gives Silvia none of Celia's passion for her wooer's emissary (or perhaps shelved it until *Twelfth Night*). He consolidates Silvia's questions and elaborates the answers supplied by Sebastian, whom the audience knew was Proteus's abandoned beloved, Julia. Regardless of gender, any performer in the role will find ways of oscillating between cheeky page and forlorn maiden, but in original performances Sebastian's self-referential pertness also highlighted the presence of the male actor and so added another dimension to the intricate speech just discussed. In short, Shakespeare discovered that he could use reflexive effects to create theatrical vibrancy and thereby to amplify the power of Julia as a character, overlaying her movements in and out of disguise with the movements of the boy actor back into and then out of his own male identity.

As a result of these reflexive effects, the soliloquy that follows the interview with Silvia, unlike the one that precedes it, permits Julia to speak with unprecedented self-assurance about her own beauty: "What should it be that he respects in her / But I can make respective in myself" (IV.ii.194–95). She also addresses Silvia's portrait in tones of vengeful anger not heard previously: "by Jove I vow, / I should have scratch'd out your unseeing eyes, / To make my master out of love with thee" (ll. 203–5).

As we have already seen, Julia virtually loses herself in her disguise as Lylian page in V.ii., her next scene after meeting Silvia, where Sebastian serves as choric commentator on Thurio's doltishness. Foreshadowing her successful intervention at the end of the play, Shakespeare makes her resume her own voice at the end of the scene in another soliloquy of resolute assertiveness: "And I will follow, more to cross that love [Proteus's for Silvia] / Than hate for Silvia, that is gone for love" (ll. 55–56).

Theatrical Vibrancy and Characterization: The Ending

In the final scene Shakespeare makes Julia discharge the theatrical power she has been building up in order to direct the events of the play toward an ending appropriate for romantic comedy. She is still in cross-gender disguise, unlike Felismena, who at this point in *Diana* had assumed the guise of a shepherdess. Julia enters as Sebastian, with or after Proteus and Silvia, and utters one line, superficially in the style of the cheeky page who can twist someone else's words into a witty rejoinder: Silvia's rebuke of Proteus—"By *thy approach* thou mak'st *me* most unhappy"—is the cue for Julia's "And *me,* when he *approacheth* to *your* presence" (ll. 31–32; emphases added). But if the verbal dexterity belongs to the smart-aleck page, the sentiment is Julia's alone. She remains silent for fifty lines until the sighlike line, also Julia's—"O me unhappy!" (l. 84)—which seems to precede her falling down and losing consciousness, as one might infer from Proteus's and Valentine's expressions of urgent concern: "Look to the *boy,*" "Why, *boy!* Why, *wag!* how now? what's the matter? Look up; speak" (ll. 86–87; emphasis added).

When Julia is played by a woman, she usually swoons and then languishes. But the text endows Julia with greater resiliency than the word *swoon* implies. It does not exist in the folio text and was first supplied in a stage direction by Pope and retained by many modern editors, evidently extrapolating from the phrase "look up." Performers or directors might make sense out of "look up" by having Julia lower her head or her gaze, but a swoon implies a state of abject helplessness.[14] But if Julia continues to play the cheeky boy rather than the forlorn cast-off maiden, then her swoon or whatever she does to attract attention must seem a deliberate stratagem to divert Proteus's attention away from Valentine and Silvia and back to herself.[15]

With similar deliberateness, Julia hands Proteus the wrong ring, that is, the same ring he had given to her when they parted rather than the one he asked Sebastian to deliver to Silvia. This "error," which some commentators see as accidental, gives her an opportunity to reveal her identity, to prevent Proteus from accepting Silvia as a token of forgiveness from Valentine, and to replace this idealized but sterile if not fatuous male bonding with two heterosexual unions.[16] It is Julia's moment of greatest power, a moment when the presentational and mimetic facets of his/her identity, the male actor's performance persona and the female character, coalesce to enable the boy heroine to seize control of the play.

Montemayor achieved a similar effect in *Diana* when Felismena changed from a character in an inserted tale to the narrator-heroine of her own story. Within her tale, she played a female page who displayed abject self-pity instead of adopting the cheeky Lylian mode. Her tale completed, Felismena resumed her role of militant shepherdess in order to rescue an unknown knight from three assailants. When this lone knight turned out to be none other than Don Felix, Felismena fell into "such a traunce she could scarce speake" (1:250). Don Felix, weakened by loss of blood but also stunned by Felismena's revelation of herself and stung by remorse, also fell "downe in a swoune at faire *Felismenas* feete" (1:251).

Whereas Montemayor could shift from one narrative plane to another, Shakespeare devised the theatrical equivalent. In *Two Gentlemen,* the precise moment of the heroine's emergence from her disguise must occur just before, during, or just after the second of her next two lines, where Sebastian explains how he came to have the ring Proteus gave to Julia and then becomes Julia before the speech is done:

> And Julia herself did give it me,
> And Julia herself hath brought it hither.
>
> (ll. 98–99)

On the modern stage, the actress—often still lying down to recover from her swoon—usually loses a cap or has someone else remove it, in the process releasing her hair, or else she unties some of the "twenty odd-conceited true-love knots" that she used to "knit it up in silken strings" (II.vii.45–46), so that a sudden and perhaps involuntary display of physical evidence of femininity becomes the means of revelation. The repetition of the phrase "Julia herself" invites a far more purposeful manner of revelation, not only under her own tight control but timed for maximum theatrical effect for both offstage and onstage audiences. The speech that follows is similarly bolstered by its rhetorical force:

> Behold her that gave aim to all thy oaths,
> And entertain'd 'em deeply in her heart.
> How oft hast thou with perjury cleft the root?
> O Proteus, let this habit make thee blush!
> Be thou asham'd that I have took upon me
> Such an immodest raiment—if shame live
> In a disguise of love!
> It is the lesser blot, modesty finds,
> Women to change their shapes than men their minds.
>
> (ll. 101–9)

If Julia is still lying down or is somewhat dazed, the speech may come across as a self-pitying whine, perhaps even a devious attempt to win Proteus by evoking his guilt. But the speech seems too forceful for such a delivery and requires more energy than such a weakened Julia might credibly muster. Although it is sometimes delivered today as a guilt-mongering whimper, this nine-line speech begins by extending Julia's moment of self-revelation ("Behold . . ."), becomes an accusation, and then shifts the responsibility for her donning male garb onto Proteus. He should blush for the shame of her donning "immodest raiment," a trivial fault compared with male inconstancy. With enough momentum behind it, the speech could also dazzle Proteus with Julia's presence and convince spectators that he truly does find her beauty no less than Silvia's, now that he sees her with "a constant eye." When Julia's revelation lacks power, Proteus's repentance seems motivated by a bad conscience. His words ring false and undermine our pleasure in their reunion and our confidence in its stability. In such productions, Julia herself often becomes no more than a token of male friendship, an "exchangeable, perhaps symbolic, property for the primary purpose of cementing the bonds of men with men."[17] On the Elizabethan stage, Julia's power in large part came from the theatrical vibrancy engineered by the reflexive allusion to the male actor and by his oscillation between multiple layers of gender identity.

After Julia reveals her identity and chastises Proteus, she joins hands with him as they exchange oaths and then falls silent for the remaining fifty-odd lines of the play. Although she is still in male attire, or mostly so, she is strongly identified as Proteus's Julia to the audience and to the other characters onstage, except for the duke, a late arrival in the scene. When Valentine asks "your Grace" what he thinks "of this page," the duke's answer may suggest puzzlement, wariness, or a shrewd guess: "I think the boy hath grace in him; he blushes" (l. 163). The blush is Julia's this time rather than Proteus's and confirms her feminine modesty, even as the duke's line renews the reflexive stress on the male performer. We do not know if it was to be imagined by the audience or supplied by the play-boy's technical virtuosity, nor do we know enough about Elizabethan usage of stage makeup to determine whether a performer's blush, if it could be summoned on cue, would have been perceptible. Whether seen or imagined, the blush allows the play-boy to ratify the restoration of Julia's femininity and the disappearance of the pert Lylian page, and in so doing to exhibit his own technical prowess.

Surprise vs. Theatrical Vibrancy: Fletcher's
The Night Walker

To a playwright in the early or middle 1590s, the cheeky servant may have seemed the most obvious role for a heroine to adopt when she donned male disguise, for the role had already been developed by earlier dramatists for male pages and coincided nicely with the imagined personality of the boy actor. Shakespeare used it extensively again only once, in *As You Like It,* where, as we shall see in chapter 6, he devised even more intricate interplay between the boy actress, the romantic heroine, and the cheeky page than he had in *Two Gentlemen.* Flashes of the cheeky page, rather than sustained use, occur in *Twelfth Night,* as when Viola, entering Olivia's house as Orsino's emissary, bristles at the mocking treatment accorded to her and, by extension, to her master. Other dramatists of the period were quick to adopt, vary, and extend the idea, among them John Fletcher, who had already written other kinds of plays about heroines in male disguise by the time he came to write *The Night Walker* (Queen's Revels? 1611?).[18]

Fletcher began writing plays around 1607 in collaboration with Beaumont and started to write for the King's Men around 1609, while Shakespeare was still the company's chief poet. Like his earlier play, *Philaster, The Night Walker* relies on a surprise revelation of the female page's female identity. That is, the audience is not explicitly told that the witty page is a disguised heroine until the end of the play, although experienced playgoers would have caught the broad hints in that direction.

The first of many such hints comes in the opening dialogue, when for no apparent reason Jack Wildbrain suddenly asks his fellow gallant, Tom Lurcher, "Where's thy young sister?" Lurcher's reply is remarkable for its lack of brotherly concern:

I know not where she is, she is not worth caring for,
She has no wit. . . .
Shee's farre enough I hope, I know not where,
Shee's not worth caring for, a sullen thing,
Shee wod not take my counsell *Jacke,* and so
I parted from her.[19]

When Wildbrain defends her as "a pretty Girle" and asks if "old *Algripe*
love[d] her?" Lurcher is vague and dismissive: "Some such thing, / But
he was too wise to fasten; let her passe" (I.i.67–69). As we learn later
on, Alathe Lurcher was contracted to marry Justice Algripe, who broke
off the agreement and now plans to marry Maria, the play's other heroine.

Before the scene is over, a youth referred to only as "Boy" engages
Lurcher in conversation. Like Bellario in *Philaster*, the boy first presents
himself as a sad and mournful victim:

> A poore distressed boy, Sir,
> Friendlesse and comfortlesse, that would entreate
> Some charitie and kindnesse from your worship.
>
> (I.ii.8–10)

Unlike Philaster, Lurcher feels no compassion for this sorrowful waif.
He finds him to be "a pretty Boy, but of too milde a breeding, / Too
tender and too bashfull a behaviour" (ll. 14–15). Fletcher then calls attention to the theatrical fashion of cheeky servants by having Lurcher agree
to hire the boy only if he promises to be dishonest and impudent. Lurcher, who has lost his lands to the same Justice Algripe who jilted his
sister, now lives by "following the Plow" (I.i.5), his euphemism for
stealing, and so interviews the boy to see if he is guileful and audacious
enough to make a worthy accomplice:

> *Lur.* I love a bold and secure confidence,
> An impudence that one may trust, . . .
> Oh mainely, mainely, I would have my boy impudent,
> Outface all truth, yet doe it piously. . . .
>   *Boy.* I scorne all hazard, . . .
> I have a thousand faces to deceive, . . .
> And impudence no brasse was ever tougher.
>
> (I.ii.22–61)

At that Lurcher hires the boy, now called "Snap," who soon satisfies
Lurcher's criterion for sauciness and larceny. He proves adept at disguise
and at one point enters carrying a gown and false beard obtained "by
my acquaintance with / The Players boyes" (IV.i.109–10), as he reflexively puts it. So talented is the boy at intrigue that by act IV he has taken

over the main role as intriguer from his master. Snap launches an independent scheme against Algripe, disguising himself as an angel in order to persuade the justice to repent his past sins of "taking forfeit of his [Lurcher's] land" (IV.v.63) and "break[ing] thy solemne vow, / Made once to that unhappy maide [herself], that weepes / A thousand teares a day for thy unkindnesse" (ll. 69–71).

Earlier, Snap had surprised Lurcher by knowing of Algripe's "vow made to another" (II.v.55). Fletcher underscored the boy's possession of this piece of information first by having Lurcher ask him how he had acquired it and then by providing a clearly makeshift response—"I overheard the women talke to night on't"—and then by having him abruptly change the subject—"But now lets lose no time sir" (ll. 68–69). A spectator who had encountered only a fraction of the many earlier narratives and plays with female pages would have had no trouble decoding hints. When the boy wrests control of the intrigue from his master in act IV and suddenly in a soliloquy remembers "my owne state" (IV.ii.3), most spectators would have understood this seemingly cryptic phrase to refer to Alathe's status as Algripe's jilted fiancée.

At the end of the play, when the reformed Algripe returns Lurcher's land to the prodigal gallant, the justice also wishes to make restitution to Alathe: "But where's thy sister? if she live I am happy, / Though I conceale our contract" (V.ii.134–35). Lurcher still has no idea of her whereabouts: "I hope she lives, but where, I cannot tell sir" (l. 139). At that moment, Snap reveals his true identity—"Even here, and please you sir" (l. 139)—accompanying the words, one presumes, with some correlative physical gesture like removing a hat or loosening hair. Alathe seems content with the reborn Algripe, who offers to embrace her even in her male attire—"*Nay, let me kisse thee in these cloathes*" (l. 149; emphasis added)—despite some apparent reluctance on her part or possibly his. Julia's retention of male clothing at the end of *Two Gentlemen* is treated as a joke on the newly arrived duke, but the kind of attention devoted to Alathe's male garb suggests greater anxiety over the layering of gender identities.

The surprise ending may explain some of the differences between *Two Gentlemen* and *The Night Walker*. Whereas spectators first see Julia, like all of Shakespeare's cross-dressed heroines, before she assumes male identity, they see nothing of Alathe in her own person until the play's closing moments. Since Snap's true identity had not been formally disclosed, the boy actor was not required to shift between heroine and cheeky page, as he was in *Two Gentlemen,* unless in production *The Night Walker* contained unscripted flashes of Alathe. Shakespeare had the play-boy cast as Julia begin by representing her in her feminine identity and provided opportunities for it to emerge even after she became Sebastian. The use of surprise enables Fletcher to underscore the page's aggressive wit *before* she is known to be a woman. After her emergence as a woman in the play's final moments, she becomes a retrospective foil for Maria, the play's more conventional romantic heroine. Maria too tries disguise, as a Welshwoman, but Snap sees through it and contrives to reunite her with her beloved.

More like a heroine of a problem play than a romantic comedy, Alathe is quite willing to marry the unsuitable Algripe, though Fletcher might easily have paired her off with Lurcher's friend Wildbrain, who had earlier admired her. Unlike Julia, Alathe serves her brother rather than the man she loves and is free to torment and humiliate Algripe, which she seems to do with glee, albeit for his own good. Among his many sins is misogyny, and at one point he sends out a servant to buy the latest antifemale tracts and ballads. Posing as an itinerant bookseller, Snap infiltrates Algripe's household, distracts the servants by distribut-ing misogynist material, binds and gags the justice, and rifles his papers in search of incriminating legal documents. Making Algripe a jilting woman hater licenses Alathe's hard-edged impudence but raises the question of just how audacious a girl might be or pretend to be and still emerge as a romantic heroine before dwindling into a wife. The question probably had particular urgency around 1611, when some women were perceived as threatening male authority by wearing selected articles of masculine attire. Linda Woodbridge categorizes *The Night Walker* with a number of other plays performed around 1610 that were sympathetic to aggressive women, a sympathy that she believes was due to the in-creasing economic influence of female spectators.[20] In several of these plays, stage misogynists receive their comeuppance at the hands of women, as in *The Night Walker,* but the coldly unromantic pairing of Alathe with Algripe also suggests that Fletcher may be scapegoating the stage misogynist in order to conceal a deeper, subtler misogyny, punish-ing Alathe for the insubordinate impudence that Snap adopted at Lur-cher's prompting.

In theory, concealing the true gender of a page created the opportu-nity for a surprise revelation toward the end of a play. But dramatists frequently hinted at the female gender of the mysterious young male

servant, as Fletcher did in *The Night Walker*. It is doubtful that many
spectators were actually surprised, for some would no doubt have heard
about the effect from earlier spectators, would have recognized female
impersonators on the stage, as Heywood claims, or would have perceived a pattern familiar from narrative literature, if not from other
plays. As Muriel Bradbrook put it, the delayed revelation of a page's
true gender had become so common in Jacobean disguised-heroine plays
that "by this time any theatrical page might be assumed to be a woman
in disguise."[21] Surprising spectators may have been less important to
dramatists than making them wonder about a page's gender, for it would
have been very difficult to tell the difference between a boy played by a
boy actor and a boy who later turned out to be a girl or woman who had
disguised herself as a boy. Shakespeare never sought to surprise or puzzle
his spectators over the gender of a page, for he always informed the
audience when his heroines were about to don male disguise. Fletcher,
by contrast, sometimes exploited the ambiguity of the page's gender,
not only in *The Night Walker* and *Philaster* but more ironically in *The
Honest Man's Fortune* (Lady Elizabeth's, 1613?), where he led the audience to anticipate a surprise revelation and even seemed to end the play
in that fashion, only to reaffirm that the boy was, after all, a boy.

In *The Honest Man's Fortune*, the relationship of gender to sexuality
is deliberately tangled, so that the presence of the play-boy is stressed
not only by the female page in male disguise but by the suggestion of
homosexual relations between boys and adult men. Although Montague's devoted page, Veramour, shows flashes of the Lylian page's
impudence, more theatrical interest is aroused by the ambiguity of his
gender. Earlier the dolt Laverdine thought he had seen through the
page's disguise: "this is a disguised whore" (249), and when Veramour
refuses to sleep with him, he feels his suspicions are confirmed: "I know
by that 'tis a woman" (250). Veramour confesses: "believe it Sir, indeed
I am a woman" (257), and Laverdine finally produces her, in feminine
attire and apparently restored to her feminine identity:

> *Lav*. This is the Gentlewoman.
> *Mont*. 'Tis my Page, Sir.
> *Ver*. No Sir, I am a poor disguis'd Lady,
> That like a Page have followed you full long for love godwot. . . .
> *Mont*. It may be so, and yet we have lain together,
> But by my troth I never found her, Lady.[22]

The spectators, no less than the characters, would surely have recognized a familiar pattern, and Fletcher even has Veramour reflexively underscore that familiarity: "I took example by two or three Plays, that methought Concerned me" (277).

But in a final twist, Veramour turns out not to be a gentlewoman but a boy bride, to the surprise of the other characters and perhaps even to those spectators who recognized the play-boy as one who often played women. The play arouses the expectation that a female character driven to conceal her gender and identity would emerge and that she would evade pursuit by the gull Laverdine in order to marry her beloved Montague. The page eventually escapes from Laverdine by revealing that he is a boy, a revelation that also cancels any notion of marriage to Montague, but only after agreeing to play the woman to put an end to gull's relentless pursuit, "to say as hee would have me," as the manuscript version puts it.[23]

Unlike the duke's innocent mistaking of Sebastian's gender at the end of *Two Gentlemen,* the manuscript version of *The Honest Man's Fortune,* even more than the folio text, underscores the idea of Veramour being used as a woman, a fate commonly believed to await young male actors in adult male companies. It is not altogether clear that Laverdine, though "asham'd of my selfe" (l. 258), has entirely abandoned sexual interest in this "masculine lady" (l. 255), even now that he knows Veramour's gender.

In *Two Gentlemen* Shakespeare established the role of romantic heroine before her resuming/assuming of cross-gender disguise as a cheeky Lylian page, thus guiding the play-boy to articulate clearly differentiated gender identities. In contrast, Fletcher (and others) sometimes created interesting effects by blurring these identities, and resolving the ambiguity only in a final revelation. In cleverly parodying this tactic in *The Honest Man's Fortune,* Fletcher achieved a startling resonance with alleged homosexual practices in the world of the playhouse.

The Limitations of Cheekiness: Massinger's *The Bashful Lover*

Heroines disguised as impudent pages appear in Caroline as well as Jacobean plays, but the tone is invariably different, as can be illustrated by Massinger's *The Bashful Lover* (King's, 1636). Whereas Fletcher's *The*

Night Walker uses an urban setting replete with such trappings of city comedy as prodigal rogues, wit intrigue, legal maneuvering, and topical satire, Massinger's play recreates the courtly pastoral atmosphere of Sidney's *Arcadia,* its primary source.

Behind these tonal differences lie cultural changes. For one thing, by 1636, Blackfriars had become the principal venue of the King's Men, whose repertory for this period displays greater responsiveness to Caroline court taste than the children's troupes had shown toward the predilections of the Jacobean court.[24] In addition, by 1636, the issues of gender politics raised by the fashion of total or partial female cross-dressing had lost some of the urgency felt during the period of the *Hic Mulier* movement a decade or two earlier. It is also possible that Massinger was simply reaping the fruit of other playwrights' experimenting with cross-dressed heroines and discovered novel innovations of his own. But the direction of his technical innovation carries ideological implications, for the heroine cannot sustain her disguise as a saucy lackey beyond the second act, and when she emerges as a woman in the third act, she becomes a handmaiden to her father as he champions her cause.

Like *The Night Walker, The Bashful Lover* relies on the dramaturgy of ostensible surprise. In Massinger's play, a cheeky boy named Ascanio is revealed at the beginning of act III to be Maria, the play's second heroine. We first see Ascanio in witty repartee with Beatrice, a waiting woman to the play's main heroine, Matilda, daughter of the duke of Mantua. They are watching one of Matilda's suitors, Galeazzo, the bashful lover of the title, as he mopes about the stage in his inamorato's melancholy, while Ascanio amuses Beatrice with a running commentary on the absurdity of lovers, whose "sighs / Are like petards, and blow all up."[25] When Beatrice protests that love never "work[ed] such strange effects" on her, Ascanio replies with the pertness of Sebastian and other Lylian pages:

> True, Madam,
> In women it cannot; for when they miss th'enjoying
> Of their full wishes, all their sighs and heigh-hoes
> At the worst breed timpanies, and these are cur'd too
> With a kiss or two of their Saint, when he appears
> Between a pair of sheets: but with us men
> The case is otherwise.
>
> (I.i. 73–79)

Ascanio's use of bawdy imagery and innuendo, as well as the boy's ironic assertion of his virility, is squarely in the Lylian tradition of wise-cracking pages. Ascanio sustains the same cheeky tone with Galeazzo himself, when the bashful lover hesitates to answer Matilda's summons:

> What a lump of flesh is this! . . .
> Move faster, sluggish Camel, or I will thrust
> This goad in your breech: Had I such a promising beard,
> I should need the reins, not spurs.
>
> (I.i.182–90)

And when Galeazzo expresses his fear of offending Matilda by looking at her, Ascanio's comment, evidently an aside to Beatrice or the audience, is in the same mocking spirit:

> A flat Eunuch!
> To look on her? I should desire my self
> To move a little further.
>
> (I.i.209–11)

Thus far, the only difference between Ascanio and other Lylian pages is his boasting or mock boasting of his own virility, and Massinger here drops no hints that this saucy lackey will be revealed to be a woman.

Such hints do come in the next scene, however, when, as the stage direction stipulates, the page inexplicably "Swouns" (I.ii.8), evidently at the sight of Alonzo, the Tuscan ambassador. In the following scene, Matilda and her waiting women discuss Ascanio's swoon, this one clearly authentic rather than calculated. They also recall the page's "witty sweetness," remarking that the cheeky servant occasionally displayed a tenderness and vulnerability and sometimes even, like Viola, mentioned a sister mysteriously wounded by love:

> *Beatrice.* . . . I have observ'd him
> Waggishly witty; yet sometimes on the sudden
> He would be very pensive, and then talk
> So feelingly of love, as if he had
> Tasted the bitter sweets of't.
> *1 Woman.*   He would tell too

A pretty tale of a sister that had been
Deceiv'd by her Sweetheart; and then weeping swear
He wonder'd how men could be false.

(II.i.17–24)

The women's reflections are pivotal, for they mark Ascanio's modula-
tion from a bold and sassy servant into another kind of "female page,"
the frail and melancholy waif.

Ascanio is next seen on the battlefield, determined to serve as squire
to Galeazzo, whom he urges to fight Alonso "to revenge / A wrong to
me done" (II.ii.35–36), a wrong he does not define. He is just as secretive
a few scenes later when he pleads with his master to spare Alonzo's life:

Alas, we foolish spleenful boys would have
We know not what: I have some private reasons,
But now not to be told.

(II.iv.19–21)

To Alonzo, Ascanio refers mysteriously to "what your entertainment
was / At old *Octavio's* house," and to "one you call'd friend, / And how
you did return it" (II.iv.27–29). In attaching himself to Galeazzo, Ascanio is reminiscent of devoted squires in Renaissance epics and romances who turn out to be women following their men off to war, but
Massinger makes it clear that the page's primary emotional focus is not
on his master, Galeazzo, but upon Alonzo, the Tuscan ambassador. The
effect of these hints was to encourage spectators to suspect (1) that Ascanio is a girl who has been in love with Alonzo and (2) that she is the
daughter of one Octavio. By the 1630s, however, these same hints might
have induced experienced theatregoers to suspect an even more surprising revelation later on: that the page was in fact male. At the very least,
such suspicions and countersuspicions kept the audience on guard and
left the gender of Ascanio an open question.

That question is abruptly resolved in III.i. Massinger begins the
scene by introducing Octavio, an exiled courtier, meditating on his fall
from grace. His ruminations are interrupted when "Galeazzo [enters]
(with Ascanio in's arms)" (III.i.28) and demands succor for the "sweet
youth" (III.i.88). Helping to revive Ascanio, Octavio recognizes the
"boy" as his daughter, Maria:

I have been
Acquainted with this voice, and know the face too:
'Tis she, 'tis too apparent; O my daughter!
I mourn'd long for thy loss.

(III.i.93–96)

To take on the role of intriguer, Octavio adopts a disguise of his own, that of a friar. So concealed, he becomes Alonzo's confessor, and in IV.ii he hears, as does the audience for the first time, that Alonzo had seduced Maria and vowed to marry her:

[He] Besieg'd her Virgin-fort, in a word took it,
No vows or imprecation forgotten
With speed to marry her.

(IV.ii.82–84)

He then broke off the relationship when Octavio fell into political disfavor. Alonzo is now deeply penitent, and when he reaffirms his vow to marry Maria, she comes to him and joins her father in forgiving her beloved.

Evidently Massinger had even graver reservations than Fletcher had in *The Night Walker* about allowing his heroine the boldness of speech appropriate to a cheeky page. Indeed, despite the diminishment of Alathe at the end of the play, Fletcher allowed her considerable impudence as Snap. Massinger reverses the same sequence by introducing Ascanio as a cheeky smart aleck who then abruptly wilts into a droopy squire before forsaking male disguise in act III. From that point on, she is Maria, the dutiful daughter of a powerful father, and it is he and not Ascanio who becomes "the Ladies champion" (II.i.25), the role to which the page had previously aspired. The collapse of Ascanio's assertiveness aligns Maria with Mathilde, the more traditional heroine of the main plot, who is fought over by three suitors.

In *Two Gentlemen,* as in his other four plays with cross-dressed boy heroines, Shakespeare introduced the female character and let the audience in on her cross-gender disguise. As a result, her assumption of male identity blended with the boy actress's resumption of his own identity, particularly when the page was represented as the familiar Lylian page. Shakespeare's reflexive stress on the actor allowed his performer the flexibility, denied to the boy actresses in Fletcher's *The Night Walker* and

Massinger's *The Bashful Lover,* to oscillate between lovelorn heroine and cheeky page instead of playing those roles in separate scenes. When such oscillation was rapid, it not only spotlighted the play-boy's virtuosity but also seemed to enhance the power of the character. Unlike Massinger's Maria, Julia could take control of the world of the play at a climactic moment, while her willingness to relinquish that control was a subtle readjustment of her various layers of identity rather than Alathe's unconditional surrender to wifely subjugation or Maria's collapse into daughterly dependency.

Chapter 5

Doubling Cross-Gender Disguise:
The Merchant of Venice

Although Shakespeare gave three different types of male identity to the three heroines in his second play to use the motif of a boy heroine in male disguise, none of them became the Lylian page of *Two Gentlemen*. Multiplying the cross-dressed heroine in a single work called attention to its artificiality as a literary convention and a theatrical construction and probably made spectators more aware of something they "always knew": the female characters they accepted as mimetic illusions in the world of the play were constructed by male performers in the world of the playhouse. In Shakespeare's time, when audiences knew full well that all performers were male, even a single heroine in male disguise like Julia could function as a sign of self-referentiality. Some playwrights, such as Sharpham and Fletcher, followed Shakespeare's lead and amplified that sign by multiplying female pages. Others, such as Middleton and Dekker in *The Roaring Girl,* contrasted a conventional female page with a more original kind of cross-dressed heroine, while still other dramatists, such as Haughton and Shirley, included both a boy bride and a female page. These repetitions and contrasts announced that cross-gender disguise was more of a dramaturgical contrivance than a mimetic representation of cross-dressing practices in the world outside the playhouse. But such variations not only encouraged parodic effects but also permitted the use of different kinds of male disguise as a way of contrasting different kinds of heroines.

Early Duplication of Cross-Gender Disguise:
Lyly's *Gallathea*

One of the first English plays to duplicate cross-gender disguise was
Lyly's *Gallathea* (1583–85), performed by the Children of Paul's at court
and probably in their own private playhouse. The idea for duplication
was evidently Lyly's, for in his source (the tale of Iphis and Ianthe in
book IX of Ovid's *Metamorphoses*), only one girl is raised as a boy, and
she is transformed into a male in order to marry the other. Lyly has *both*
girls, Phillida and Gallathea, disguised as boys and then makes them fall
in love with each other but leaves open the question of which one Venus
will change into a boy.

This uncertainty preserves the symmetrical balance between the two
heroines, symmetry being as central a feature of Lyly's dramaturgy as
euphuism is of his prose style. In parallel scenes, Lyly shows that each
girl has been disguised as a boy by her father so that she will not be taken
as "the fairest and chastest virgine in all the Countrey" (I.i.42–43), who
must be sacrificed to Neptune. At the beginning of act II, Lyly brings
the two disguised heroines together. From this point, they are always
onstage at the same time and usually speak and act as mirror images of
one another. Each girl has fallen in love with the boy that the other
pretends to be and so feels trapped within her own cross-gender disguise.
In their second meeting, each one hints at her true gender, and they do
so with such success that they suspect each other of being a girl in male
disguise:

> *Phil.* Suppose I were a virgine (I blush in supposing my selfe one)
> and that under the habite of a boy were the person of a mayde, if I
> should utter my affection with sighes, manifest my sweete love by
> my salte teares, and prove my loyaltie unspotted, and my griefes
> intollerable, would not then that faire face pittie thys true hart?
> *Galla.* Admit that I were as you woulde have mee suppose that
> you are, and that I should with intreaties, prayers, othes, bribes, and
> what ever can be invented in love, desire your favour, would you
> not yeeld?
> *Phil.* Tush, you come in with "admit."
> *Galla.* And you with "suppose."
> *Phil.* (*Aside.*) What doubtfull speeches be these? I feare me he is
> as I am, a mayden.

Galla. (Aside.) What dread riseth in my minde! I feare the boy to be as I am a mayden.

(III.ii.17–31)

Continuing in the same parallel fashion, Lyly makes each girl try to deny the growing suspicion that the other is also a girl. Their confessions that they both prefer "a fonde boy" (l. 55) to any of Diana's nymphs throw the relationship into a quandary, as Phillida acknowledges in the last speech of the scene: "Come let us into the Grove, and make much one of another, that cannot tel what to think one of another" (ll. 58–59).

In their next scene, they seem to have vanquished these fears and have returned to the starting point of their relationship, each believing that the other is male. Once again they speak in parallel:

> *Phil.* I marvell what virgine the people will present, it is happy you are none, for then it would have falne to your lot because you are so fair.
> *Galla.* If you had beene a Maiden too I neede not to have feared, because you are fairer.

(IV.iv.1–5)

Their exaggerated relief suggests a strained effort to deny what they fear. Within a few lines, Phillida tells Gallathea that "I love thee as a brother, but love not me so," and Gallathea readily declares that "I cannot love as a brother" (IV.iv.12–14). Phillida then proposes for the sake of "showe" that one of them pretend to be a woman, as Rosalind will offer to do to cure Orlando of his lovesickness in *As You Like It:*

> Seeing we are both boyes, and both lovers, that our affection may have some showe, and seeme as it were love, let me call thee Mistris.

(IV.iv.15–17)

This asymmetry is of short duration and balance is quickly restored when both admit fear of attending the sacrificial rite.

Lyly is sometimes compared unfavorably to Shakespeare for preferring to manipulate his characters into intricate patterns instead of exploring their psychological states. For G. K. Hunter, who emphasizes the debate structure underlying Lyly's plays, their artistry lies in the juxtaposition of contrasting attitudes toward a central issue:

Where all the characters are arranged to imitate one another, and where the focus of interest is on the repetition and modification and rearrangement of a basic pattern of persons, we do not ask how the persons will develop individually, but how the situation can be further manipulated.[1]

In *Gallathea,* where the central debate topic is the relative superiority of love or chastity, several strands of plot serve, in Anne Lancashire's words, "to balance against one another different modes of loving."[2] The chaste and miraculously fulfilled love of the two disguised heroines is contrasted with two other plots: (1) Cupid inflames Diana's nymphs with lust for the two girls disguised as boys before he is punished by the Goddess of chastity and returned to his rightful place under the dominion of his mother, Venus; and (2) Rafe and his brothers outwit a series of pedantic dolts, but in displaying the cynical and bawdy wit typical of Lyly's pages, they also lightly suggest the impossibility of chastity as an ideal for human beings.

The complex interlacing of these plot lines is accompanied by an equally complex use of theatrical reflexivity. In choosing to double the heroine in male disguise, and also to make Cupid disguise himself as a nymph, Lyly highlights the presence of boy actors in female roles and so stresses the artificiality of his design. But at the same time, the multiple gender identities of male actors and female characters, and of male disguises in the cases of Phillida and Gallathea, create additional confusions of gender. The competing claims of love and chastity may also be perceived in terms of the tensions between homosexual desire and intense but Platonic friendship. These ambiguities of gender identity created by cross-gender casting and cross-gender disguising add poignancy to what Ellen Caldwell defines as the overriding question of the play: is there a kind of love that does not violate chastity, one that allows union with another without loss of self?[3]

From this viewpoint, there need be no contradiction between the ingenuity of Lyly's design and the urgency of the problem he is exploring. By act V, where both heroines are revealed by their fathers to be girls, sexual relationships in the play have become so tangled that they can only be resolved by the intervention of divine power, as in Ovid. Diana and Neptune propose to resolve the problem by ending what seems to them an unnatural relationship. But Lyly makes Venus, her supremacy over Cupid reestablished, approve Phillida's and Gallathea's relationship as an example of Love and Faith triumphing over Nature and Fortune. When they swear to her that their "loves [are] unspotted, begunne with trueth, continued wyth constancie, and not to bee altered tyll death," she overrules Diana and Neptune and promises to "turne one of them to be a man" (V.iii.133–40). She does not specify which one.[4] In the world of the playhouse, where both characters have always been boys, the indeterminacy of the ending echoes the love between Gallathea and Phillida before Venus's intervention transformed it into a conventionally heterosexual relationship.

Lyly's playful and sophisticated duplication of cross-gender disguise is rare for the mid-1580s and does not recur in his later works. Nor does such duplication occur in the 1590s in the first plays of adult troupes to use the heroine in male disguise, Greene's *James the Fourth* and Shakespeare's *The Two Gentlemen of Verona*.

Duplication in *The Merchant of Venice*

In writing his second play with a heroine in cross-gender disguise, Shakespeare discovered the technique of varying the motif through repetition. Shakespeare had already discovered the efficacy of replication in writing *The Comedy of Errors* (Strange's, 1591?), where he doubled Plautus's single set of twins in order to multiply opportunities for confusion. There, because such doubling is so obviously mechanical, it helps to create an atmosphere appropriate for farce, a genre requiring a world apparently governed by equally mechanical principles that nevertheless baffle characters caught up in them precisely because they are so arbitrary and rigid.[5] In adding a second and a third woman in cross-gender disguise to *The Merchant of Venice* (Chamberlain's, 1596–98),[6] Shakespeare transcended the simple duplications of farce, but used repetitions to achieve more sophisticated kinds of cross-referencing. Nerissa's disguise is part of a simultaneous shadowing or echoing of Portia's cross-gender disguise. Jessica's disguise is part of a sequential arrangement, offering an abbreviated and ironic preview, or what Joan Hartwig calls a "proleptic parody," of what is to come. Jessica's disguise as a torchbearer or page also contrasts with Portia's disguise as a much more powerful male, a highly educated and assertive doctor of the law.[7] These parallels and contrasts not only underscore the conventionality of the literary motif but also evoke awareness of the three play-boys and appreciation of their theatrical skills.

These additional cross-gender disguises do not occur in the narrative sources. Shakespeare added Nerissa's cross-gender disguise to the pound of flesh plot, novella 3.1 of Ser Giovanni's *Il Pecorone* (1378), perhaps taking a hint from Anthony Munday's *Zelauto* (1580), where both maid-servant and mistress don male disguise. Whatever its genesis, Nerissa's presence in the courtroom as clerk to Portia's "young doctor of Rome" (IV.i.153) results in the presence onstage of a second female character in male disguise. Using Nerissa's disguise as an echoing or shadow effect calls attention to the conventionality of a familiar motif, especially when the spectators have already seen another heroine—Jessica—appear in male disguise.

Jessica's disguising is also "Shakespeare's addition," as Kenneth Muir puts it,[8] to the elopement of the usurer's daughter, in number 14 of Masuccio Salernitano's *Novellino* (1476) or in Munday's *Zelauto*. Jessica's escape in "the lovely garnish of a boy" (II.vi.45) is a particularly gratuitous addition, for the plot supplies the slenderest of reasons for Jessica to disguise herself—to attend Bassanio's feast undetected by Shylock. But in fact her plans for the disguise are laid even before Shylock receives the invitation to dinner.[9] Earlier, Lorenzo tells friends he was "provided of a torch-bearer" (II.iv.23) and spoke to Gratiano of a "page's suit she hath in readiness" (II.iv.32). When we next see Jessica, in III.ii in Belmont, she seems to have resumed female attire and no subsequent mention is ever made of her having worn a page's suit when she eloped from Shylock's house. Extraneous with respect to plot, Jessica's brief appearance in male attire invites directors to make a theatrical and thematic point. The romantic quality of the cross-gender disguise was underscored by the lavish visual spectacle added to the scene in the nineteenth century, while modern productions use it to establish Jessica's vulnerability.[10]

Jessica's adoption of male disguise underscores the precariousness of her situation but does not, like Julia's or Alathe's, allow her the compensating wit of a saucy lackey. That precariousness is suggested even before Lorenzo arrives, when Gratiano and Salerio, commenting on his tardiness, suggest that their friend's "obliged faith" lacks the passion of "love's bonds new made" (II.vi.6–7). Her short exchange with Lorenzo questions the reliability of men's love for women like herself and Portia, who are "richly left." In response to Lorenzo's call, "Ho! who's within?" (II.vi.25), Jessica—located "above"—asks that he identify himself with "more certainty, / Albeit I'll swear that I do know your tongue" (ll. 26–27), evidently finding his voice alone, or perhaps his words, not sufficient basis for trust. Lorenzo answers by name and styles himself "thy love," but Jessica wonders "whether I am yours?" (ll. 29, 31). His reply, "Heaven and *thy* thoughts are witness that thou art" (l. 32; emphasis added), has a slightly evasive tone, while her action, "Here, catch this casket, it is worth the pains" (l. 33), may indicate a desire to secure Lorenzo's love by means of a self-granted dowry, an impulse repeated a few lines later in her offer to "gild myself / With some moe [*sic*] ducats" (ll. 49–50).

The scene also raises other questions about Lorenzo's commitment to Jessica. While she descends, Lorenzo expresses his love for her to Gratiano in "a figure of words" artificial enough to cast doubt on the sincerity or depth of his feelings. Whether or not Lorenzo's "On, [gentleman,] away!" includes his torchbearer, perhaps as affectionate teasing,[11] more urgent attention is directed toward his male friends and their rendezvous with Bassanio: "But come at once, / . . . we are stay'd for at Bassanio's feast . . . Our masquing mates by this time for us stay" (ll. 46–48, 59). Unlike Bassanio's constancy, Lorenzo's is never tested, although it is challenged, bitterly or in jest, in the mythological "out-nightings" that begin act V.[12]

Finally, although Jessica comments on the impropriety and possible shame of wearing male attire, she is willing to join other lovers in committing such "pretty follies" (l. 37), risking her reputation for the sake of her beloved. Wearing male attire although not yet actually in her male identity, Jessica hesitates—either banteringly or thoughtfully—at the idea:

> *Jes.* What, must I hold a candle to my shames?
> They in themselves, good sooth, are too too light.
> Why, 'tis an office of discovery, love,
> And I should be obscur'd.
> *Lor.*   So are you, sweet,
> Even in the lovely garnish of a boy.
>
>   (ll. 41–45)

Lorenzo's last words are rich in significance, for "garnish," according to the OED, can mean "outfit [or] dress," as well as "embellishment or decoration in general," although he later uses the word to disparage Launcelot's new livery or "army of good words" (III.v.65–70). In reassuring Jessica that her disguise is impenetrable enough to prevent her being shamed by discovery, Lorenzo seems also to be saying that in his eyes it embellishes her natural loveliness. In Shakespeare's day, the entire passage might also have reminded the audience that Jessica's appearance in male disguise was indistinguishable from the play-boy's resumption of his own identity. Unlike the speaker in Donne's elegy, "On His Mistres," who prefers his beloved to "Be my true Mistris still, not my faign'd Page,"[13] Lorenzo's delight in finding Jessica's female identity "obscur'd" may also have suggested to some spectators a stronger sexual interest in the play-boy than in the female character.

Jessica's vulnerability as a powerless female page highlights the more assertive version of male identity of "worthy doctor" (V.i.222) that Shakespeare and his sources assigned to Portia. Whereas most other disguised heroines serve men as youthful companions, Portia invents a role that will give her authority over the men in the play. To quote Catherine Belsey, in the guise of a "civil doctor" (V.i.210) "Portia fights Bassanio's legal battles for him—and wins."[14] Portia is also the only one of Shakespeare's heroines to adopt and relinquish male disguise "not under pressure of events from outside . . . but by her own choice of time and circumstance."[15] From the moment Portia broaches the idea of male disguise in III.iv, she reveals an energy, vitality, and playfulness that will enable her to control all relationships in the play. Whereas her counterpart in *Il Pecorone* dominates by inviting her suitors to bed and then drugging them, Portia manipulates events by the audacity and wit she displays while in male disguise, both in her legal battle with Shylock and in the ring episode that follows.

Portia in Belmont

Portia's first words in the play seem to echo Antonio's melancholic opening of the previous scene: "By my troth, Nerissa, my little body is a-weary of this great world" (I.ii.1–2). The scene goes on to explain the source of this weariness—Portia's husband will be selected by a lottery devised by her late father, who was, as Nerissa reminds her, "ever virtuous, and holy men at their death have good inspirations" (I.ii.27–28). Her only release is purely verbal—a satiric cataloging of her wooers according to national stereotypes—and is as conventional as Lucetta's catalog of Julia's suitors in I.ii of *The Two Gentlemen of Verona*. It permits

Portia to exercise her wit upon her suitors, one of whom will win her hand in accordance with her father's dictates. The mood is abruptly changed by Nerissa's innocent or teasing inquiry as to whether or not she remembers a visitor "in your father's time, a Venetian, a scholar and a soldier?" (I.ii.112–13). Portia's reply—"Yes, yes, it was Bassanio—as I think, so was he call'd" (ll. 115–16)—contains a rush of enthusiasm followed by some sort of second thought, perhaps an attempt to appear nonchalant, even though neither the folio nor the first two quartos include the midline dash. She is reminded of her father's scheme by the servant's announcement of the departure of "four strangers" and the arrival of "a fift [sic], the Prince of Morocco" (ll. 123, 125).

Unless stage business to the contrary is added, the casket scenes themselves stress Portia's helplessness. Submissive to the will of her dead father, she has even less control over these events than does her counterpart in the tale in Gesta Romanorum, who is herself forced by the emperor to choose the vessel that will prove her a suitable bride for his son. As she tells Morocco, she is barred from the "right of voluntary choosing" and "hedg'd ... by his [her father's] wit" (II.i.16, 18). Relieved when Morocco and Aragon make wrong choices, she is hopeful at the news of Bassanio's arrival but reveals considerable anxiety at their first meeting:

> One half of me is yours, the other half yours—
> Mine own, I would say.
>
> (III.ii.16–17)

She makes an adroit recovery, for the slip is not coyness but indicates her fear that she might either lose Bassanio forever or succumb to the temptation to violate her father's will. Unable to persuade Bassanio to delay his choice, she identifies herself with "the virgin tribute paid by howling Troy / To the sea-monster," and adds a declaration of complete passivity: "I stand for sacrifice" (III.ii.56–57). Nevertheless, although some critics and directors think she steers Bassanio toward the leaden casket, her conduct during the casket scenes, according to the text, is ritualistically correct.[16]

After Bassanio's choice, many critics sense an emergence of self-assertiveness in Portia, and some find it enhanced by the planning and donning of disguise. Richard Wheeler notes a hint of Portia's power

where others see only submissiveness: "when her likeness emerges from
the lead casket, Portia, like the jinni emerging from the wonderful lamp,
puts herself in the absolute service of 'her lord, her governor, her king'"
(III.ii.165).[17] Lynda Boose describes Portia's speech as a "showpiece
demonstration of... deferential rhetoric" and notes how this "unles-
son'd girl, unschool'd, unpractic'd" (l. 159), exploits advantages of birth
and wealth to usurp male prerogatives:

> [She] deftly proceeds to appropriate the husband's role and the hus-
> band's ring vow as she endows Bassanio with all *her* worldly goods
> inside a contract to which she appends conditions for converting the
> vows of wifely obedience into a wife's "vantage" and a husband's
> ingratiated debt.[18]

Shakespeare makes Portia flex her power more explicitly when she
hears of Antonio's plight, for as several critics have pointed out, she
recognizes Antonio as her rival for Bassanio. Whereas Ansaldo (Antonio) of *Il Pecorone* is the childless godfather of Giannetto (Bassanio), who
has often asked the young man's real father to send him his godson,
Shakespeare makes him a friend of unspecified age.[19] The text is open
enough to allow one to explain Antonio's love melancholy as stemming
from one of several forms of male love: the jealousy of a homosexual
lover, the frustration of an unacknowledged homoerotic attraction, or
the possessiveness of a clinging friend.

At the very outset of the play, moreover, as Ruth Nevo has observed, marriage to Portia is presented as the way for Bassanio to clear
himself of indebtedness to Antonio.[20] Up until Antonio's reversals, he
has given Bassanio generously of his wealth and recklessly of his credit,
but his inability to pay Shylock, as he makes clear in the letter he sends
to Bassanio, forces him to make explicit demands on his friend's love.
His farewell speech in the courtroom scene is a challenge to Portia, for
in sacrificing his life for Bassanio he levies an unpayable claim on Bassanio, a gift that his living wife can neither match nor repay. Only by
saving Antonio's life can she prevent that drain on her husband's emotional capital. To do so, she must encounter her adversary not as his
female rival but as his male deliverer.

Her first move, however, is to consolidate her position as Bassanio's
wife before he returns to Venice, even if consummation must be deferred
until later, as it is not in *Il Pecorone:*

First go with me to church and call me wife,
And *then* away to Venice to your friend.

(III.ii.303–4; emphasis added)

Boose points out that Portia's entire speech, beginning with "What, no more?" (l. 298), exhibits a sudden shift in Portia's rhetorical style: "In the space of sixteen lines she uses thirteen imperative verbs and four times subjugates male options to the control of her authoritative 'shall.'"[21]

In her next scene, Portia informs Nerissa that they will see their husbands "in such a habit / That they shall think we are accomplished /With what we lack" (III.iv.60–62), a clear reminder to Elizabethan spectators that the boy actors onstage were already so equipped. Unlike Jessica's shameful but necessary disguise as Lorenzo's torchbearer, this second scheme of male disguise is first envisaged as the occasion to parody outrageous excesses of swaggering masculinity:

I'll hold thee any wager,
When we are both accoutered like young men,
I'll prove the prettier fellow of the two,
And wear my dagger with the braver grace,
And speak between the change of man and boy
With a reed voice, and turn two mincing steps
Into a manly stride; and speak of frays
Like a fine bragging youth, and tell quaint lies,
How honorable ladies sought my love,
Which I denying, they fell sick and died.
I could not do withal. Then I'll repent,
And wish, for all that, that I had not kill'd them;
And twenty of these puny lies I'll tell,
That men shall swear I have discontinued school
Above a twelvemonth. I have within my mind
A thousand raw tricks of these bragging Jacks,
Which I will practice.

(III.iv.62–78)

We never see these "raw tricks," for once Portia enters the court-room disguised as Balthazar, she conducts herself with the gravity befitting a precocious legal scholar. The speech is a release of frustration, an eruption of high spirits. From now on, Portia's wit is no longer her recompense for helplessness before men but an instrument for taking over the male domain of the law. Her ridicule of men for their competitive rivalries, as well as for exaggerating their sexual prowess, indicates the superior sophistication that will bring her victory over Shylock in the legal arena and over Antonio in the battle for her husband's deepest loyalty.

But the speech has important theatrical effects. Whether given by a boy or a woman, it invites broadly parodic vocal and bodily mannerisms, certainly at "I could not do withal," perhaps in the style of the cheeky Lylian page. Portia answers Nerissa's question, "Why, shall we turn to men?" by pointing up the sexual innuendo in "turn," a subtler joke than Julia's and Lucetta's remarks about breeches, farthingales, and codpieces. On the Elizabethan stage, the phrase had rich reflexive possibilities, for the boy actors had not yet themselves become men or had only recently done so, and so might be understood to be asking about their future as female impersonators or to be wondering, perhaps with mock horror or mock innocence, whether they should turn sexually to (toward) men. Such ironies could have transformed Portia's mimicry of swaggering virility into self-parody by a young male performer, reflexively alluding to his presence even before Portia's appearance in male disguise.[22]

Portia as Doctor Balthazar

Such reflexivity gives Portia considerable power when she actually enters the courtroom, not as the theatricalized cheeky page, but as the sober legal prodigy. As Keith Geary puts it, the boy actor discarded the mannerisms of Portia, along with female costume, donned a lawyer's gown, and simply played Balthazar, a young doctor of laws.[23] For most of the trial scene, to look only at the text, Shakespeare does seem to submerge Portia in the fused male identities of Balthazar and the young male performer. In this regard, Portia differs from Julia and Rosalind, who have numerous asides both as themselves and as their male alter egos, as well as from Viola and Imogen, who address the audience as themselves in soliloquies while in male garb. In her own person and as Balthazar, Portia has no soliloquies nor obvious asides, nor are there any unconscious reversions to female identity, "no funny, foolish slips when she plays the man; . . . no charming lapses into girlhood," as Chris Hassel puts it.[24] If Portia was physically absent on Shakespeare's stage during the courtroom scenes, the female character was nonetheless present in the minds of the spectators, just as they remained conscious (at some level) of the play-boy while Portia's female persona monopolized the stage.

Although the trial scene contains many nonverbal opportunities for the performer to oscillate between female character and male persona, Portia's absent presence is explicitly invoked only once, in a digression from the legal proceedings, a two-line remark on the willingness of husbands to sacrifice their wives. No such remark occurs in *Il Pecorone,* but Shakespeare seems to have added it not only to sharpen the rivalry between Portia and Antonio, but also to counterbalance the heavy emphasis on the male performer and male disguised persona by granting the female character a moment of rapport with the audience.

This crucial section begins with Antonio's farewell to Bassanio, which contains an explicit challenge to Portia:

> Commend me to your honorable wife,
> Tell her the process of Antonio's end,
> Say how I lov'd you, speak me fair in death;
> And when the tale is told, bid her be judge
> Whether Bassanio had not once a love.
>
> (IV.i.273–77)

Bassanio's reply is an equally passionate elevation of male love over any other value, especially marriage:

> Antonio, I am married to a wife
> Which is as dear to me as life itself,
> But life itself, my wife, and all the world,
> Are not with me esteem'd above thy life.
> I would lose all, ay, sacrifice them all
> Here to this devil, to deliver you.
>
> (ll. 282–87)

Bassanio's rhetoric includes Portia, not by her name but merely by the generic title of "wife."

Portia's response, if spoken as an aside, may have authorized the male performer to revert briefly to the mannerisms of the female character, but whether he did so or continued to play the doctor of law, the lines bring Portia's presence to the audience's mind:

> Your wife would give you little thanks for that
> If she were by to hear you make the offer.
>
> (IV.i.288–89)

The lines, which chastise Bassanio for offering to sacrifice his wife in order to free Antonio, can be spoken by Balthazar directly and perhaps only to Bassanio, but they might also be spoken aside to Nerissa, or to the audience. With or without a performer's explicit return to Portia, the lines point up Portia's presence. On the early modern stage, reminders of the female layer of identity probably underscored the virtuosity of the male performer in negotiating such rapid shifts and may thus have added depth or resonance to the character as well.

Bassanio's sacrificial offer is echoed in Gratiano's wish that his wife were in heaven to "entreat some power to change this currish Jew" (IV.i.292), just as Portia's (or Balthazar's) is echoed by Nerissa (or the clerk), who may address Gratiano directly, or offer an aside to Portia, or to the audience:

> 'Tis well you offer it behind her back,
> The wish would make else an unquiet house.
>
> (ll. 293–94)

The whole discussion is rounded off by Shylock's contemptuous reflection, "These be the Christian husbands!" and sealed shut by his demand that the court no longer "trifle time [but] . . . pursue sentence" (ll. 295–98).

This thirty-line segment, embedded in the trial scene, is the only scripted opportunity for Portia to remind the audience of her female identity. Elsewhere in the trial scene, Portia might find other occasions to exchange knowing glances with Nerissa, to mime a hurried consultation with her clerk, to allow her disguise to slip, or in other ways to play upon the audience's awareness of her layered gender identity. For example, she can react nonverbally to Bassanio's eagerness to pay double and then ten times the sum Antonio owes, offering money Portia gave him before he left Belmont. While Giannetto in *Il Pecorone* made only one offer to reimburse Shylock, Bassanio twice more offers to pay off the loan. Each time Bassanio does so, Balthazar insists that Shylock has chosen justice. From a thematic point of view, Portia's legal tactics are part of a theological debate with Shylock over the claims of mercy and justice, in which she will maneuver him into a trap created by strict interpretation of an obscure statute.[25] But the immediate effect of rejecting Bassanio's several offers to repay the loan is to bring her into direct confrontation with her husband over the use of money she bestowed upon him.

Despite the deliberate blurring of Balthazar with the boy actor, the trial scene also reminded spectators of Portia's presence, whether or not the performer chose to embellish such signals nonverbally. When a performer of either gender acknowledges such reminders, spectators usually find it amusing, enjoying their superior knowledge vis-à-vis the characters, although making the effect too overt or too frequent can tilt any scene toward farce. During the trial, Shakespeare relied less on his heroine's movement in and out of cross-gender concealment and more on subtler reminders of her presence. He used more obvious reminders of Portia's feminine identity after the conclusion of the legal proceedings, when Portia, still in male disguise, discovers that Bassanio is still emotionally bound to Antonio.

Balthazar Obtains Bassanio's Ring

However one imagines the atmosphere during the trial, a sense of relaxation and relief must follow Shylock's departure and that of "the Duke and his train" seven lines later. Bassanio and Antonio, instructed by the duke "to gratify" Balthazar, linger onstage with the lawyer and, one assumes, her clerk. At this point, in a moment of informality and intimacy, Shakespeare releases the comic, almost carnivalesque, potentialities of cross-gender disguise that had been hinted at but kept more or less bottled up during the actual legal proceedings.[26] Explicit play on Portia's multiple sexual identities begins when Bassanio addresses his wife as a "most worthy gentleman." Whether or not the performer chooses to respond to this mode of address in any way that indicates Portia's reaction, the audience's awareness of her presence would provide a strong undercurrent of irony. Such irony may arise from the casual posttrial atmosphere that encourages Bassanio to stand closer to Portia than he was when he offered to pay Shylock. Similarly, during the actual trial, the text required Portia to distribute her attention not only to him, but also to the lawbooks, to Shylock, to the duke, to Antonio, and possibly in other directions as well. In this segment of some forty lines until she leaves the court, she speaks almost exclusively to Bassanio.

Again Bassanio is lavish with his wife's money. His initial offer of the three thousand ducats due to Shylock to "freely cope your courteous pains withal" (l. 412) is immediately seconded by Antonio's offer of "love and service to you evermore" (l. 414). Portia refuses both gestures, but it is not clear to whom she addresses the line, "I pray you know me when we meet again" (l. 419). The line could point in several directions: a polite but ironic wish for further acquaintance directed to Antonio, an implicit challenge to Bassanio to recognize her, and, as the context activates bawdy connotations, both a wish and a dare that Bassanio sleep with her at their next encounter. Balthazar tries to take his leave but is prevented by Bassanio. In a gloss on Bassanio's next line, "Dear sir, of force I must attempt you further" (l. 421), one editor imagines that "Bassanio now runs after Portia, and the ensuing dialogue gains its effect from the audience knowing that they are husband and wife."[27]

At the equivalent point in *Il Pecorone,* the reader is also playfully reminded of the real identity of the judge (Portia). In refusing Giannetto's (Bassanio's) offer of money, the judge says, "Keep it, so that your lady may not say that you have squandered it." When Giannetto replies that his lady is "so kind and generous . . . that if I spent four times as much as this, she would not mind," the judge asks him if he is "happy with her." He answers that "she is as beautiful and wise as anyone Nature ever made" and invites him to come home with him to see for himself.[28] When the invitation is refused, Giannetto again offers the money, at which point the judge notices the ring and asks for it. The narrative provides no indication of the reactions of Giannetto's wife underneath her male disguise but simply assumes that readers' awareness of her presence will allow them to savor the irony. Similarly, Shakespeare also relied on the audience to supply the presence of Portia, whether or not the male performer chose to make that presence visible through nonscripted shifts in and out of the female character.

But Shakespeare expanded the moment in adapting it to the stage, perhaps to give greater opportunities to the actor moving between Portia and Balthazar. In an addition to the source material, Shakespeare makes Balthazar refuse a cash payment for his services and ask instead for a pair of gloves before requesting the ring:

Give me your gloves, I'll wear them for your sake,
And for your love I'll take this ring from you.

(ll. 426–27)

The gloves can belong to either Antonio or Bassanio. If they are Antonio's, "your sake" would refer to him and "your love" to Bassanio, creating a playable antithesis that builds up to the request for the ring. If they are Bassanio's, Portia's focus on her husband's gloves, which he holds, or perhaps wears and removes, leads her to notice the ring on his finger.[29] Unlike Gianetto, Bassanio refuses to part with a ring "given me by my wife" (l. 441) and Portia's last speech in the scene plays as wittily upon her hidden identity as her counterpart in *Il Pecorone* does:

And if your wife be not a mad woman,
And know how well I have deserv'd this ring,
She would not hold out enemy for ever
For giving it to me. Well, peace be with you.

(ll. 445–48)

Unlike the judge in the narrative, she accepts Bassanio's refusal as definitive, disappointed as Balthazar but undoubtedly pleased as Portia, and leaves the stage, presumably with Nerissa.

In *Il Pecorone*, Giannetto (Bassanio) fears that his wife will believe "I have given it [the ring] to some other woman . . . and fallen in love elsewhere" (1:474). The judge seems to defend the wife but reiterates her doubts: "I am sure that she must love you well enough to believe you when you tell her that you gave it me. But perhaps you wanted to give it to one of your old loves here?" (1:474–75). Challenged to prove both his own fidelity and his faith in his wife's perfection, Giannetto gives the ring to the judge.

Shakespeare defers the surrender of the ring until after Portia leaves, in order to make Antonio pressure Bassanio into giving it to the lawyer, again pitting male lover against wife:

Let his deservings and my love withal
Be valued 'gainst your wive's commandement [*sic*].

(ll. 450–51)

Shakespeare invented a short scene in which Gratiano delivers the ring to Balthazar. Portia begins the scene by speaking to Nerissa, but the performer must abruptly shift back to Balthazar mannerisms when Gratiano addresses the lawyer as "Fair sir" (IV.ii.5). When Balthazar accepts the ring, Nerissa as the clerk asks for a private conference with the lawyer: "Sir, I would speak with you" (l. 12). Drawing Portia away from Gratiano, Nerissa proposes to get her husband's ring and clearly succeeds in doing so offstage while still disguised as a boy. Shifting gender identities, as the text did not require them to do during the actual trial, both women now resume their male attitudes, Nerissa turning back to Gratiano—"Come, good sir" (l. 19)—to request directions.

Portia's Return to Belmont

In the resolution of the ring plot in the final scene, the male performers represent Portia and Nerissa rather than the lawyer and clerk, although these male identities are as strongly present in the audience's memory as the female characters were in the courtroom. The audience's awareness of the male performers is also piqued throughout the scene by bawdy innuendoes, most of which refer to markers of male gender. Gratiano is the agent of the most overt bawdry, whether threatening to "mar the young clerk's pen" (l. 237) or vowing to "keep . . . safe Nerissa's ring" (l. 307).[30] Portia first announces her intention to "have that doctor for [my] bedfellow" (l. 233) and within thirty lines confesses that "the doctor lay with me" (l. 259). Nerissa echoes both statements with regard to "that same scrubbed boy, the doctor's clerk" (l. 261), quoting Gratiano's earlier description of the clerk. When the men learn that they gave their rings to their own wives, they join Portia and Nerissa in jests about the maleness of doctor and clerk, which are also playful allusions to the gender of the two actors:

> *Gra.* Were you the clerk that is to make me cuckold?
> *Ner.* Ay, but the clerk that never means to do it,
> Unless he live until he be a man.
> *Bass.* Sweet doctor, you shall be my bedfellow—
> When I am absent, then lie with my wife.
>
>   (ll. 281–85)

Unlike the trial scene, which depended on the audience's multicon-sciousness of actor, character, and disguise, the final scene derives its humor and its thematic force from explicit allusions to the heroines' various gender identities, and also from frequent use of bawdry—not as a conventional gender marker but to highlight all of the layers of gender in play.

Despite these differences, the final scene, like the trial scene, draws on the dexterity and energy of the performer in the world of the play-house to enhance Portia's power as a character in the world of the play. Unlike other heroines in male disguise, she retains her authority when she returns to Belmont and resumes her identity as Bassanio's wife, and she uses her power to seal her victory over Antonio once and for all.[31] As in the case of Julia in *The Two Gentlemen of Verona,* a female charac-ter's power can be reinforced by the theatrical vibrancy produced when opposing layers of gender identity are invoked on stage or actively evoked in the spectators' minds.

Unaware that it was his wife who canceled his debt to his friend, Bassanio introduces Antonio to Portia as the "man . . . to whom I am so infinitely bound" (ll. 134–35). Portia's reply revives Shylock's insistence on the literal terms of his *bond:*

You should in all sense be much *bound* to him,
For as I hear he was much *bound* for you.
(ll. 136–37; emphasis added)

Antonio's disclaimer, "No more than I am well acquitted of" (l. 138), even if genuinely self-effacing rather than smugly self-satisfied, cannot eradicate Bassanio's sense of obligation to the man who offered to sacrifice his life on his friend's behalf. To rescue Bassanio from his wife's displeasure over the parting with the ring, Antonio makes an even more extravagant offer:

I once did lend my body for his wealth,
. . . I dare be bound again,
My soul upon the forfeit, that your lord
Will never more break faith advisedly.
(ll. 249–53)

Seeming to accept Antonio's offer to be her husband's "surety" (l. 254),[32] Portia then undercuts it: she makes Antonio her unwitting agent by asking him to deliver to Bassanio a second ring, which her husband recognizes as the first. After some teasing, Portia explains all, reducing Antonio to a three-word statement of speechless wonder, "I am dumb" (l. 279), his next-to-last speech in the play. Shakespeare invents two more trump cards for her to play: her news for Antonio that "three of your argosies / Are richly come to harbor suddenly" (ll. 276–77), followed by her gratuitously mystifying refusal to tell Antonio how she acquired this information: "You shall not know by what strange accident / I chanced on this letter" (ll. 278–79). By restoring her rival's wealth, as Monica Hamill comments, Portia "removes the last vestige of Antonio's role as martyr."[33]

In addition to endowing Portia with an aura of mystery, Shakespeare also gives her a final use of legal terminology to recall her appearance in the courtroom, and perhaps to allow the performer a momentary reversion to Balthazar:

> Let us go in
> And charge us there upon inter'gatories
> And we will answer all things faithfully.
>
> (ll. 297–99)

Whether Balthazar is also invoked by vocal or physical traits, as well as linguistically, the legalistic "inter'gatories" represents a final allusion to Portia's male disguise and so ends the play by calling attention to the layered complex of boy actor, female character, and male disguise. In the trial scene, male disguise reflexively illuminated the play-boy and also transformed the female character into a Bradamante or a Britomart jousting in the courtroom rather than in the lists or on the battlefield. In the final scene, rather than allow her to dwindle into a wife, Shakespeare not only endows her with superior knowledge but makes frequent and lively play with her complex identity as a boy heroine recently in male disguise, having already italicized this convention by using it proleptically and contrastively with Jessica and simultaneously with Nerissa. Shakespeare reminded his audience of the presence of several talented play-boys, one of whom represented both the loving, powerful, and now mysterious lady of Belmont and her alter ego, the witty and resourceful doctor of law. In so rich a field of theatrical play, I believe that many spectators would have noted the destabilization or disruption of gender roles but would have had difficulty extracting a single, consistent attitude toward the role and status of women.

Replicating the Female Page: Fletcher's *Love's Pilgrimage*

Lyly's twin heroines in *Gallathea* may seem difficult to differentiate, but in Edward Sharpham's *The Fleire* (Queen's Revels, 1605–6), acted by one of the children's troupes, nearly all characters are pairs of clones.[34] In addition to two gallants (Sparke and Ruffel), two corrupt would-be gallants (Piso and a knight, Sir John Havelittle), and two courtesan sisters (Florida and Felecia), the play includes two romantic-heroine sisters (Nan and Susan). These women disguise themselves as pages in order to disrupt relations between the courtesan and the gallants, whom they love and wish to marry. Unlike the world beyond the playhouse, especially as it appeared to Bridewell magistrates, where female cross-dressing was associated with prostitution, Sharpham makes it the emblem of pure-hearted romantic heroines. The duplication here seems rather mechanical, as it does in Fletcher's *The Pilgrim* (King's, 1621), where farcical possibilities are multiplied, when both a heroine and her maid adopt a bewildering succession of disguises, some of them male.

But in a slightly earlier play, *Love's Pilgrimage* (King's, 1615–16), Fletcher multiplied disguised heroines more ingeniously: he placed one cross-dressed–heroine plot inside the other, and he used surprise; that is, he made spectators wonder for a short time whether the pages were young male characters or female characters in male disguise. As in his source, Cervantes's tale of "The Two Damsels" in his collection of *Exemplary Novels* (pub. 1613; Fr. trans. 1615), when the first page orders a room in an inn and insists upon absolute privacy, spectators may have suspected him of being a female page, but they were not told that the character is a woman, whose name is Theodosia, until she confesses, "I am a most unfortunate lost woman" (I.ii.48) to the man brought to share her room, who turns out to be her brother, Philippo. When the siblings encounter a page called Francisco, Theodosia anticipates or articulates the audience's suspicion that "this is no boy" (II.ii.188). Under Theodosia's interrogation, Francisco confesses to being Leocadia, the daughter of a neighbor, in love with, contracted to, and abandoned by a man named Mark-Antonio, the same man who had won, betrothed, and abandoned Theodosia. As in the source, Theodosia does not reveal *her* identity to Leocadia, who is fuming with anger at a woman named Theodosia for stealing her beloved. Although willing to succor Leocadia in her distress, Theodosia fears that her rival may have a stronger legal and emotional claim to Mark-Antonio.

Theodosia preserves the secret of her rival's disguise, revealing Leocadia's gender only to Philippo, who claims he suspected as much and who is obviously attracted to her:

> I ghest it was a woman, and a fair one.
> I see it through her shape, transparant plain.
>
> (III.ii.226–27)

His confidence in making this assertion must have seemed ironic to an audience aware that Leocadia, like his sister, was played by a play-boy.

Leocadia remains in disguise and joins Theodosia and her brother in their travels. They reach Barcelona in time to see Mark-Antonio wounded, the sight of which causes Theodosia to faint and Leocadia to run off, pursued by Philippo. The three are reunited at the governor's house, where Mark-Antonio has been taken for medical treatment. First Leocadia and then Theodosia reveal themselves to the wounded man. He gives preference to Theodosia, and once again Leocadia flees and once again is pursued by Philippo, who overtakes her and persuades her to accept him as a more loyal and trustworthy lover and husband than Mark-Antonio. She accepts, but Fletcher tops Cervantes by making her flee yet once more when the two women's fathers discover them and believe Philippo to have abducted her. For the third time, he dashes off to find her, miserable until she is brought on stage with Theodosia by Eugenia, the governor's wife, who reunites both couples and reconciles all parents and children.

Fletcher is at his most playfully self-conscious when first Leocadia and then Theodosia reveal themselves to Mark-Antonio. When Leocadia, Fletcher's second heroine, emerges from her disguise, Mark-Antonio rejects her and, not realizing Theodosia is there, declares her "my wife this half hour whilst I live." Theodosia answers eagerly and in so doing reveals herself, "That's I, that's I, I'me *Theodosia*" (IV.iii.181–82). Neither heroine's revelation is a surprise to the audience, but Leocadia is stunned to find herself trumped in her bid for Mark-Antonio by the young man she took to be her protector and confidant.

Cervantes' prose tale stresses the astonishment of the onlookers in a single sentence: "The rest of those present stared in each others' faces in speechless amazement at these extraordinary occurrences."[35] Fletcher underscores the theatricality of the moment with Eugenia's remark that the two young men, Mark-Antonio and Philippo, may also reveal themselves to be cross-dressed women:

> I am afraid they wil all four turn women
> If we hold longer talk.
>
> (IV.iii.191–92)

Apart from Leocadia's tendency toward flight, there is very little to distinguish her character from Theodosia's. Whereas Sharpham duplicates the heroine in male disguise mechanically, Fletcher's sequential and nested doubling of the female page places them on different planes of reality until Theodosia's undisguising. Theodosia, like Portia, possesses the knowledge to give her an edge over everyone else in the play, but her power is diluted in several ways. It is entirely dependent on Mark-Antonio's decision to consider himself contractually bound to her, which like Bertram's acceptance of Helena in All's Well That Ends Well, is made under sufficient pressure to call its authenticity into question. Nor is her power reinforced by the kind of frequent invoking of multiple gender identities found in the last act of The Merchant of Venice. Finally, whereas the cross-dressings of Jessica and Nerissa are different enough from Portia's to accentuate her status as the central female protagonist, Theodosia's status is reduced by the presence of a double, who takes over the primary romantic interest once Theodosia has won Mark-Antonio. The governor's wife, rather than either cross-dressed heroine, asserts the authority of a Portia in the conclusion of the play.

Fletcher's duplication of the boy heroine in male disguise diverts attention from the multilayered gender identity of a single female protagonist and accents the ingenuity of the play's structure. In Lyly's Gallathea, such replication creates a balanced symmetry of attitudes, while in Sharpham's The Fleire, a more mechanical duplication of nearly all of the major figures creates parodic effects. In Fletcher's fugal deployment of two female pages, the emphasis falls not on the wit and energy of a single, multilayered figure like Portia, but on the dramaturgical dexterity of the playwright himself.

Contrasting Boy Brides with Female Pages

Although Shakespeare multiplied and contrasted the female characters in male disguise and occasionally used the boy-bride motif, he never had both male and female characters don cross-gender disguise in the same play. Other playwrights did so, as in such plays as *The Wars of Cyrus, George a Green* (Sussex, c. 1593–94), Marston's *Antonio and Mellida,* Fletcher's *Love's Cure, or The Martial Maid* (King's, 1605–13?), and Henry Glapthorne's *The Hollander* (Queen Henrietta's, 1636), where a "mock" marriage between a female page and a boy bride turns out to be valid.

Such pairing of a female page and a boy bride also occurs in William Haughton's *Englishmen for My Money* (Admiral's, 1598).[36] Haughton may well have written the play in response to *The Merchant of Venice,* for the play triples the motif of the elopement of the usurer's daughter.[37] The Shylock figure, a Portuguese usurer named Pisaro who lives in London with three daughters, demands that they marry three "strangers"—French, Dutch, and Italian—instead of the Englishmen they love. Two daughters outwit their father by donning cross-gender disguise, but Haughton made greater use of the farcical potentialities of the boy bride. An English suitor gains entrance to Pisaro's house by disguising himself as a neighbor's daughter, fends off the usurer's sexual overtures, and remains "in Womans attire" (l. 2654) at the end of the play.

Parodic effects come close to burlesque in plays that double both types of cross-gender disguise, as in Nathan Field's *Amends for Ladies* (Queen's Revels, c. 1611), a private theater play that Linda Woodbridge labels as "a *tour de force* of transvestism."[38] Others might claim that title for one of James Shirley's early plays, *The School of Compliment, or Love Tricks* (Lady Elizabeth's, 1625), which uses two boy brides to counter-balance a heroine who appears in two male disguises. In the main plot of the play, derived from the Lelia story, a brother, Antonio, is mistaken for his sister, Selina, known to have donned male disguise to avoid an unwanted marriage. He goes along with the error by disguising as a girl and is married off to the old man who courted his sister and whom he then beats up on their wedding night. The female disguise also gives him access to the old man's daughter, with whom he has fallen in love. In Gorgon, Antonio's servant, Shirley adds another boy bride, a farcical figure who becomes the play's conduit for coarse sexual humor.

Shirley combines such reflexive effects with a large dollop of burlesque. Following *As You Like It,* Shirley makes Selina escape to the country in "shepherd's weeds,"[39] accompanied by her sister, disguised as a shepherdess. Instead of playing the saucy lackey or Lylian page, Selina complains of being "lost in a masculine habit" and cut off from Infortunio, the man she loves. When Infortunio follows her to the country but cannot penetrate her disguise, she promises to "fetch Selina to you" but returns instead in a second male disguise, this time as her brother "habited like Antonio" (1:77). Like Orlando, Infortunio proposes that the boy represent his beloved:

> And will you be my mistress then, and teach me
> How to forget myself?—What sayst [thou] boy?
> Shall I be shepherd too? I will live here,
> And have thy company, thou art like my love.
>
> (1:79)

Selina then shifts Infortunio's love from this "boy" back to "that virgin . . . that you first loved" simply by announcing her true identity, "Look on thy Selina" (1:82), perhaps reinforcing the line by removing a hat or allowing her hair to fall. Because Infortunio again refuses to believe this "jugling boy" (1:83), Selina must again prove her identity and does so in a recognition scene with her brother, as both siblings emerge from cross-gender disguises. Whereas Shakespeare repeated cross-gender disguise to heighten Portia's theatrical vibrancy and so permit her to dominate the play, Shirley's Selina joins with Antonio in multiplying cross-gender disguise to burlesque conventions that Shirley evidently felt had lost their power to be used more vigorously, as they had been in *The Merchant of Venice.*

Chapter 6

Layers of Disguise: *As You Like It*

Even more ingenious than adding a second or third heroine in cross-gender disguise, as Shakespeare did in *The Merchant of Venice,* is having the cross-dressed heroine take on a second cross-gender disguise. It would be as if Balthazar, Portia's disguised male alter ego, adopted female disguise. Such a second cross-gender disguise would reverse the direction of the gender change of the first and intensify what was already a highly reflexive situation, for in representing a woman, the female page would be repeating in the world of the play what the male performer was doing in the world of the playhouse. In *As You Like It,* Shakespeare has Ganymed pretend to be a woman and at moments invites the performer to play broad female stereotypes but stops well short of a second cross-gender disguise. No play of the English Renaissance exploited the full potentiality of this variation, probably because of the technical difficulty of dramatizing two disguisings and undisguisings. The usual solution was to conceal the heroine's initial cross-gender disguise from other characters and ostensibly from the audience until the end of the play.

Second Disguise as Undisguising: Heywood's *The Four Prentices of London*

Freeburg uses the term "retro-disguise" to describe plays in which female pages adopt a second disguise as a woman, although it should properly be reserved for plays in which the second disguise is perceived as a return to her original female identity.[1] Freeburg cites sixteenth-century examples of plays using retro-disguise from the tradition of *commedia erudita,* such as Porta's *La Cintia* and its Latin adaptation *Laby-*

rinthus, performed at Cambridge in 1599. The earliest example in English, probably acted several years before *As You Like It,* is Heywood's *The Four Prentices of London* (Admirals, 1592–94).[2]

Four apprentices, actually sons of the earl of Bulloigne, enlist in the Crusades, but one of them, Guy, is shipwrecked on the shores of France. He wins the love of "the Lady of France," as the king's daughter is called, who announces, in a short soliloquy, that she plans to follow Guy when he returns to the wars as commander of her father's army. She neglects to say how she will do so, but spectators familiar with chivalric romance, Renaissance epic, and folk ballad would have anticipated her reappearance as a page or squire. Such suspicions are confirmed several scenes later, when his page (later called Jack) speaks a soliloquy, preceded by the stage direction "Manet the French Lady," revealing himself to be the princess, who, "Under the habite of a trusty Page" (53, l. 1131), has become Guy's close companion:

> My love and Lord, that honoured me a woman,
> Loves me a youth, employes me every where. . . .
> And now I have learnt to be a perfect Page,
> He will have none to trusse his points but me,
> At boord to waite upon his cup but me:
> To beare his Target in the field, but me.

Such fondness has led to an awkward and unsatisfying intimacy:

> Nay, many a thing, which makes me blush to speak,
> He will have none to lie with him but me.
>
> (53, ll. 1135–44)

In the world of the play, the passage registers the female character's embarrassment at having to impersonate a boy and perhaps at being used sexually as one, as play-boys were alleged to be in the world of the playhouse.

But Heywood, more than most writers of late chivalric romances and Renaissance epics, also allows the disguised heroine to articulate her sexual frustration at this emotional intimacy and physical proximity afforded to her in and because of her cross-gender disguise:

> I dreame and dreame, and things come in my mind:
> Onely I hide my eyes; but my poore heart

Is bar'd and kept from loves satiety.

(53, ll. 1145–47)

She can only experience "love[']s satiety" as a woman, although the reflexive effect of male disguise has also made the audience highly aware of the play-boy as a performer, and perhaps as a sexual object.

In the confusion of battle Jack runs off and is taken prisoner by Eustace, one of Guy's brothers, and asks permission to "cloath me like a Lady" (82, ll. 1832, 1846) so that he might evade his master's displeasure when they meet. But Eustace informs Guy that Jack intends to appear before him disguised as a woman and asks his brother to forgive the errant page:

The poore boy, brother, stayes within my Tent,
But so disguis'd you cannot know him now,
For hee's turn'd wench: and but I know the wagge,
To be a boy, to see him thus transform'd,
I should have sworn he had bene a wench indeed.

(111, ll. 2518–22)

Jack's appearance in female attire is interpreted in several ways. Eustace, who is privy to Jack's plan, sees a boy bride. Most of the other characters, taken in by the disguise, see a strange woman. Guy and the audience see this second disguise as an undisguising, as the reappearance of the lady of France.

As the princess had hoped, Guy recognizes her at once and embraces her. The onlookers, who believe this woman to be Jack in female disguise, are astonished to see Guy "kisse a boy, . . . a Page, a wagtaile by this light" (112, ll. 2533, 2536), although, as many spectators would have realized, that is precisely what was happening in the world of the playhouse. Eustace's "error" in taking Jack as male articulates the audience's awareness of the male performer beneath the female role. Eustace's warning to his brother about this maid is not altogether off the mark:

Do not mistake the sex man, for he's none,
It is a rogue, a wag, his name is *Jack*,
A notable dissembling lad, a Crack.

(112, ll. 2539–41)

Guy sheepishly explains that "she hath beene my bedfellow / A yeare
and more, yet had I not the grace—" (112, ll. 2543–44). Unable or
perhaps unwilling to continue his explanation, he takes her as his bride.

The second cross-gender disguise, though brief in duration, heightens possibilities of "discrepant awareness"[3] and offers the spectators a
choice of several erotic possibilities. At the nexus of this tangle is the
play-boy representing a woman and by means of reflexive allusion to his
male identity generating the theatrical vibrancy that enhances the princess's power to reclaim her beloved, just as it did Julia's in *Two Gentlemen*.

As You Like It: Rosalind, Ganymed, and "Rosalind"

No one can say whether Shakespeare noted the use of a second cross-
gender disguise in Heywood's *The Four Prentices* or in earlier academic
or commercial plays. Nevill Coghill theorizes that a second cross-gender
disguise reversing the direction of gender switch of the first occurred to
Shakespeare as a permutation of his or others' previous work: "A boy
can present a girl; a boy can present a girl presenting a boy; a boy can
present a girl presenting a boy presenting a girl."[4] Ganymed's representation of Rosalind also occurs in Lodge's *Rosalynde* (pub. 1590), the
primary narrative source for *As You Like It* (1599),[5] but the suggestion
of a second cross-gender disguise may be one of the features that attracted Shakespeare to this prose pastoral romance.

In the play, as in Lodge's romance, Rosalind, disguised as the page
Ganymed, meets Orlando in the forest, and offers to pretend to be
"Rosalind." Because Ganymed never goes so far as to adopt female
disguise, as does Heywood's Jack in *The Four Prentices,* "Rosalind" exists
only as a pretense for as long as Orlando chooses to accept it. Neither
he nor anyone else mistakes Ganymed for "Rosalind," as happens in
plays using retro-disguise, but the pretense of "Rosalind" resembles a
disguise on top of a disguise by giving the performer a second, female
layer of identity beyond the original female character and her first disguise as Ganymed. As a result of this triple layering, the text provides
rich opportunities for the performer to shift abruptly from one layer of
gender identity to another.

An audience would be confused unless the performer, regardless of
gender, made it clear when Rosalind herself was speaking, when the
character was speaking as Ganymed, and when Ganymed was posing as

the stereotyped "Rosalind." In the minds of the audience and the performer, all three of these layers are understood as forming the complex amalgam of the female character, but an attempt to convey them simultaneously would produce confusion. Instead, I suggest that the boy actor did what most actors do when called upon to play multiple layers of identity: he committed himself fully to one layer of identity at a time as suggested by the script or determined in rehearsal, perhaps occasionally suggesting connections and oppositions between layers, or trusting the audience to do so. In moving from layer to layer, the performer could probably also count on spectators to maintain awareness of the play-boy and to admire his virtuosity.[6] Once the play shifts to the Forest of Arden, the text invites the performer to invent a different mode or style for each of these three separate and distinct layers of identity—Rosalind, Ganymed, and "Rosalind."

The original layer, the voluble and high-spirited Rosalind, is in love with a man she barely knows and is aware of the risks in loving. In I.iii, after the duke has decreed Rosalind's banishment and left the stage, Celia assumes the dominant role in the relationship, proposing that they both flee the court, while Rosalind replies in monosyllabic half-lines. But in response to Celia's suggestion that they don "poor and mean attire . . . [and] with a kind of umber smirch" their faces, Rosalind takes the initiative, beginning with the idea of her donning masculine apparel:

> Were it not better,
> Because that I am more than common tall,
> That I did suit me all points like a man?
>
> (ll. 111–16)

Within the world of the play, the mere idea of playing a man releases for Rosalind the same kind of wit and verbal energy it did for Julia and Portia; within the world of the playhouse, the passage allowed recognition of the fact that a boy actor, taller than most women, was performing the role and that his excessive height was cleverly woven into the fabric of the play. Shakespeare's Rosalind, like Portia, also imagines herself burlesquing male swaggering once she is dressed as a man:

> A gallant curtle-axe upon my thigh,
> A boar-spear in my hand, and—in my heart
> Lie there what hidden woman's fear there will—

We'll have a swashing and a martial outside,
As many other mannish cowards have
That do outface it with their semblances.

(I.iii.117–22)

This speech indicates a capacity for antiromantic wit, which finds
expression through her adoption of male identity. But although Rosalind
had already decided to take the name of "Jove's own page" (I.iii.124),
she discovers her true Ganymed voice to be that of a Lylian page only
after Orlando appears, well into III.ii, when she decides to "speak to him
like a saucy lackey, and under that habit play the knave with him"
(III.ii.295–97). After over a hundred lines of Lylian wit, Ganymed proposes to adopt yet another layer of identity by pretending to be
Orlando's beloved: "I would cure you, if you would but call me Rosalind, and come every day to my cote and woo me" (III.ii.426–27). Before
Ganymed impersonates "Rosalind," he gives Orlando and the audience
a preview of this female role by describing how he took it on once before
in order to cure another *inamorato:*

> He was to imagine me his love, his mistress; and I set him every day
> to woo me. At which time would I, being but a moonish youth,
> grieve, be effeminate, changeable, longing and liking, proud, fan-
> tastical, apish, shallow, inconstant, full of tears, full of smiles; for
> every passion something, and for no passion truly any thing, as
> boys and women are for the most part cattle of this color.
> (III.ii.407–15)

Slightly less variable than this sketch, Ganymed's "Rosalind" is a blend
of such misogynistic stereotypes as the scold, the fickle or cruel Petrarchan mistress, and the shrewish cuckold maker.

Although I believe that the text invites the performer to establish
these three distinct layers of identity, it is not obvious at every moment
which one should be played. Different performers will make different
choices. In analyzing a sample passage, IV.i.171–200, I want to show
how these distinctive tones might be articulated and how quickly they
change.

Ganymed has been offering "man-to-man" advice to Orlando on
the behavior of wives, has suggested the possibility of infidelity, and
reaches a crescendo of exuberant cynicism in celebrating the wit of

women to "make her fault her husband's occasion." Orlando is either dumfounded or disappointed and, perhaps in order to break off this misogynistic diatribe, recalls his duty to the duke: "For these two hours, Rosalind, I will leave thee." Unaware that the real Rosalind is present, he addresses "Rosalind," the image of his beloved constructed by Ganymed, but it might well be the real Rosalind and not the coy or imperious "Rosalind" who replies, "Alas, dear love, I cannot lack thee two hours!" She could then cover this involuntary revelation of her true feelings in her next speech by resorting to tones usually associated with "Rosalind," first the contemptuous dismissal of "Ay, go your ways, go your ways" and then the extravagant self-pity of "'Tis but one cast away, and so come death!" But the very next sentence is Rosalind's anxious attempt to verify the time of Orlando's return, while the breezy response to Orlando's "Ay, sweet Rosalind" is Ganymed's stern warning to his friend that he dare not be late lest he be unworthy "of her you call Rosalind." At these and similar points in the play, different performers will make different decisions, but the text invites anyone playing the role to act each moment in one of these three distinct modes, to move rapidly between them, and to invent ways to negotiate the transitions.[7]

Nancy Hayles comments perceptively on Rosalind's "on-layering" and "off-layering" of disguise and pretense, suggesting that these multiple identities are established and dismantled in linear sequence.[8] Broadly speaking, she is right, but closer inspection, I would argue, suggests that a rigidly linear pattern is disrupted not only by textual signals for the performer to change abruptly from one identity to another, but even more forcefully in Shakespeare's day by reflexive allusions to the gender of the boy actor. As in *Two Gentleman,* the saucy lackey called Ganymed is a Lylian page, a theatricalized version of the wit and audacity Elizabethans attributed to and sometimes cultivated in boys. Although we do not know the name of the play-boy who acted Rosalind, Heywood assures us that most Elizabethan spectators did. Whatever the real personality of that boy, it must have been difficult for spectators to separate the play-boy from the pert and cheeky adolescent, even if the pert and cheeky adolescent was, in the world of the play, a disguise adopted by a female character. Instead of existing at a further remove from reality, Ganymed would probably have seemed as much a figure of the audience's world, the world of the playhouse, as of the fictive world of the play. To add yet another dimension of reflexivity, Ganymed's representation of "Rosalind," replicated within the world of the play exactly what the audience saw in the world of the playhouse: a boy impersonating Rosalind.[9] Hayles's linear sequence of on- and off-layering produces a concentric model of roles nested within roles, but the intricacy of the text and the reflexive effects produced by the presence of a male actor suggest a far more complicated scheme.

Once Rosalind is in male attire, the play makes many more references to her concealed feminine identity than *Two Gentlemen* or *The Merchant* did and often encourages the performer to oscillate between female and male layers of identity with lightning speed, whether Rosalind is playing Ganymed or Ganymed is pretending to be "Rosalind."[10] On Shakespeare's stage, these oscillations became even more dazzling in the light of spectators' dual consciousness of the boy actor producing all of these abrupt shifts. These multiple layers of identity and the swift movements from one to another produced a theatrical vibrancy that engaged audiences in the illusion that an amalgam constructed of multiple and discrete layers of identity represented a unified character.

Shakespeare's Adaptation of Lodge's *Rosalynde*

In Lodge's narrative, Rosalynde is one of three women in love, whose stories he tells one at a time, at more or less equal length, and "on the same plane of courtly, artificial sentimentality."[11] Shakespeare turned Rosalind's into the main plot, into which he wove the other stories, and made her the dominant figure in the entire play. Not only does Shakespeare enable her to outtalk any of the other characters,[12] but he makes her motives more enigmatic. Whereas Lodge simply tells the reader that his heroine offers to pretend to be Rosader's beloved to entice him to stay with her a bit longer, Shakespeare is far less explicit. He allows us to ascribe that motive to Rosalind, if we wish, in spite of Ganymed's antiromantic offer to cure Orlando of love. The play is similarly ambiguous as to whether Orlando, who really does not want to be cured, is accepting a dare or finding himself drawn to this strange youth.[13] Shakespeare also makes more theatrical use of his heroine's multiple layers of identity than Lodge does by making her jump from one to another and by exploiting the additional layer of identity of the boy actor, obviously not available to Lodge or his readers. As Bruce Smith writes, "We are never tempted to forget that Rosalynde is a woman; the Orlando-figure never takes her for anything but a man. All of Lodge's sexual jokes turn . . . on keeping that distinction clear."[14]

Cross-gender casting permits Shakespeare to treat these layers of identity more fluidly. He makes the heroine sometimes play Ganymed and sometimes "Rosalind," as we have seen. He also highlights the contradictions between Rosalind and Ganymed, especially between the heroine's self-confessed unfathomable love for Orlando and the saucy lackey's antiromantic cynicism. Shakespeare also develops this contrast in snatches of dialogue between Rosalind and Celia, the only other character besides Touchstone who knows Ganymed's real identity. Here too Shakespeare developed ideas present in his source. Lodge's *Rosalynde*, for example, underlines the opposed genders of her dual identity by commenting on gendered articles of clothing and on the radically different attitudes toward women she considers appropriate to each layer of her sexual identity:

> Thus (quoth *Ganimede*) I keepe decorum, I speake now as I am *Alienas* page, not as I am *Gerismonds* daughter: for put me but into a peticoate, and I will stand in defiance to the uttermost that women are courteous, constant, vertuous, and what not. (2:181)

Shakespeare's Rosalind also contrasts conventional gender roles in similar terms:

> *Ros.* I could find it in my heart to disgrace my man's apparel and to cry like a woman; but I must comfort the weaker vessel, as doublet and hose ought to show itself courageous to petticoat; therefore courage, good Aliena.
>
> (II.iv.4–8)[15]

Lodge sometimes makes Aliena comment on Ganimede's male clothing as a betrayal of Rosalynde's true female identity:

> Leave off (quoth *Aliena*) to taunt thus bitterly, or els Ile pul off your pages apparell and whip you (as *Venus* doth her wantons) with nettles. (2:182)

Shakespeare echoes this rebuke, adding anatomical innuendoes to the gender-based sartorial details:

> You have simply misus'd our sex in your love-prate. We must have
> your doublet and hose pluck'd over your head, and show the world
> what the bird hath done to her own nest. (IV.i.201–4)[16]

Adding sexual innuendoes not found in Lodge underscored the various
layers of gender identity held in suspension in such scenes.

Shakespeare further departs from his source in using Celia, whether
or not she speaks, to accentuate Rosalind's presence beneath her disguise
as Ganymed. In other plays, Shakespeare has his heroines in male disguise
convey their female identities in soliloquies or asides.[17] In *As You Like
It,* he makes Rosalind play off of Celia, who knows the truth of her
identity. Rosalind, or more precisely the performer playing the role, can
shift from Ganymed to Rosalind by turning to Celia in the midst of
scenes involving other characters. Several scenes begin with a dialogue
between Rosalind and Celia, before they are joined by other characters
and become Ganymed and his sister Aliena. Shakespeare makes Ganymed
by far the more active of the two in those portions of the scenes, but as
long as Celia is present the two performers can activate the audience's
knowledge of their other identities merely by glancing toward one another, as Lodge cannot make them do on the printed page without directly
or indirectly narrating such an action.

The first time Ganymed pretends to be "Rosalind" in a scene with
Orlando, Celia, who had much to say to her cousin before Orlando's
appearance, suddenly turns mute. When Celia does speak, after some
forty lines, she seems to be trying to prevent "Rosalind" from giving
away the presence of Rosalind:

> *Orl.* Virtue is no horn-maker; and my Rosalind is virtuous.
> *Ros.* And I am your Rosalind.
> *Cel.* It pleases him to call you so; but he hath a
> Rosalind of a better leer than you.
>
> (IV.i.63–67)

Celia's fear that Rosalind will reveal herself to Orlando articulates to the
audience the layers of identity involved in the world of the play and
points up the presence of the talented play-boy who constructs and
juggles them all.

The second time Celia speaks while Orlando is present is about sixty
lines later during the "wedding ceremony." Whereas Celia proposes the

mock marriage in Lodge's novel, and Rosalynde "changed as redde as a rose" (2:214), in the play Rosalind suggests it, and Celia seems so shocked either at the sacrilege or at Rosalind's audacity in realizing her deepest fantasy that she "cannot say the words" (IV.i.128).[18] She seems irritated by Ganymed's prompting "Go to!" but does get out one line of the priest's part—"Will you, Orlando, have to wife this Rosalind?" (IV.i.130–31)—and then remains silent for about seventy more lines until Orlando leaves.

Some stage productions have Celia recede into the background and come forward only to deliver her lines. In the BBC version the camera usually frames its shots so as to exclude her. Her two scripted intrusions into the duet between Rosalind and Orlando suggest that her function is to provide the performer playing her cousin with a focal point for reestablishing the presence of her female identity as Rosalind. Similarly, when Ganymed attempts to disentangle himself from Phebe, some of his utterances to Aliena will be understood by the audience as communication between Rosalind and Celia as well, as in III.v, where Ganymed's three separate exit lines to "sister" indicate an increasing urgency, an urgency that reminds the audience of the heroine's female identity even if the performer chooses not to indicate it.

Lodge often reminds his readers of his heroine's female layer of identity by describing such involuntary physical reactions as blushing and weeping. Shakespeare dramatized only one such moment: Celia, having mentioned "a chain, that you once wore, about his neck," notices that Rosalind blushes: "Change you color?" (III.ii.181–82). As in *Two Gentlemen,* Shakespeare either expected his boy actress to blush on cue or hoped that the verbal suggestion would create the illusion in the spectators' minds. Shakespeare also amplified Rosalynde's involuntary reaction to Rosader's wound. Lodge's heroine is "busie dressing up the wounds of the Forrester" (2:222) and later reacts more emotionally. Even when her feelings are stirred, she continues to administer first aid:

> *Ganimede* had teares in her eyes, and passions in her heart to see her *Rosader* so pained, and therefore stept hastely to the bottle, and filling out some wine in a Mazer, shee spiced it with such comfortable drugs as she had about her, and gave it him. (2:224)

Shakespeare dilates and complicates this moment. Rosalind listens to Oliver's account of Orlando's injury, presumably without betraying her own emotional response, but when Oliver shows her the napkin stained with his brother's blood, she swoons. Possibly suspicious of Ganymed's gender, Oliver charges the "page" with "lack[ing] a man's heart" (IV.iii.164). Rosalind seems to confess—"I do so, I confess it"—while Ganymed (or a weakened version of him) quickly retracts Rosalind's admission by claiming "this was well counterfeited! I pray you tell your brother how well I counterfeited. Heigh-ho!" (IV.iii.165–68).[19] Whereas Lodge exploited the techniques available in prose narrative to remind his readers of the heroine's true gender, adapting the material for the stage required Shakespeare to provide moments for the performer to evoke the heroine's female identity with economy and precision.

In modern productions, the actress's swoon also emphasizes the presence of Rosalind behind her disguise but does so by narrowing the gap between the heroine and the female performer. As Mary Hamer has observed, playgoers and performers from the mid-eighteenth century on have often conspired to reduce this distance at such moments, in order to create an illusion of Rosalind's innate feminine delicacy. As embodiments of a "myth of femininity," most Rosalinds of that period had to display such tenderness of feeling in order to counterbalance such "female vices" as volubility and bossiness.[20] On the Elizabethan stage, moments like the swoon would have been perceived as opportunities for the boy actor to construct the illusion of Rosalind's femininity.

Avoiding Intimacy in *As You Like It*

An even trickier moment for the Elizabethan boy actor occurs later in the play, in V.ii, when Shakespeare brings Rosalind and Orlando alone on stage for the first time. Orlando refers to "my Rosalind" (l. 16) and Oliver greets the page as "fair sister" (l. 18), but these remarks seem playfully addressed to Ganymed's "Rosalind," as neither brother elsewhere shows any sign (to me) of having seen through Rosalind's disguise.[21]

During this sixty-line duet with Orlando, Rosalind has no Celia to restrain her or to play off of as herself. In her opening line, an expression of pity from "Rosalind," she seems inadvertently to betray the presence of Rosalind: "O my dear Orlando, how it grieves me to see thee wear thy heart in a scarf!" (ll. 19–20). To his matter-of-fact correction, "It is my arm" (l. 21), she offers a line that can be delivered as a continuation of Rosalind's concern, as Ganymed's nonchalant attempt to cover the

error, or as "Rosalind's" wide-eyed mock confusion: "I thought thy
heart had been wounded with the claws of a lion" (ll. 22–23). Orlando's
reply marks a resumption of his earlier lovesickness, "Wounded it is,
but with the eyes of a lady" (l. 24), but it puts enough emotional pressure
on Rosalind to drive her hastily into Ganymed's sauciest mode: "Did
your brother tell you how I counterfeited to sound [swoon] when he
show'd me your handkercher?" (ll. 25–27). He then launches into a long
account of Oliver's and Celia's courtship spoken with Ganymed's Lylian
pertness, an amused account of the other couple's wildfire passion.

Reminded by their good fortune of his own "heart-heaviness,"
Orlando's self-pity prompts Rosalind to ask an ambiguous question containing a common bawdy innuendo: "Why then to-morrow I cannot
serve your turn for Rosalind?" (ll. 48–49). If the "I" is "Rosalind," the
line becomes a veiled offer, a test to see if Orlando wants to continue the
game they have been playing, and his reply, "I can live no longer by
thinking" (l. 50), indicates that he has exhausted such playful fantasies
and now desires the real Rosalind. If the "I" is Ganymed, the sexual
meaning of "serve your turn" may be activated in a way that provokes
Orlando to declare an end to their innocent pastimes for fear of what
they may lead to. In either case, she is pleased that Orlando has tired of
"thinking" and wants her rather than the "Rosalind" he believes was the
pretense of a boy, if not the boy himself. As Philip Traci argues, the
name Ganymed evokes the idea of a homoerotic relationship.[22] But
whereas *Twelfth Night* explores that possibility by granting Orsino and
Cesario several scenes alone and emphasizing their growing closeness,
As You Like It allows Orlando and Ganymed only one brief moment
alone onstage. Nor does the play refer to offstage intimacy between
master and page as does Heywood's *The Four Prentices*. Although a
production of *As You Like It* might suggest a degree of homoerotic
attraction between Orlando and Ganymed, the language of the text generally keeps the tone of their relationship teasing and light, rather than
somber and intense. In Ganymed's next speech, he takes control of the
scene and, assuming Orlando is serious about marrying Rosalind, offers
to use his magic to "set her before your eyes to-morrow" (ll. 66–67).

In addition to avoiding intimacy between Orlando and Ganymed,
Shakespeare also avoided a spectacular disclosure of Rosalind's identity,
such as he had used at the end of *The Two Gentlemen* when Julia
"swooned." Whereas the sudden onstage transformation of sexual identity would remain a feature of plays employing heroines in male dis-

guise, Shakespeare makes Rosalind's off-layering occur offstage, as he did Portia's in *The Merchant of Venice*. Ganymed leaves the play for the last time at l. 25, while Duke Senior and Orlando remark on his resemblance to Rosalind. Rosalind returns ceremoniously at l. 107 as herself, escorted by Hymen, if not in her wedding dress at least "not furnish'd like a beggar" (epilogue, ll. 9–10). Having divested herself of both Ganymed and his creation "Rosalind," she appears in the rest of the scene simply as Rosalind. Unlike Julia and Viola, who never remove male attire, Rosalind is restored to female garb as well as female identity, reaffirmed as daughter to the duke and now given as wife to Orlando.[23]

Reversibility of Gender Roles: The Epilogue

The play ends with four marriages, familial reunion and reconciliation, and restoration of political authority. Within the world of the play, all of these gestures depend on a stable sense of individual identity, particularly gender identity. But the epilogue, the only one we have for Shakespeare's five plays with cross-dressed heroines, begins by dissolving characters' identities as it invokes the world of the playhouse:

> It is not the fashion to see the lady the epilogue; but it is no more unhandsome than to see the lord the prologue. If it be true that good wine needs no bush, 'tis true that a good play needs no epilogue. (ll. 1–5)

Although the speaker, still presumably wearing Rosalind's wedding gown, identifies herself as "the lady," a change in gender is indicated by "If I were a woman." One suspects that this change was signaled or accompanied by a physical gesture such as the removal of a wig or some article of female attire.[24]

Most Elizabethan epilogues reminded audiences of what they always knew, that all of the characters are roles for performers, but this one goes further. Before the spectators' eyes it refracts the figure they had accepted as Rosalind into the various layers of gender identity adopted by a boy actor. Recent commentators regard this stress on the male performer as commentary on the politics of gender, although there is a difference of opinion as to its precise meaning. From a psychoanalytic viewpoint, Janet Adelman sees the emergence of the play-boy as the reinstatement of an androgynous ideal, whereas Peter Erickson regards it as a dilution of Rosalind's female power. Juliet Dusinberre argues that the return of the play-boy is really the return of Rosalind "as insouciant as ever in her breeches," while Catherine Belsey sees it as yet another disruption of sexual difference, a final gesture toward the arbitrariness of gender roles, for the play-boy if not for the audience he had just divided according to their gender and perhaps their sexual preference.[25]

Another group of critics sees the epilogue's shifts in gender as movements between planes of illusion, what Keir Elam calls "a species of linguistic tightrope-walking between different ontological zones."[26] In such readings, the epilogue is not the play's final word on sexual politics but an attempt to place the world of the play in some relation to the world of the playhouse. For Kent van den Berg, the splitting of character from performer "affirms . . . the boundary that separates her fictive world from the reality of the audience," while Albert Cirillo sees Rosalind "stepping out of the play, as if out of the fiction, [to] exercise . . . the genuine force of her magic on us by bringing us *into* the fictional . . . [so that] the play is our Arden."[27]

My own inclination is to take the epilogue as theatrical play rather than social polemics. What both groups of critics fail to consider is that the text instructs the performer to end the epilogue with a gesture toward femininity, if not a complete return to female identity, inviting the men "when I make curtsy, [to] bid me farewell" (ll. 22–23).[28] The performer's male gender emerges clearly at "if I were a woman," but the flirtatiousness with both men and women that follows could either be taken as a homoerotic come-on or a movement back toward the fictive female role, as *you* (the Elizabethan playgoer) like it. The emergence of the play-boy dissolved all three of the heroine's layers of gender identity, but the return of a fictive female character, as implied by mention of the curtsy and perhaps by the coyness which follows, would have been a kind of curtain call, the virtuoso repeating the trick for the audience's admiration even after showing them the secrets that made it possible.

Double Undisguising: Heywood's *Wise Woman* of *Hogsden*

Whereas Shakespeare had Ganymed merely pretend to be "Rosalind," Heywood used a second full cross-gender disguise in *The Wise Woman of Hogsden* (1603–5).[29] Instead of presenting the heroine, Second Luce, as herself and then dramatizing her decision to don male attire, Heywood has her come onstage for the first time already disguised as a page. She is described in a stage direction as "a yong Countrey Gentlewoman, in the habit of a Page" (93, ll. 352–53), and reveals her identity and her motives a few dozen lines later in soliloquy:

> Heigh hoe: have I disguis'd my selfe, and stolne out of the Countrey thus farre, . . . To this Gallant was I poore Gentle-woman be-troathed. . . . After him come I thus habited. (ll. 385ff.)

The gallant in question is Chartley, who jilted her for another girl, also named Luce. The soliloquy informs spectators that they are watching the familiar plot of a young woman who dons male apparel in order to pursue the man she loves.

Under the name Jack, she enters the service of the title character, who is also something of a matchmaker. The Wise Woman asks Jack to disguise himself as a woman and to substitute for Chartley's bride, a third girl named Gratiana:

> *Wisewo[man].* Thou shalt be tyred like a woman; can you make a curtesie, take small strides, simper, and seeme modest? Methinkes thou hast a womans voice already.
>
> (ll. 589–91)

Second Luce's reply, "Doubt not of me, Ile act them *naturally*" (l. 592; emphasis added), ironically highlights the artful complexity of the boy actor playing a woman disguised as a page now about to adopt yet another layer of cross-gender disguise. When another character, seeing Jack half into his female disguise, asks if he is a "Girle or Boye," he replies:

> Both, and neither; I was a Ladd last night, but in the morning I was conjured into a Lasse. And being a Girle now, I shall be translated to a Boy anon. (ll. 1038–40)

The speech baffles the other character, but to the audience it not only describes Jack's plan to stand in for Chartley's bride during the wedding ceremony but also alludes to the play-boy's impersonation of a female character for the entire play. Whereas Shakespeare invoked Rosalind's multiple identities by having the actor shift abruptly from one layer to another, Heywood depends less on the actor than on his own writing, using ambiguous speeches and frequent asides as authorial winks to the audience.

Like Heywood's French princess, as well as Shakespeare's Julia, Portia, and Rosalind, Second Luce shares the secret of her identity with the audience, and thereby acquires the theatrical power to make her control of the play seem convincing. Her plan is to fulfill the Wise Woman's scheme. Whereas Chartley thinks he has married Gratiana, and the Wise Woman plans to reveal the marriage later as a fraud, for Second Luce the ceremony is real and binding.

But Heywood delays her revelation. After the wedding, Second Luce resumes her identity as Jack for the remainder of the play, and Heywood avoids the problem of staging two distinct revelations of two different disguises. When Chartley is confronted by his two other fiancées, Second Luce rescues him by declaring herself his wife and reveals herself as his original betrothed:

> You and I have bin better acquainted and yet search mee not too farre least you shame mee, looke on me well, nay better, better yet, ile assure you I left off a petticoate when I put on these breeches. What say you now? (ll. 2304–8)

The stage direction that follows, "Shee skatters her hayre,"[30] suggests the sudden release of hair that has been tied up or concealed by a hat. The moment deliberately recalls Ariosto's Bradamante, Tasso's Clorinda, and Sidney's Parthenia, who became known as women when their tresses were revealed as their helmets fell off or were removed. The Wise Woman registers astonishment at Jack's metamorphosis: "My boy turn'd girle—I hope shee'l keepe my counsell; from henceforth, ile never entertaine any servant but ile have her searcht" (ll. 2311–13).

Unlike Rosalind and Portia, whose actual undisguisings occur offstage, Second Luce's scattering of her hair creates an instantaneous and highly theatrical revelation of her gender. To the audience, aware from the opening scene that Jack is Second Luce, the cascade of hair fulfills a long-held expectation, but to the characters on stage it is a complete surprise. In prose narratives, whether expected or not, such a gesture comes at the climax or denouement, signifies an end of disguise, and reveals the emergence of the female character in her own identity.

To playhouse spectators, it was also a climactic moment in the world of the play, but, prompted by frequent use of theatrical reflexivity, they also perceived another level of illusion, this one created by a young male actor probably wearing a wig. The emotional power of the moment was enhanced rather than undermined by this self-conscious display of dramaturgical ingenuity, an invitation to the audience to become engaged in a familiar female-page plot brought to life by the playwright's juggling of four distinct layers of gender identity—the boy actor, Second Luce, Jack, and the false bride.

Surprise and Parody: Chapman's *May Day*

Performed by a reactivated children's troupe at the newly reopened Blackfriars theater, Chapman's *May Day* (Chapel, 1601–2)[31] strives for novel treatments of cross-gender disguise. The play is an adaptation of Piccolomini's *Alessandro* (1544), a variant of the Lelia tradition, in which each member of a separated couple adopts cross-gender disguise.[32] Chapman gives the heroine a second cross-gender disguise on top of the first, the latter a surprise to the spectators, who are not told until the end that Lionell, a page, is really Lucretio's beloved Theagine, although they watch him deceive some of the characters in his disguise as a "Gentle-woman."

Because the first disguising is hidden from the audience, Theagine/Lionell/gentlewoman is not nearly as central a figure as Rosalind was, and she pretends to be a woman not to gain her own ends but to serve the designs of others. Yet Chapman extracts considerable theatrical self-referentiality from Lionell's second, or female, disguise, when his master, Leonoro, introduces him to the roistering Captain Quintiliano, who immediately sees the boy as a potential female impersonator, singing to him as to a woman, and perhaps inquiring about his homoerotic experience:

> Afore heaven 'tis a sweete fac't child, me thinks he should show well in womans attire: *And hee tooke her by the lilly white hand, and he laid her upon a bed.* Ile helpe thee to three crownes a weeke for him, and she can act well. Ha'st ever practis'd, my pretty *Ganimede*?[33] (III.iii.202–5)

For Chapman's spectators, the prospect of seeing Lionell "act well" as a woman would replicate what they were seeing in the theater—a play-boy portraying a female character. The captain's sexual interest in the boy may have been another reflexive allusion to the world of the playhouse, where boy actors were frequently thought to serve as "ganymedes."

A few scenes later, Leonoro tells Lionell that he must be "disguis'd like a woman" in order to gull Quintiliano's lieutenant, Innocentio: "thou shalt dance with him, we will thrust him upon thee, . . . come *Lionell* let me see how *naturally* thou canst *play* the woman" (IV.iv.29–36; emphasis added). As in *The Wise Woman of Hogsden,* words like "naturally" and "play" illuminate the layers of artifice involved. The plot to discomfit Innocentio is never developed beyond a brief self-referential passage in the final scene.

At the climax of the play, Lucretio, no longer in cross-gender disguise as "Lucretia," looks about for Theagine but fails to recognize her. Chapman even has him ask this "Gentlewoman" if she knows Theagine. Unlike Heywood's French princess, whose second, female disguise revealed her presence to her beloved Guy, Theagine's double disguise impedes the revelation of her real identity and so dilates the moment for theatrical effect. She addresses the forlorn Lucretio: "It seemes you will not know her" (V.i.238), until he suddenly recognizes her as "the Gentlewoman to whom . . . I was betroth'd" (ll. 245–46).

May Day was the first play to achieve a surprise ending by concealing the identity of the heroine from the audience beneath the first of her disguises. In *As You Like It* and *The Wise Woman,* where the audience is at all times fully aware of the real gender and identity of the female page, the second layer of pretense or disguise increases the depth and resonance established by the first, and she comes across as complex and ingenious. But in *May Day,* which achieves surprise by concealing a female character's identity, she seems part of other characters' schemes or the playwright's design or both, "a puppet" rather than "a sentient shaper of self," to use Paula Berggren's apt terms.[34] Chapman's innovative use of surprise, which he added to his source, extended Heywood's and Shakespeare's idea of the boy heroine's second gender-reversing disguise in the direction of parody. He may have taken into account the real or self-styled sophistication of his private theater audience as well as the tendency of children's troupes to burlesque plays of adult troupes.[35]

In Chapman's cleverest parody of cross-gender disguise, a married woman named Franceschina, about to have an affair, dresses as a man to conceal her identity. Her husband, the play's miles gloriosus, sees her and immediately recognizes her as a woman, but not as his wife:

Upon my life the hindermost of them, is a wench in mans attire, didst thou not marke besides his slabbering about her, her bigge thighs and her splay feete? (IV.v.106–8)

In the next scene, he concludes that she must be an adulteress, "some honest mans wife of the Parish . . . drest like a Page" (IV.vi.15–20). Unlike the boy actor playing Lionell, who represents a girl who can pass for a boy in the world of the play, the boy actor playing Franceschina represents a woman supposedly incapable of passing for a boy!

Surprise and Satire: Middleton's *The Widow*

The main action of *The Widow* (King's, c. 1616)[36] dramatizes the story of Valeria, a widow who protects her estate from predatory suitors and finally marries the one she chooses on her own terms. To Linda Woodbridge it demonstrates a sympathetic and undoctrinaire position toward widows, perhaps in response to the growing influence of women at the box office.[37] The title character, Valeria, is a strong-minded widow capable of fending off unwanted suitors, including a widow-hunting gallant who claims, fraudulently, that she has promised herself to him. Like the duchess of Milan in the main plot of *More Dissemblers,* and widowed duchesses in several other plays, Valeria preserves her chastity, her dignity and her independence, and marries the one suitor who wants her for herself, not for her wealth.

The play also parodies women and male stereotypes of women. Just as Ganymed's "Rosalind" is a male's impression of the Petrarchan mistress and the willful shrew, so Middleton, in the second scene of *The Widow,* has one gallant help another practice wooing techniques. To do so they take turns playing the woman and comment on each other's acting. One plays a coy flirt, while the other enacts a scornful shrew and contrives the illusion of femininity so skillfully that his friend tries to "stop *her* mouth with kisses" (emphasis added)—until the spell is broken, with some difficulty and some regret: "A bots on thee, thou dost not know what injury thou hast done me; I was i' the fairest dream (I.ii.141–42)."

The subplot of *The Widow* is an even more explicit reworking of female-page plays like *As You Like It* that use or imply a second cross-gender disguise. Halfway through the play, Ansaldo first appears, and the audience does not know but may well have suspected that he is a girl. Alert spectators might have anticipated that a disguised heroine would turn up when someone refers to a runaway daughter named Martia. Questions about Ansaldo's gender might have arisen from his reaction, when he is stripped to his shirt during a robbery and a highwayman threatens bodily search. Ansaldo's timidity and youthfulness also might have furthered suspicions of his gender, for he is described as "a sweet young gentleman" (III.iii.29) who has "never a hair on's face" (IV.ii.75). Ansaldo's shyness and delicacy are the very qualities that attract Philippa (the young wife of an old magistrate), whose first choice for an adulterous liaison, Francisco, has failed to keep the rendezvous.

Middleton goes beyond *As You Like It,* for whereas Ganymed never fully adopts the persona of Orlando's Rosalind, Ansaldo is at one point dressed as a woman, dazzling all of the men who are present with her feminine beauty. This new woman especially charms Francisco, Philippa's paramour, who woos her ardently and takes her offstage to get married. Thinking Ansaldo is a man, Philippa behaves as if she is directing a boy-bride play, and intends to complete her revenge on Francisco by revealing to one and all that the gallant has pledged himself to marry a boy. But Martia's father recognizes this boy bride as his long-lost daughter. Whether or not spectators anticipated that Ansaldo was Martia, they would have enjoyed the satiric reversal of seeing the trickster tricked. Middleton's combination of surprise with double cross-gender disguise achieves exactly this kind of satiric discomfiting, an effect not found in any of Shakespeare's disguised-heroine plays.

Within the world of the play, the joke is on Philippa and her servant, but within the world of the playhouse they share another joke with the audience, for Francisco's bride really is a boy and they themselves are boy actors too. There is no logical reason Middleton could not have added yet another revelation, that Ansaldo is not really the long-lost Martia, a girl, but (say) a long-lost son named Martin, who disguised himself as Martia, who disguised herself as Ansaldo, and so forth. Like the epilogue to *As You Like It,* with its easy reversibility of gender, the series of undisguisings at the end of *The Widow* implies the possibility, at least in the theater, of an infinite regression of gender reversals.

Around the time of *The Widow,* plays with heroines in male disguise also acquired special resonance from extratheatrical sources, especially from the modified forms of cross-dressing that flourished roughly be-

tween 1610 and 1620. Like real women wearing masculine attire, cross-
dressed theatrical heroines directly challenged the dress codes that helped
to reinforce established gender roles, but unlike cross-dressed women
in the street and in the audience, female pages on the stage were played
by male performers. For that very reason, while the figure of the female
page amplified challenges to the culture's rigid conception of gender
roles, an awareness of the boy actor could undercut the female characters
who made those challenges. Middleton exploited the interest in a hot
issue without taking a position in the debate. As in *The Roaring Girl*,
Middleton is here aware of gender politics, but as a playwright rather
than a pamphleteer he embedded them in a field of ingenious and subtle
theatrical play.

Surprise and Romance: Jonson's *The New Inn*

In one of his last plays, *The New Inn* (King's, 1629),[38] Jonson also combined a second cross-gender disguise with surprise. He did so not to
produce the kinds of satiric discomfitings noted in *May Day* and *The
Widow*, but rather to create an ending in the spirit of Shakespeare's
romances and Fletcher's tragicomedies. Female cross-dressing, which
Jonson had lampooned in the Collegiate Ladies of *Epicoene*, could now
be integrated into a tragicomic vision.

Following the examples of Chapman and Middleton rather than
Heywood and Shakespeare, Jonson waited until the end of the play to
inform his audience that the host's boy, Frank, is a woman named Laetitia Frampul. Nor are the spectators ever told that the secret of Frank's
identity is bound up with other secrets: the host, called Goodstock, is
really Lord Frampul, and the Irish nurse who sold "Frank" to him is
really his own wife, who left home with Laetitia and has disguised the
girl as a boy. By 1629, few spectators would have been surprised by such
revelations of gender or kinship. Jonson has both the host and the nurse
hint at who they are, makes "Frank" unwittingly pun that he descends
"of a right good stock" (II.vi.23),[39] and mentions a long-lost daughter
of the Frampul family named Laetitia.

Like Chapman and Middleton, Jonson makes the disguised heroine,
Frank, the site of theatrical reflexivity. When Frank, who is "a bashfull
child" (II.ii.11) rather than a saucy lackey, is compared to a "play-boy"
(I.iii.5), the audience is pointedly reminded that it may be watching
either a boy actor playing a boy disguised as a girl, or a boy actor playing

a female character disguised as a boy disguised as a girl.[40] The issue is not settled until the final scene.

Like Chapman and Middleton, Jonson also reinscribes female impersonation into the world of the play when Frances, the host's daughter, agrees to help "Frank" pass as a "gentlewoman," as a joke on the gallants who are visiting the inn. Unaware that Frank is her sister, she observes that his name is the male equivalent of hers (II.ii.19–23) and proposes that they "call him Laetitia, by my sister's name" (II.ii.56). The sisters establish a Court of Love, a pastime that enables Frances and Lovel to express the love for one another that they cannot otherwise acknowledge. As Jon Lawry has written, "Theatricality . . . [can] express truth as well as concealing or degrading it."[41] A tone of sadness overcomes the play when Frances's chambermaid, Pru, proclaims "the Court's dissolv'd, remov'd, and the play ended" (IV.iv.247).[42] Lovel, echoing Pru's theatrical metaphor, reverts to despair and misery, while Pru disparages her "courtly" apparel as "this play-boyes bravery" (IV.iv.321). Lovel and Frances will eventually be reunited, not through the wit of a heroine in male disguise, or of any other character, but by sheer dramaturgical ingenuity lightly masked as chance.

In what seems at first to be a more farcical key, Laetitia pairs off with Beaufort, an Ovidian sensualist among a group of Neoplatonists. Their relationship survives the dissolution of the Court of Love, and they go through a wedding ceremony. Eager to consummate the marriage, the lusty bridegroom begins to disrobe, but his ardor is squelched by the host, who tells him that he "ha' married, / Your hosts sonne, and a boy" (V.iv.45–46). Like the end of Middleton's *The Widow*, the host's revelation ridicules the man who appears to have married a boy bride. By dissolving the last surviving trace of the Court of Love, this disclosure also helps establish a more wistful tone.[43]

The roles played out by the lovers during the Court of Love have led only to evanescent and broken relationships, but a deeper level of theatricality, engineered by the playwright himself, now begins to restore those visions to actuality. Undoing the effects of the revelation of Frank's role as "Laetitia," Jonson now makes the Irish nurse reveal that this boy is really a girl. As in *The Widow*, the marriage is binding after all, and Beaufort's attraction to "Laetitia" is validated. Other revelations follow: when Beaufort churlishly balks at a marriage to so evidently lowly born a spouse, the nurse reveals that the girl is Laetitia Frampul, and that she herself is the girl's mother. If this disclosure satisfies

Beaufort, it astonishes the host, who announces that he is Lord Frampul, now reunited with his wife and both daughters. The revelations of the heroine's two fabricated layers of identity have provided the hinge on which the ending of the play pivots from satiric discomfiture toward the "Jonsonian equivalent of Shakespearean wonder."[44]

In *As You Like It,* Shakespeare allowed the audience to share the performer's perspective from the outset, and as the boy actor moved like quicksilver from one layer of identity to another, his nimbleness and skill in differentiating these various gender identities somehow seemed to endow the character of Rosalind with sufficient energy or power to control the world of the play, even as his epilogue enabled the boy actress to take control of the world of the playhouse. Dramatists like Chapman and Middleton, as we have seen, deprived the disguised heroine of her centrality and her power but carried the heroine's second cross-gender disguise to greater lengths for satiric discomfiting of comic gulls and for demonstrating their own dramaturgical virtuosity. Jonson tried to transcend satire by integrating surprise and double disguise into a romancelike central plot. Perhaps inspired by Shakespeare's last plays, Jonson deployed familiar devices defensively to forestall ridicule by acknowledging the play's artificiality and then invited the disarmed audience to enter an obvious if fragile fantasy of wish fulfillment and to enjoy an artistic tour de force.

Chapter 7

Anxieties of Intimacy: *Twelfth Night*

Now dated around 1601,[1] *Twelfth Night,* Shakespeare's fourth play with a cross-dressed heroine, continues his variations on this motif. Indeed, after *Two Gentlemen* each play of this type seems to be a deliberate variation on its predecessor(s). Three earlier plays stress the masculine side of the boy heroine's disguised identity. Two use pert Lylian pages and the third a doctor of the law. In part, the vigor of these male personas supports the assertiveness the heroine needs to control the outcome of the play. In *Twelfth Night,* Shakespeare enlarged the male persona that the boy heroine assumed along with male disguise. At times, the actor playing Viola displays Ganymed's audacity if not Balthazar's commanding resourcefulness. At other times, the role calls for different aspects of boyishness—delicacy and shyness. The two sides of Cesario's personality represent Viola's tendencies toward assertiveness and vulnerability, modulated to suit a young male servant. Cesario's double nature is underscored farcically by his terror of dueling but more interestingly by his appearance in highly charged duet scenes both with the man he serves and has come to love and with a woman who has fallen in love with him. In *Twelfth Night,* more explicitly than in previous plays involving heroines in male disguise, Shakespeare exploited the play-boy's dexterous articulation of layered sexual identities by accenting the very sexuality of these identities. Some subsequent playwrights, such as Barry, Middleton, and Brome, picked up this variation and in turn modified it in characteristic ways, while Shirley alone surpassed Shakespeare in exploring the anxieties created by the homoerotic potentialities of the play-boy/female page.

The Staging of Intimacy

Although Viola plays a page who is at different moments both cheeky and shy, who attracts a woman and who is attracted to a man, the complex figure of male actor/female character/male disguise did not, I believe, fuse into a single androgynous entity. The young male performers who specialized in female roles were not genderless but boys or young men, not yet but potentially adult males. They were androgynous only in the sense that they might be sex objects both to some men and to some women. When they played romantic heroines, they must have been capable of representing sexually mature and responsive young women. In plays in which such women adopt male disguise, these same performers probably played female and male identities in contrasting ways. Indeterminacy of gender in disguised heroine plays occurred only when dramatists like Fletcher, Chapman, or Middleton wished to create uncertainty, if not actual surprise, in their audiences by withholding explicit knowledge of the page's female identity. As separate moments in a play highlighted the discrete layers of sexual identity belonging to actor, heroine, and disguised persona, various images of hetero- and homosexual intimacy crossed the consciousness of individual spectators, arousing types of anxieties peculiar to their own personal histories. Antitheatrical writers object to the images of women being represented on the stage, to the effeminization of the male performer, and to his use as an object of erotic excitement. Given the lack of reliable data and the probable heterogeneity of playhouse audiences, it seems impossible to specify which particular responses were elicited in which spectators by which types of theatrical combinations. Nor is it necessary to do so, for nearly any likely response to the representation of intimacy added excitement and risk to the form of play known as play going.

Some psychoanalysts suggest that spectators respond to theatrical representations of intimacy as primal fantasies, like children imagining that they are watching their parents in sexual intercourse. Such representation in Shakespeare's day might have included scenes of kissing, caressing, and embracing, as well as scenes depicting emotional relations implying or leading to sexual exchange. The psychoanalytic model suggests a rich mixture of responses, possibly including elements of desire, pleasure, jealousy, embarrassment, guilt, or fear. Because the precise components of this mixture vary widely among individuals, I refer to it by the general term *anxiety*.

As readers may recall from their own (early) experience, such moments of theatricalized intimacy may also test spectators' identification with protagonists. Juvenile audiences, one recalls, would snicker, hoot, and groan whenever their role models strayed into love scenes, even if these sexual exchanges were carefully stylized and stopped far short of implying intercourse, let alone representing it. Adult spectators may feel similar anxieties but rarely express them as open derision. Although the precise nature of the anxiety may vary with one's gender, social status, and personal experience, dramatized portrayals of sexual and emotional intimacy can be troubling because exciting and exciting because troubling. One adult defense against such anxieties is to dismiss what is happening on screen or stage as "only a film" or "only a play," that is, to use aesthetic distance as a psychological barrier.

But one of the theater's most potent effects is precisely the blurring of boundaries between art and life, an effect easily created when spectators are in the physical presence of live actors who are publicly saying words and occasionally performing actions usually reserved for secluded situations. By means of conventions and codes, theater also blurs the distinction between physical and emotional intimacy, for what actors do and say onstage may be intended to imply far greater physical or emotional intimacy than what is being enacted.[2]

The codes and conventions of Shakespeare's day, more restrictive than those of the late twentieth century, implied what could not be shown or what one was to imagine might be about to take place offstage. Passionate scenes between lovers and would-be lovers that seem tamely decorous to modern spectators might well have evoked stronger responses in the period and might have served as the equivalent of theatricalized primal scenes. Often the language surpasses the stage action in emotional intensity, as in Robert Greene's *James the Fourth,* where a woman who falls in love with a female page speaks of her "insatiate lust" even though her behavior, to judge from the text, is chastely self-restrained. Because of its unusual reliance on intimate duet scenes, *Twelfth Night,* which even by Elizabethan standards is restrained in the ways it dramatizes sexual attraction, needs to be understood in a context of theatrical representations of both sexual and emotional intimacy.

In the Renaissance theater, cross-gender casting added another set of anxieties because of the culture's official condemnation of homosexuality and the obsessive focusing of Puritan antitheatrical attacks on theatrical transvestism. Scenes of heterosexual physical intimacy in the world of the play could be seen as involving homoerotic acts in the world of the playhouse. How pervasive this view was among actual audiences is debatable, for very few plays do anything to authorize a puritanical response, but it seems likely that many spectators were aware of the condemnation of theatrical cross-dressing expressed in antitheatrical treatises and elsewhere throughout the period.

Addressing just such anxieties over the plays he produced at Christ Church College, Oxford, between 1582 and 1592, William Gager denied that his staging of heterosexual love scenes involved any actions that could be construed as homoerotic:

> As for the danger of kissinge bewtifull boyes, . . . it is un-trwe, . . . that owre Eurymachus did kisse owre Melantho. I have enquyred of the partyes themselves, whether any suche action was used by them, and thay constantly denye it; sure I ame, no suche thinge was taught. If you conjecture there was kissinge because Melantho spake this verse, *Furtiva nullus oscula Eurymachus dabit,* . . . yet, therby no kissinge can be proved agaynst us, but that rather, that thinge only in wordes was expressed.[3]

If Gager's attitude is representative, university productions did not *enact* sexual passion but rather *indicated* it through words alone, perhaps accompanied by chastely stylized stage business, as in some scholastic productions today. Gager also differentiated academic productions, ostensibly done for pedagogic purposes, from those of the commercial theater.[4]

Unlike Gager's pupils, Elizabethan professional troupes did not hesitate to dramatize moments of physical intimacy, and apparently did so with greater naturalism and intensity. J. G. B. Streett's catalog of examples suggests that English Renaissance plays call for considerably more kissing, caressing, and fondling than earlier scholars wished to acknowledge.[5] One example comes from Kyd's *The Spanish Tragedy* (c. 1588–90), a play written long before the alleged decadence of the late Jacobean and Caroline periods. In the famous bower scene, Horatio and Bel-Imperia sit down ("for pleasure asketh ease") and then graphically describe their progression from hand-holding to footsie, kisses, close embraces, and finally—just before his killers interrupt them—to Horatio's plea that Bel-Imperia "stay a while, and I will die with thee."[6] Gager's argument, that verbal expressions of emotional and physical intimacy need not necessitate physicalization, would not seem to apply to so explicit a listing of gestures.

It is hard to imagine the actors not doing what the characters say they are doing. By our standards, the actors might have seemed detached, but even if stylized or coded the physical gestures represent the sexual expression of passionate love, in this case a clandestine tryst rather than the simple kiss of Gager's example. Moments like this one aroused the ire of William Prynne, who was hardly an objective source and who probably relied on secondhand reports. Nevertheless Kyd's play provided a graphic example of what a Puritan like Prynne, in his antitheatrical tract entitled *Histrio-Mastix* (pub. 1633), called *"those immodest gestures"* or *"those reall lively representations of the actors of venery,"* which attend and set out Stage-playes."[7]

Such representations of heterosexual sexual activity, however naturalistically staged, probably evoked or accented the presence of the male actors, especially if, as Heywood claims, they were easily recognized by spectators. The aesthetic defense against anxiety caused by scenes of heterosexual intimacy—"it's only a play"—led to another source of anxiety by activating audiences' dual consciousness of play-boys and female characters and so evoking concern over (and sometimes interest in) what the male actors were doing with their own bodies.

Although most plays do not activate dual consciousness by explicit allusions at such moments, boy-bride plays do so by incorporating female impersonation into the world of the play, so that the audience finds itself in the position of those characters who are in on the joke, that is, watching a boy make other men believe he is a woman. If consciousness of the play-boy was accented by the reflexive effect of male disguise, then any intimate scenes involving a female page may have further underscored the homoerotic nature of the relationship at the metatheatrical level.

Staging Male Homosexual Intimacy: Farrant's *The Wars of Cyrus*

This complex of anxieties over the presentation of intimacy at both mimetic and theatrical levels can be illustrated by the subplot of *The Wars of Cyrus*. The play was probably written by Richard Farrant for the Chapel Children and performed in the first Blackfriars theater in the late 1570s, although it was not published until 1594. Both the subplot, adapted from Xenophon's *Cyropaedia,* and the main plot are variants of the captive-heroine motif often used in plays performed by the children's troupes in the 1570s and 1580s.[8] Alexandra, the heroine of the subplot, escapes from captivity by exchanging clothing and identities with her page, Libanio. Both mistress and page are played by two young male actors capable of depicting boys or women equally well. One plays a woman impersonating a boy, a female page; the other a boy impersonating a woman, a boy bride.

Libanio impersonates his mistress well enough to excite Dinon, their guard. As Alexandra, Libanio initially protests that "I am too young to love" (l. 894), while Dinon offers to buy her favors, but she then coyly implies that it is not the offer of wealth but passion itself that makes her "blush to say I love my Lord" (l. 935). When Dinon presses further—"And when thou blushes[t] *Dinon's* heart is fired; / Therefore to quench it give a gentle grant" (ll. 936–37)—Libanio parries by seeming to redefine "grant" in purely verbal terms: "My honor being preserved, my grant is given" (l. 938).

It is not clear from the text exactly how Dinon understands Libanio's ambiguous reply, nor whether he understands "honor" to mean reputation or virginity. Perhaps verbal capitulation is enough to satisfy him, or perhaps it is intended as a symbolic indication of sexual submission. In either case, he quickly falls into a state of lassitude, asking Libanio to "lull me asleep with sweetness of thy voice" (l. 942). In the context of this play, the song might have functioned as a symbolic indicator of sexual intimacy—the equivalent of the closing of the bedroom door in films of an earlier day. Although the song seems to put Dinon into state of repose, in describing this encounter to other men later in the play, Libanio disingenuously attributes the guard's sleepiness to other causes: "long continued talke, / And heate of sunne reflecting on the bankes, / Or happlie with the ratling harmonie / [of] Euphrates his gliding streames" (ll. 1112–15).

Whether or not the page's sexual submission was symbolically indicated, the boy bride immediately resumes his male identity. Having compromised his manliness by the assumption of female disguise and by allowing Dinon to see and perhaps to use him as a woman, Libanio now moves to redeem his own virility. The moment Dinon falls asleep, Libanio prepares to kill him with the guard's own sword, "the sworde that hangde loose dangling by his side" (l. 1120), but which he appropriates as his own in the soliloquy preceding the murder:

Sleep, *Dinon!* Then, *Libanio,* draw thy sword
And manly thrust it in his slumbering heart!
. . . Now *Dinon* dies! Alas, I cannot strike!
This habit makes me over pitiful.
Remember that thou art *Libanio*—
No woman, but a bondman! Strike and fly!

(ll. 944–57)

To reaffirm his own masculine identity, Libanio rejects both compassion
and self-pity as feminine attributes induced by his wearing of women's
garments, and he commits an act of "manly" violence. Only such an act
will cleanse him of the shame of being "taken" as a woman, and permit
him to accept the title that other men later bestow on him, "president
of manly fortitude" (l. 1128), in which there may have lurked a further
irony depending on the age of the play-boy cast in the role.

This subplot betrays considerable uneasiness about the risk to male
sexual identity when boys or young men impersonate women too successfully. Within the world of the play, Libanio's impersonation of Alexandra reflects exactly what young male actors often did in the world of
the playhouse—portray women who aroused the sexual interest of male
characters and, so it was said, of male spectators as well. In most plays,
such anxieties are unacknowledged and remain confined to the
metatheatrical level. Boy-bride plays like this one, however, bring such
concerns to conscious attention. Most of them, like *Epicoene,* focus ridicule on the man who mistook the boy bride for a woman. *The Wars of
Cyrus,* however, sees the "mistake" from the point of view of the boy,
dramatizing underlying concerns about the effects of cross-gender casting on male sexuality. That concern was brought to the surface more
subtly in plays like *Twelfth Night,* where, instead of reinscribing female
impersonation within the world of the play, cross-gender disguise reflexively underscored the presence of the male actor in the female role.

Staging Intimacy between Women: Greene's *James the Fourth*

Unlike *The Wars of Cyrus,* which dramatizes the attraction of a man to
a boy bride, Greene's *James the Fourth* (Queen's? c. 1590)[9] depicts a
woman's infatuation with a female page. As such it is a precursor of
Twelfth Night, the only one of Shakespeare's disguised heroine plays to

explore the relationship between the protagonist and another woman. Greene makes far more of Lady Cuthbert Anderson's desire for the disguised Dorothea, queen of Scots, than Cinthio did in the source (*Hecatommithi* III.i). Cinthio's novella denies any sexual basis to the relationship between Arenopia and her rescuer by informing the reader that "the wife of the knight [who nurses the female page back to health] liked her very much indeed, not lasciviously but . . . as a brother."[10] Greene devotes parts of two scenes to Lady Anderson's "insatiate lust" for the disguised Dorothea, yet does so with restraint. In V.i., the presence of Nano, Dorothea's dwarf, prevents Lady Anderson from wooing her patient too ardently. Six lines before the end of the scene, Dorothea sends Nano away and Lady Anderson is finally alone with the object of her affections for the first time. Their brief dialogue is formalistically intensified by rhymed stichomythia but nevertheless gives intimacy a very wide berth:

> *L. And.* Now, sir, what cheer? Come, taste this broth I bring.
> *Dor.* My grief is past, I feel no further sting.
> *L. And.* Where is your dwarf? Why hath he left you, sir?
> *Dor.* For some affairs; he is not travelled far.
> *L. And.* If so you please, come in and take your rest.
> *Dor.* Fear keeps awake a discontented breast.
>
> (ll. 94–99)

In another context, Lady Anderson's invitation might sound seductive; here it resembles the professional solicitude of a hospital nurse.

In V.v, Nano is again present and forces Dorothea to reveal her identity by offering to wager with Lady Anderson that "My master here will prove a married wife" (l. 21). Blushing but relieved, Dorothea verifies Nano's claim, while Lady Anderson, deeply stung, modulates from anger to shame and does so not in asides or soliloquy but in conversation with Nano and Dorothea:

> *L. And.* Deceitful beauty, hast thou scorned me so?
> *Nano.* Nay, muse not, madam, for she tells you true.
> *L. And.* Beauty bred love, and love hath bred my shame.
> *Nano.* And women's faces work more wrongs than these;
> Take comfort, madam, to cure your disease.
> And yet she loves a man as well as you,

Only this difference, she cannot fancy too.
L. And. Blush, grieve, and die in thine insatiate lust!

(ll. 46–53)

Then, in response to Dorothea's offer of friendship, still referring to the queen as "my lord," she expresses her continued love ("although not as I desired"), acknowledges her "false heart," and asks "pardon [of her] most gracious princess" (ll. 56–60). These rapid transitions skate quickly over Lady Anderson's complicated emotional states.[11] Her reactions result from her having made amorous advances toward a character she has discovered to be of her own sex, a situation inversely reflected in the fact that both actors were male, as Dorothea's cross-gender disguise would have reminded the audience.

Shakespeare's Staging of Intimacy between Women: Viola and Olivia

In *Twelfth Night,* Shakespeare puts greater pressure on the relationship between mistress and female page than either Lyly or Greene had done. In his earlier disguised-heroine plays, he did not allow any of his female pages to play intimate scenes with female characters, even though the source for *Two Gentlemen* had explored just such a relationship. In *Twelfth Night,* Shakespeare keeps Olivia and Viola together alone on stage three times in order to dramatize Olivia's deepening passion.

Each of these encounters begins by announcing a private rendezvous. In their first meeting, I.v, Olivia finds herself intrigued by this stranger, who had been saucy at her gates but who now seems respectful, if resolute.[12] Her interest piqued, Olivia dismisses her attendants: "Give us this place alone, we will hear this divinity" (ll. 218–19). Olivia's scorning of Orsino's suit, coupled with her pride and vanity, drive Cesario to declare what he would do "If I did love you in my master's flame" (l. 264), a declaration that for the first time in the scene diverts Olivia's attention away from her own role as the "cruel fair" and on to the person standing before her: "Why, what would you?" (l. 267). Cesario's answer, the energetic (and perhaps urgent) "willow cabin" speech, keeps Olivia's attention riveted on this audacious youth: "You might do much. / What is your parentage?" (ll. 276–77). In Olivia's next speech, she abruptly modulates from haughtiness toward Orsino to seductive charm toward Cesario:

> Get you to your lord.
> I cannot love him; let him send no more—
> Unless (perchance) you come to me again
> To tell me how he takes it.
>
> (ll. 279–82)

This first exchange, ending with Olivia's realization that she has caught the "plague," compresses and dramatizes what Shakespeare's probable source, Riche's "Of Apolonius and Silla," reports took place only after Julina (Olivia) had "many tymes taken the gaze of this yong youth." Julina is straightforward in revealing her feelings to the duke's emissary: "it is enough that you have saied for your maister; from henceforthe, either speake for your self or saie nothyng at all."[13] In two other duet scenes, Shakespeare dramatized Olivia's growing infatuation, and her attempts both to conceal and expose enough of it to extract a reciprocal response from Cesario.

Privacy is again stressed in the second meeting, when Cesario returns to woo on Orsino's behalf. He asks to speak alone with Olivia, who sends the other characters off: "Let the garden door be shut, and leave me to my hearing" (III.i.92–93). Her next words imply a desire for even closer contact: "Give me your hand, sir." She asks the servant's name but becomes angry when Cesario reopens Orsino's courtship, and then—as tactfully as she can—points out that she has virtually thrown herself at Cesario:

> To one of your receiving
> Enough is shown; a cypress, not a bosom,
> Hides my heart.
>
> (ll. 119–21)

Unable to make Cesario acknowledge her feelings, let alone reciprocate them, Olivia orders him to leave but then abruptly orders him to "Stay!" (l. 137). In one of the most reflexive moments in the play, each character accuses the other of not being "what you are" (l. 139). In their first meeting, Cesario had denied being a "comedian" but admitted "I am not that I play" (I.v.184), alluding both to the female character and metatheatrically to the performer. Here the line is repeated in revised form—"I am not what I am" (l. 141)—and underscores both of those layers of identity, as well as seeming to point beyond them to more profound ontological realms. But the dialogue returns abruptly to the mimetic level with Olivia's wish that "you were as I would have you be" (l. 142), Viola's "contempt and anger" (l. 146), and Olivia's aside, followed by her formal Petrarchan declaration of passion in rhymed couplets:

> Cesario, by the roses of the spring,
> By maidhood, honor, truth, and every thing,
> I love thee so, that maugre all thy pride,
> Nor wit nor reason can my passion hide.

(ll. 149–52)

In matched rhymed couplets, Cesario refuses to accept any woman's love, and the scene ends with one last plaintive appeal from Olivia—"Yet come again." But the urgent command is retracted, seemingly restated in less imperious but passionate terms ("for thou perhaps mayst move"), until it is masked by the duplicitous hint of her receptivity to Orsino's suit ("The heart which now abhors, to like his love" [ll. 163–64]). Olivia's entreaty to a social inferior plus her sudden abandonment of her vow of mourning, however lightly held, is a sure sign that powerful forces of sexual attraction are stirring in her.

More than in any of the possible sources and analogues, the scene emphasizes the desperation of Olivia's wooing, however restrained by decorum, as well as stressing Viola's confused mixture of embarrassment and anger. An Italian dramatic treatment of the same source material, Gl'Ingannati, avoided such delicate feelings in favor of franker physicalization of the mistress's "insatiate lust" framed by coarse onstage commentary.[14] In II.vi, the only duet scene between Isabella (Olivia) and Lelia (Viola) in her disguise as Fabio (Cesario), the lady reveals her attraction to the page by inviting him to "Come into the doorway a little" (2:308). She kisses him, just offstage, according to two voyeuristic servants, after which Lelia returns to offer her own cynical and self-absorbed appraisal of the situation: "On the one hand I am having fun at the expense of her who believes me a man, on the other I should like to get out of this scrape" (2:309). Viola is never approached as directly as this, nor is she amused by Olivia's plight: "Poor lady, she were better love a dream" (III.ii.26). Instead of Isabella's advances and Lelia's mockery, Shakespeare offers Olivia's enthrallment by the mysterious servant, an enthrallment she barely checked by her upper-class self-restraint. Less physically explicit than *Gl'Ingannati, Twelfth Night* suggests deeper wells of sexual passion and adds Viola's empathy with one she finds no less a victim of this bizarre triangle than herself and Orsino.

The third duet scene between Olivia and Cesario, embedded in III.iv, compresses their encounter into fifteen lines. Olivia does not need to demand privacy, as Fabian sees her coming with Cesario and warns Maria and Sir Toby to "give them way" (ll. 196–97). Jettisoning aristocratic reserve, Olivia complains that she has acted dishonorably in flinging herself at Cesario in order to bind him to her, while Cesario tries to make her empathize with Orsino's feelings of rejection so that he can renew Orsino's courtship. In each of these encounters, insistence on privacy leads one to expect physical intimacy, as in *Gl'Ingannati*, but Shakespeare dramatizes the emotional entanglements—Olivia's desire, vulnerability, and humiliation; Viola's bewilderment, irritation, and embarrassment. As in *James the Fourth*, the audience witnesses an intense interaction between two women, while the theatrical level involves the interaction of two male performers.[15]

Male Disguise and the Representation of Heterosexual Intimacy

Shakespeare's willingness to explore the problems of intimacy in scenes between a heroine in male disguise and the man she loves is all the more remarkable considering how few precedents he had to draw on in narrative or dramatic treatments of the material. In many narrative versions, particularly those in the chivalric tradition, the disguised heroine serves as faithful page or squire to her lover or husband. The emotional pressure of such proximity is rarely explored, even though she may sleep in the same room or bed, or on the same plot of ground, although Boccaccio and other writers of novelle develop the erotic possibilities of such scenes of intimacy.[16]

Until the Jacobean period, even when English playwrights dramatized moments of heterosexual intimacy, they rarely did so in scenes involving a heroine in male disguise, probably because of the reflexive power of the assumed male identity to call attention to the gender of the play-boy and so raise the kinds of anxieties alluded to by Gager and exorcised by Farrant in *The Wars of Cyrus*. Before *Twelfth Night*, stage heroines in male disguise are denied scenes of emotional intimacy with their husbands, lovers, or other men. Neronis, disguised as a page in

Clyomon, meets her beloved, the title character, alone in the woods, but, as he too has concealed his identity, they fail to recognize each other. Once Dorothea, the heroine of *James the Fourth,* dons male disguise, her only private encounter with a man, the assassin Jacques, is violent but is not sexual. Once Julia and Portia don male disguise, they have no duet scenes with Proteus or Bassanio. As Ganymed, Rosalind has one such moment with Orlando, but, as was noted, it was broken off in part because it suggested more intensity of feeling than either of them wished.

When Italian dramatists brought the disguised heroine and her beloved onstage, they usually sought broad comic effects, just as they did when the disguised heroine is wooed by another woman. In *Gl'Ingannati,* for example, Flamminio (Orsino) tells Fabio (Cesario) that he once loved "one named Lelia who I have often wished to say is the very image of you" (2:303). But when Flamminio repudiates Lelia in another duet, he fails to grasp the significance of the page's visible reaction:

> *Flamm.* You have lost your colour. Go home; have a hot cloth on your chest and a rub behind the shoulders. . . . What strange accidents befall us men! . . . he seems to love me so much that if he were a woman I should think him lovesick for me.
>
> (2:310)

Whereas the author of *Gl'Ingannati* stresses the comic effects of Flamminio's inability to see through Lelia's disguise, Shakespeare achieves quite different effects in *Twelfth Night,* in part because he stresses the female page's femininity rather than her boyishness. Alexander Leggatt observes that such stress on the female page's femininity is unusual: "Normally, when another character describes one of these disguised heroines, the emphasis is on the pert boyishness one imagines as a quality of the boy actor himself."[17] Viola is also less self-assertive than Julia, Portia, or Rosalind. Although she initially displays a brisk resolve to take control of her life, as the play unfolds she feels herself trapped by events she cannot subdue to her will, and she soon throws herself on the mercy of Time to untangle the knot that is too hard for her to untie.

The circumstances of Viola's disguising also accentuate her relative helplessness. The other three heroines arrange their disguisings. Viola's depends on the cooperation of the captain, and she sees in male disguise no possibilities for parodying male folly. By the end of II.ii, she regards "disguise" as "a wickedness / Wherein the pregnant enemy does much" (ll. 27–28). Neither a doctor of law nor the saucy lackey, Viola instructs the captain to "present me as an eunuch" (I.ii.56).[18]

Viola is also more isolated than Shakespeare's other heroines in male disguise. Her confidant, the captain, never returns after his initial appearance, leaving her with no Celia or Nerissa on stage through whom she can activate her identity as a woman. She therefore speaks in riddles to the other characters—"I am not that I play" (I.v.184), "I am not what I am" (III.i.141), and "I am all the daughters of my father's house, / And all the brothers too" (II.iv.120–21), and she frequently turns to the audience for soliloquies and asides, as neither Portia nor Rosalind need to do. While these moments establish a strong rapport with the audience, they do not "mock or undermine others, as comic asides conventionally do," but rather express her feelings of impotence and evoke pathos. She may take over the play, but she cannot control the plot.[19]

Intimate moments between the disguised heroine and the man she loves are lightly sketched in Riche's "Of Apolonius and Silla," where the page rises to the status of trusted valet: "Silvio [Cesario] pleased his maister so well that above all the reste of his servantes aboute hym he had the greatest credite, and the Duke put him moste in trust" (2:350–51). Leslie Hotson suggested that Shakespeare amplified and intensified Riche's narrative to make his Duke Orsino resemble Elizabeth's visitor of the same name from Italy.[20] Whatever the reasons, Shakespeare deviated not only from his source, but also from contemporary theatrical treatments of the heroine in male disguise and from his own previous treatments of the motif. He placed Viola, disguised as Cesario, in two scenes (one of them divided into two subscenes) with Orsino; and he dramatized the duke's growing attachment to his new "male" servant.

These scenes necessarily included material Riche had already narrated in earlier episodes. Silla had fallen in love with the duke when he visited her father and travels by sea to the duke's court so that "she might againe take the vewe of her beloved Apolonius" (2:348). Viola, shipwrecked by fortune, recalls hearing of Orsino when the captain mentions him as the local ruler. By denying Viola any previous involvement with Orsino, Shakespeare had to dramatize her falling in love with him at some point after she had taken on the identity of Cesario.

In fact, Orsino's attraction to Cesario is presented first. In the opening lines of their first scene together, I.iv, Valentine, one of Orsino's servants, paraphrases Riche's description of their rapidly developing intimacy:

> If the Duke continue these favors towards you, Cesario, you are like to be much advanc'd; he hath known you but three days, and already you are no stranger. (ll. 1–4)

He then dramatizes this relationship directly. Orsino's entering line, "Who saw Cesario, ho?" (l. 10), implies a sense of urgency, and his order to his other servants when he notes Cesario's presence—"Stand you awhile aloof"—is a demand for privacy that emphasizes the intensity of the bond that has suddenly grown between them. His next lines make the point explicitly:

> Cesario,
> Thou know'st no less but all. I have unclasp'd
> To thee the book even of my secret soul.
>
> (ll. 12–14)

The text inscribed in this book is Orsino's self-induced love for Olivia, which Shakespeare parodies as Petrarchist narcissism. In this mode, Orsino three times urges Cesario to plead "the passion of my love" (l. 24) to Olivia, while each time the page tries to point out the futility of the errand. Cesario's appeal to his youth and immaturity calls forth from Orsino a protest that plays reflexively across the various layers of Viola's identity:

> Dear lad, believe it;
> For they shall yet belie thy happy years,
> That say thou art a man. Diana's lip
> Is not more smooth and rubious; thy small pipe
> Is as the maiden's organ, shrill and sound,
> And all is semblative a woman's part.
>
> (ll. 29–34)

No less a victim than Olivia of Viola's cross-gender disguise, Orsino may without knowing it be responding to the woman beneath the disguise, but he takes Cesario to be what the audience knows the performer is—a pubescent male, or as Malvolio puts it, "not yet old enough for a man, nor young enough for a boy" (I.v.156–57).

As several critics observe, Cesario has the same effect on Orsino that he has on Olivia, drawing both characters out of self-absorption by riveting their attention onto himself.[21] But whereas Olivia was attracted by the audacity of one who dared to be "saucy at my gates" (I.v.197), Orsino finds himself drawn to the feminine qualities of his page. By making Cesario appear both as an effeminate boy and as a saucy lackey, Shakespeare guided the boy actor toward a fresher treatment of the heroine's male disguise. Based on the view expressed by Rosalind that "boys and women are for the most part cattle of this color" (III.ii.414–15), Cesario's feminine male persona, like the image of the master-mistress of sonnet 20, must have made Orsino's attraction to him both more understandable and more troubling.[22]

But unlike the speaker at the end of the sonnet, Orsino never explicitly dissociates himself from a sexual relationship with Cesario, and the actor can choose whether or not to make the duke self-conscious about his attachment to the youth.[23] As elsewhere in the play, the text gives him several opportunities to shift his focus away from Cesario by redirecting the conversation to his "love" for Olivia. Here, the transition from intense focus on the page to the resumption of Petrarchist posturing may occur gradually through the next line and a half—"I know thy constellation is right apt / For this affair"—or may be abruptly signaled by the phrase that follows, an imperiously vague command to his servants—"Some four or five attend him"—which in turn is followed by more Petrarchist self-dramatization—"All, if you will, for I myself am best / When least in company" (I.iv.35–38). After a short exhortation to Cesario, he leaves, allowing Viola an aside, a rhymed couplet that ends the scene and that is the first time the audience knows she has fallen in love with her master: "Yet a barful strife! / Whoe'er I woo, myself would be his wife" (ll. 41–42).

Cesario and Orsino are once again in intimate conversation in II.iv, a scene that has no equivalent in Riche's tale. Riche simply announces that the duke has chosen Silvio [Cesario] "to bee his messenger to carrie the tokens and love letters to the Ladie Julina [Olivia]." In *Twelfth Night*, this second conversation is interrupted by Feste's song and then resumed with even greater intensity. Both parts of the conversation, moreover, repeat the rhythm of I.iv: they begin with Orsino's insistence on privacy with Cesario, they require him to oscillate between his self-indulgent passion for Olivia and his troubled but intense absorption in Cesario, and they present that absorption in terms that reflect and activate the spectators' sense of Viola's multiple identities and hence of desire's possibilities.

In the first part of II.iv, Orsino sends Curio away to seek Feste and then summons Cesario to "Come hither, boy" (l. 29).[24] But again, the message he offers in this private moment is in fact a self-indulgent gesture toward himself as the model for "all true lovers" (l. 17), and again it is Viola/Cesario whose genuinely wistful response to the music attracts his focus on to him/her rather than on his own alleged passions:

> *Duke.* Thou dost speak masterly.
> My life upon't, young though thou art, thine eye
> Hath stay'd upon some favor that it loves.
> Hath it not, boy?
> *Vio.* A little, by your favor.
> *Duke.* What kind of woman is't?
> *Vio.* Of your complexion.
> *Duke.* She is not worth thee then. What years, i'faith?
> *Vio.* About your years, my lord.
> *Duke.* Too old, by heaven. Let still the woman take
> An elder than herself.
>
> (ll. 22–30)

Orsino's interest in Cesario's melancholy response to the music initiates an inquiry into the experience that underlies it. Dale Priest notes how that experience reaches out to implicate Orsino himself, as when Cesario implies to Orsino that the "favor" that his eye lingers lovingly upon is the duke's countenance.[25] Cesario's concentration on Orsino's complexion and years causes the duke to assume an avuncular tone, as if he is evading or resisting this deepening involvement with this mysterious creature "That can sing both high and low" (II.iii.40–41).

After Feste's song, Orsino again demands to be left alone with his page: "Let all the rest give place" (II.iv.79). Once more, his first words are a Petrarchist exhortation to "get thee to yond same sovereign cruelty" (l. 80), which lead again to an insistence on the preciousness of his feelings:

> Make no compare
> Between that love a woman can bear me
> And that I owe Olivia.
>
> (ll. 101–3)

Viola's incomplete response "but I know—" may be deliberately un-
finished or broken off by Orsino. The choice determines whether his
question, "What dost thou know?" (l. 104) indicates rapt curiosity or
scornful dismissal. Viola's next speech introduces herself in thinly veiled
form:

> My father had a daughter lov'd a man
> As it might be perhaps, were I a woman,
> I should your lordship.
>
> (ll. 107–9)

As if enchanted, Orsino is drawn further into the story: "What's her
history?" Viola tells how "she pin'd in thought" and how "she sate like
Patience on a monument, / Smiling at grief" (ll. 109, 112, 114–15). Like
Rosalind, she breaks the spell herself by abruptly altering her tone,
speaking as Cesario, himself "in standing water, between boy and man"
(I.v.159), on behalf of "we men." But Orsino remains spellbound: "But
died thy sister of her love, my boy?" Viola's riddling answer alludes to
her layered genders:

> I am all the daughters of my father's house
> And all the brothers too—and yet I know not.
>
> (II.iv.119–21)

She then once more assumes the brisk tones of Cesario—"Sir, shall I to
this lady?"—and this time Orsino follows her lead, ending the scene by
resuming his Petrarchist guise:

> Ay, that's the theme,
> To her in haste; give her this jewel; say
> My love can give no place, bide no denay [*sic*].
>
> (II.iv.221–24)

In the modern theater, the audience's knowledge of Cesario's identity, which gives it the advantage of dramatic irony over Orsino in these duet scenes, is reinforced by the "theatrical irony" of the presence of a female performer in the role of the disguised heroine. Orsino found Cesario "semblative [of] a woman's part" (I.iv.34), but his failure to perceive Viola's female presence often makes him a more absurd figure than he was originally. On the Elizabethan stage, however, where Viola's assumption of male disguise blended with the play-boy's resumption of male identity, Orsino was protected from such ridicule. But the play then generated anxiety about homoerotic intimacy at the metatheatrical level, between an adult male actor and one of the troupe's apprentices.

Similar anxieties were evoked at its mimetic level by Antonio's selfless and reckless passion for Sebastian, which Shakespeare added to the material he adapted from Riche's tale. Antonio echoes Orsino's eroticized friendship with Cesario, and for some spectators probably evoked the homoeroticism that enemies of the stage associated with the playhouse.[26] Although most critics claim that Antonio, like his namesake in *The Merchant of Venice,* loses his friend to marriage, enabling the play to create "a context in which sexual ambiguity presages fulfillment rather than damnation," Joseph Pequigney argues that Sebastian never casts off Antonio's love and that a homosexual liaison is consistent with "the diverse bisexual fictions that make up *Twelfth Night,*" as well as an even more explicit replication of alleged homoeroticism within the acting company.[27]

Twelfth Night: The Final Scene

The intimate scenes between Orsino and Viola contrast sharply with the crowded, bustling farce of the low-comic scenes, as Jean Howard has observed in her study of the play's varying tonalities.[28] They also help to prepare the spectator for the violence of Orsino's outburst when he hears that Cesario has married Olivia. That outburst was anticipated by Antonio's reaction to Sebastian's evident duplicity, in which he compared "that most ingrateful boy" to "a witchcraft" (V.i.76–77).

The strength of Orsino's outrage indicates a wound deeper than his alleged affection for Olivia. When she enters, he observes her presence (instead of greeting her) in a single line of Petrarchan cliché, "Here comes the Countess, now heaven walks on earth" (V.i.97). Abruptly resuming his interrogation of Antonio, he then fails to answer her direct question addressed to him ("What would my lord . . . ?" [l. 101]), a failure that would be either the result or the cause of her immediately turning to Cesario. His first direct address to her in the play, "Gracious Olivia—" (l. 105) either runs out of steam or is cut short by Olivia. By contrast, his discovery of Cesario's apparent betrayal of him elicits an explosion of homicidal vengefulness nominally addressed to Olivia but in fact aimed primarily at his page: "Why should I not (had I the heart to do it), . . . Kill what I love?" (ll. 117–28).[29] While Olivia remains the "marble-breasted tyrant" she has always been in his Petrarchist fantasy, Cesario, whom he tendered dearly, has shocked him with an act of betrayal. He then turns to the page, whom he orders to the slaughter:

> Come, boy, with me, my thoughts are ripe in mischief.
> I'll sacrifice the lamb that I do love,
> To spite a raven's heart within a dove.
>
> (ll. 129–31)

Viola/Cesario's reply, matching Orsino's concluding couplet, meets the duke's homicidal threats with a martyr's eagerness:

> And I most jocund, apt, and willingly,
> To do you rest, a thousand deaths would die.
>
> (ll. 132–33)

Turning to Olivia, the page explains himself in couplets that are the most direct sentiments Viola has uttered about Orsino since the brief soliloquy following their first meeting:

> After him I love
> More than I love these eyes, more than my life,
> More by all mores than e'er I shall love wife.
>
> (ll. 134–36)

Accentuated by rhyme, these impassioned speeches articulate in public the nature of the relationship Orsino and Viola have played out in and between the lines of their intimate scenes together. As John Russell Brown has noted, Orsino's agonized sense of betrayal arises more from the loss of Cesario than from the loss of Olivia, a reaction that permits the audience to accept his love for Viola when her true sex is revealed.[30] Even after that revelation, Orsino twice refers to her as if she were male. On the theatrical level she still was and always would be male, but on another level Orsino wants to establish continuity with their earlier moments of intimacy:

> *Duke.* Boy, thou hast said to me a thousand times
> Thou never shouldst love woman like to me.
> *Vio.* And all those sayings will I over swear,
> And all those swearings keep as true in soul
> As doth that orbed continent the fire
> That severs day from night.
> *Duke.*   Give me thy hand,
> And let me see thee in thy woman's weeds.
>
> (V.i.267–73)

A few lines later, he speaks to her in her female identity, and then offers his own hand ("Here is my hand") to "your master's mistress" (ll. 325–26).[31] Orsino ends the scene by announcing that "a solemn combination shall be made / Of our dear souls" (ll. 383–84) and turns once more to his beloved:

> Cesario, come—
> For so you shall be while you are a man;
> But when in other habits you are seen,
> Orsino's mistress, and his fancy's queen.
>
> (ll. 385–88)

Although using the page's name may represent a wish to retain the relationship with his male servant, the final couplet restates the desire to see Viola dressed "in her woman's weeds" and can therefore define Orsino's final attitude more as impatience or relief than as uncertainty or disappointment about her gender.[32] Whether Viola removes a hat or releases bound-up hair, like Julia, she remains in male attire despite her resumption of female identity and the performer's resumption of whatever mannerisms, if any in this case, were used to signify it. Her page's apparel may in fact now accentuate her feminine identity, but Orsino's comment on the gender specificity of her clothing and his use of the name Cesario, whatever his own attitude, underscored the presence of the boy actor for the audience.

Such reflexive allusion to the actor's maleness generated emotional crosscurrents counter to the play's drive toward heterosexual union. This prospect is always potentially present in the world of the playhouse when heterosexual intimacy is portrayed by an all-male company, but usually remains dormant unless something reflexive—like continued verbal reference to the abandoned but still visible cross-gender disguise—calls attention to the principle of layers of gender identity and so keeps spectators alert to *all* of the layers involved.

In modern productions, the allusions to Viola's male identity are comic rather than reflexive or metatheatrical, and the marriages that end the play seem "natural"; that is, the genders of the characters match those of the performers. But in the original production, these final allusions to the male component of Viola's identity actually underscored the existence of another level of pretense, in which the two brides-to-be in the play were young male actors. Calling attention to that pretense, which the audience had thought it had agreed to accept without question, now threatened to undercut the conventional ending in heterosexual union. For some spectators, the play's exposure of its own artificiality might even have implied another and very different ending based on the gender of the actors, and perhaps on suspicions that boy actors served as catamites within all-male companies. For other spectators, the stress on the play-boy's presence simply demonstrated with more explicitness than usual what they "always knew" a play to be—a theatrical illusion they had paid to see and could see again, along with others like it, whenever they sought diversion from "the wind and the rain."

In *As You Like It,* a similar movement toward the world of the playhouse, which also stresses the gender of the boy actor, is delayed until the epilogue. In *Twelfth Night,* by contrast, Viola remains in male attire, is still referred to as "boy" by Orsino—either out of habit or with self-conscious irony or possibly both, seriatim. In the absence of an epilogue, the audience's final impression of Viola includes her still contending with disguise as "a wickedness."[33] G. K. Hunter's summation of the general differences between the heroines also applies to the boy actresses in their final appearances: "Rosalind is able to use her disguise as a genuine and joyous extension of her personality; Viola suffers constriction and discomfiture in *her* role."[34] Hunter may be right about

Viola, but not about the performer, for in the absence of sequential off-layering, the male garb proclaims the simultaneous presence of all three layers of identity. The movement from play to playhouse negotiated by the epilogue in *As You Like It* occurs in *Twelfth Night* in Feste's final song. Alone onstage, Feste sings a kind of autobiographical sketch, tracing a few stages in a life cycle to suggest that pain and suffering are as inevitable and relentless as the "rain it raineth every day," and have been so since "the world begun" (V.i.405). With its surprisingly self-referential third line—"But that's all one, our play is done—" the last stanza sets the song's darker vision in the context of yet another vision— one that redefines the play just performed as a compassionate even if commercial effort to provide solace for the gloominess of the human condition: "And we'll strive to please you every day."[35]

Female Pages and Sensationalized Intimacy: Four Variations

Most other English dramatists who took up the heroine in male disguise followed *James the Fourth* rather than *Twelfth Night* in that female pages appear in intimate scenes only with female characters. Within the world of the play there is never any suggestion of lesbianism (evidently too threatening or incredible an idea for the commercial stage of the period), so that the pursuing women are simply foolishly mistaken about the object of their affections. Unlike Shakespeare, other English dramatists not only ridicule the lady's obsessive infatuation with the shy page, but frequently heighten the farcical effects by multiplication and "surprise," as well as by coarsening the tone of intimate scenes. Four of these plays rework intimate moments or relationships found in *Twelfth Night*.

Ram Alley

Lording Barry's *Ram Alley* (King's Revels, 1607–8), is one of the first plays to multiply intimate moments by having the female page interact with more than one female character. The heroine, Constantia, who has donned male attire to follow the man she loves, enters his service as a page and beholds him wooing the wealthy Widow Taffeta. Like Orsino, Boutcher does not pursue his intended with genuine fervor, but instead of serving as his emissary, as Viola does, the page, presumably adopting a man-about-town air, advises him to approach the mistress by way of her servant, "for you must know / These waiting-maids are to their mistresses / Like porches unto doors: you pass the one / Before you can have entrance at the other."[36] The equivalent in *Twelfth Night* would be to have a suavely urbane Cesario urge Orsino to make love to Maria in order to obtain Olivia. The page recoils, however, when the Maria figure, of course depicted by another play-boy, attempts to seduce *him:*

> A pretty knave, i'faith! Come home tonight,
> Shalt have a posset and candi'd eringoes,
> A bed if need be too. I love a life
> To play with such baboons as thou.
>
> (ll. 817–20)

The bawdy tone of these passages typifies the coarseness of the play. For example, Barry makes Constantia fear not that she will be shamed if discovered wearing male attire but that her own sexual excitement at seeing male apparel will give her away:

> Lord, how my feminine blood stirs at the sight
> Of these same breeches! Methinks this codpiece
> Should betray me.
>
> (ll. 7–9)

Writing for a minor boy company when the vogue for children's troupes was ending, Barry burlesqued the conventions of cross-gender disguise by turning tactful scenes of intimacy into sexual farce.[37]

No Wit, No Help Like a Woman's

For the main plot of *No Wit, No Help Like a Woman's* (Lady Elizabeth's? c. 1611), Middleton adapted an Italian academic comedy, Porta's *La Sorella*,[38] but the subplot, which is entirely his invention, is a farcical reworking of the Viola-Olivia relationship in *Twelfth Night*. It is also a female version of his own early city comedies, in which a "prodigal daughter," Kate Low-water, outwits a greedy widow, Lady Goldenfleece, who, together with her late husband, had bilked Kate and *her* husband of their estate. Early in this play, Kate enters the widow's house disguised as "a gallant gentleman, her husband like a serving-man after her" (II.i.169). As a swaggering gallant, Kate drives away the rival suitors and hopes to regain her property by winning the widow's heart. The plan goes beyond the verbal audacity with which Viola unintentionally arouses Olivia's love. Kate will "put her to't, i'faith" (II.iii.94), that is, gain the widow's heart by all but conquering her body. Kate instructs her husband to stand by, ostensibly to rescue the widow from rape but really to prevent the disclosing of Kate's gender. But the widow is taken with Kate's exhibition of macho bravado and declares that she will marry this "beardless youth": "with this kiss / I choose him for my husband" (ll. 186–87). As in *Twelfth Night*, a twin brother, split off from the heroine, arrives to provide a match for the widow and to facilitate Kate's undisguising: "You can but put me to my book, sweet brother, /And I've my neck-verse perfect, here and here" (ll. 343–44). Exactly where the performer locates his "neck-verse" is not clear from the text. The editor of the Regents edition here adds a stage direction, "Removes her disguise, revealing her bosom," along with a note to the effect that "Mistress Low-water's neck-verse . . . is her breasts" (125), without explaining how this effect might have been created by a young male actor.

Far coarser than Shakespeare's duets between Cesario and Olivia, Middleton here achieves broad comic effects: one play-boy oscillates between Kate's feminine modesty and a brazen male persona, while the other depicts the tension between the widow's feigned coyness and her genuine sexual excitement. Kate's impersonation of a brash youth evokes the presence of both male performers, again articulating the separate layers of gender identity in the enactment of both roles, highlighting the artistry required to negotiate them, and exaggerating the well-worn roles of cheeky female page and lusty, avaricious widow into opportunities for theatrical virtuosity.

Anything for a Quiet Life

Further elaboration of situations first found in *Twelfth Night* is illustrated by *Anything for A Quiet Life* (1619), where Middleton used an intimate scene between mistress and page in a drastically abbreviated subplot. To make the page's revelation of gender a surprise to the audience, or at least to cloud it in uncertainty, Middleton does not reveal that Selenger, Lord Beaufort's servant, is Mistress George Cressingham.

Selenger, who is pursued by Mistress Knavesby, is a shy rather than a saucy version of the page, a mere pawn of the clever wench in control of the intrigue. Unlike Olivia, who is truly infatuated with Cesario,

Mistress Knavesby is merely using the page to discourage Lord Beaufort from trying to seduce her. She literally entangles Selenger in her intrigue by asking the page to hold a skein of yarn for her to unwind and then grasping it in such a way as to hold him her "prisoner":

> for, look you, you are mine now, my captive manacled, I have your
> hands in bondage. (III.i.42–44)

Both characters use the stage business as a conceit for sexual entrapment and resistance that threatens at one point to become more than a conceit:

> *Mis. G. Cres.* . . . pray you, release me now.
> *Mis. Kna.* I could kiss you now, spite of your teeth, if it please
> me.
> *Mis. G. Cres.* But you could not, for I could bite you with the
> spite of my teeth, if it pleases me.
>
> (ll. 47–51)

They spar until Lord Beaufort enters, seeking his prey. He takes in the sight with exquisite politesse, simply observing that "you are busy" (l. 85), and offers to withdraw. Mistress Knavesby frees her captive, who leaves with a smutty masculine retort: "I'll ne'er give both my hands at once again to a woman's command; I'll put one finger in a hole rather" (ll. 92–93).

In the final scene, when Beaufort tells Knavesby that his wife has slept with the page, Mistress Knavesby confesses that "we lay together in bed" (V.ii.218), but Middleton then directs the audience's attention to the presence of "Mistress George Cressingham in female attire" (l. 214), to use the words of the stage direction. The revelation may or may not have surprised the audience, but her undisguising was either cut from the text or, given the audience's familiarity with the motif, could have been assumed to take place offstage.

A Mad Couple Well Matched

Richard Brome's *A Mad Couple Well Matched* (Beeston's Boys? 1636?) involves the heroine in male disguise with three different women. Although Brome never informs the audience that "this beardless Bellamy" is a woman, enough hints are furnished to arouse suspicion.[39] In a scene reminiscent of the first meeting between Olivia and Viola, a citizen's wife named Alicia Saleware is the first woman to fall for Bellamy. She receives this "handsome youth," an emissary of his employer, Lord Lovely, willfully misinterprets his remarks, kisses him, and fawns over him. In a subsequent scene, Lady Thrivewell, who has also fallen for young Bellamy, is seen in intimate conversation with the page. Mistress Crosstill, a widow, is the third woman to fall for Bellamy and tries to woo him even at the same time she herself is being wooed by a widow-hunting gallant.

Toward the end of the play, her brother, Fitzgerrard, suddenly appears, demanding that Lord Lovely produce his sister Amy, who left home two years ago to attend his Lordship. Bellamy then enters "in a woman's habit" and explains that she adopted "a masculine boldness" to be near the man she loved but feared she could never marry (V.ii.246–47). Unlike Orsino, Lovely did not find himself attracted to Bellamy, but he is as quick as the duke of Illyria was to propose to his former page.

Male Homosexuality Sensationalized: Shirley's *The Grateful Servant*

Not until Shirley's *The Grateful Servant* (Queen Henrietta's, 1629) did another playwright explore the anxieties that an Orsino might feel about his attraction to his page. To stress the point, Shirley made the audience wait until IV.iii for explicit revelation of the gender of the page, a delicate lad named Dulcino, who attracted not one but two adult males and appeared in duet scenes with each of them.

The first of these Orsino figures is Foscari, whom the page serves out of gratitude for having been "rescued . . . from the Banditti." Although Foscari claims to love Cleona, he is so strongly attached to Dulcino, this "sweet-faced thing, . . . [with whom] some ladies / Might change their beauties" (21). In a scene that recalls Orsino's avuncular advice about women to Cesario, Foscari warns Dulcino against the wiles of "some wanton lady [who] hath beheld thy face" (19), and, fearing that this "boy, so young and beautiful, / [is] apt to be seduced" by some court lady, he promotes him from his servant to "my companion" (20). Dulcino carries Foscari's messages to Cleona, who never becomes infatuated with the messenger as Olivia does with Cesario, and Shirley even has Cleona's comic servant spy upon the lady and the page in order to keep their duet at the level of farce. When Foscari decides to take monastic vows, he insists that Dulcino accompany him. The page agrees and is later extricated from this plight not through the removal of disguise but through the intervention of Father Valentio, who recognizes him as Leonora, the missing princess of Milan.

The second Orsino figure is the duke of Savoy, who had fallen in love with Leonora from her picture and hoped to marry her, but hearing of her father's plans for another match half-heartedly decides to court Cleona, Foscari's beloved. While visiting Cleona, however, he first sees Dulcino and is lovestruck by the sight: "What boy is that?... It is no common face" (31). Shirley points up the contrast between the duke's perfunctory wooing of Cleona and his excited discovery of Dulcino with an abrupt midline shift:

> There is a virtuous magic in your eye,
> For wheresoe'er it casts a beam, it does
> Create a goodness; [to Cleona] you've a handsome boy.
>
> (32)

In act III, when told that Cleona is ill, he first inquires for "the pretty boy I told thee of" before announcing that "we are resolv'd to comfort her" (50–51).

In the opening soliloquy of IV.ii, the duke tries to deny any sexual interest in the missing Dulcino but recognizes the nature of his "foolish passion":

> Our hot Italian doth affect these boys
> For sin; I've no such flame, and yet methought
> He did appear most lovely; nay, in his absence,
> I cherish his idea; but I must
> Exclude him while he hath but soft impression;
> Being removed already in his person,
> I lose him with less trouble.
>
> (64)

Only in Dulcino's absence can the duke maintain a platonic attitude toward the page. Shakespeare hinted at such anxieties in Orsino but never allowed him to pine for Cesario so explicitly nor to express relief when the page he loves turns out to be a woman. Shirley's duke is more direct:

I'll do my heart that justice to proclaim
Thou mad'st a deep impression; as a boy
I loved thee too; for it could be no other,
But with a divine flame; fair Leonora,
Like to a perfect magnet, though enclos'd
Within an ivory box, through the white wall
Shot forth embracing virtue: now, oh now,
Our destinies are kind.

(90–91)

Foscari is astonished—"This is a mystery, Dulcino!"—but resumes his courtship of Cleona, the second choice to Dulcino of both men throughout the play. One almost wishes that Leonora's twin brother would wander on stage to provide a match for Foscari.

In *The Grateful Servant,* as in *Twelfth Night,* adult male characters feel themselves attracted to a shy and delicate page whom they discover to be a female character, played as always by a male actor. Although reflexive allusions to the performer's gender are, as we have seen, inherent in virtually any play with a cross-dressed heroine, these two plays, and some of the others surveyed in this chapter, are exceptional. Their uniqueness lies in their linking the intimacy between characters in the world of the play to possibilities of intimate homoerotic relations between performers in the world of the playhouse.

In Shakespeare's previous disguised-heroine plays, we noted fleeting glances at male homoerotic behavior involving play-boys as cross-dressed female characters, as in the use of the name Ganymed, or in Nerrisa's offstage success while disguised as a clerk in obtaining Gratiano's ring. Given the allegations that play-boys were catamites, such glancing allusions must have produced a modicum of resonance. In *Twelfth Night,* Shakespeare brought these extradramatic resonances more fully into the world of the play than he had in previous works, and he was followed in this regard, albeit in different ways, by such dramatists as Barry, Middleton, and Brome. Shirley went further than Shakespeare by doubling the Orsino figure and by making one of the two worry about his sexual inclinations, thus articulating what in *Twelfth*

Night had been confined to a possible subtext of the master-page relationship.

It was at least seven years before Shakespeare wrote another play with a heroine in male disguise, and that work, *Cymbeline,* moved in yet another direction. There the short-lived relationship between eroticized female page and master, that is, between Fidele and the Roman general, Lucius, is treated more explicitly than in the plays before *Twelfth Night,* even if it has less structural and thematic centrality than the mutual infatuation between Cesario and Orsino.

Chapter 8
_____

From Center to Periphery: *Cymbeline*

Despite some resemblances to Viola, Imogen, the heroine of *Cymbeline* (King's, 1608–9)[1] and the last of Shakespeare's cross-dressed female characters, differs radically from those already discussed. All of the others are central figures. Three of them use male disguise to control the action and manipulate other characters, while the fourth, Viola, who is almost as powerless as Imogen, gains theatrical prominence through asides and soliloquies and intimate duet scenes. Imogen, an assertive woman who holds a central position in the opening scenes of the play, becomes one of many characters buffeted about by providential events and dramaturgical ingenuity. Fidele, her male persona, is not a cheeky Lylian page but a frail waif.

In plays like *Cymbeline,* as in some narrative treatments of the motif, the powerlessness of the heroine in male disguise accompanies a deemphasis of her role. Some are pawns in other characters' intrigues and appear only in brief subplots. While male disguise may embolden heroines in comedies, it does little to empower cross-dressed heroines in plays in the romance tradition, where the weakening and marginalization of cross-dressed female characters might even have been perceived as a rebuke to women who wore male apparel.

When the heroine's true gender and identity are a "surprise," that is, are not explicitly revealed to the spectators, she is unable to make the audience privy to her scheme, share with them any of the dramatic irony of cross-gender disguise, or entertain them with rapid moves between layers of identity. Even after the surprise effect was weakened by overuse, the ambiguity surrounding the page's sex could have been exploited theatrically, but such treatment would probably have forestalled the audience's sympathetic engagement either in her witty audacity or in the

173

pathos of her plight. In plays derived from the romance tradition, the cross-dressed heroine became less of a focus of attention in her own right and more of a figure in the dramatist's design.

Diminishing the Cross-Dressed Heroine: *The Maid's Metamorphosis*

One of the first plays acted by one of the newly revived children's troupes, *The Maid's Metamorphosis* (Paul's, c. 1600) keeps the female page at the center of the play but treats her as a victim of circumstance rather than as an active intriguer and uses male disguise to stress the powerlessness of the cross-dressed heroine. As the title suggests, the heroine Eurymine does not really don a disguise but is transformed into a boy by Apollo, at her own entreaty, to avoid the god's lustful advances. The metamorphosis, which is reversible, is functionally equivalent to cross-gender disguise. Interestingly, the moment of the first transformation is simply Apollo's flat assertion, "I grant thy wish, thou art become a man,"[2] really a sign to the audience that henceforth this boy actor, onstage and still dressed as a woman, is to be thought of as a boy. If the actor played the transformed heroine as a boy, it was not as a saucy lackey, the role here taken by Joculo, a truly Lylian page who attends Ascanio, her beloved. Eurymine, who changes from girl to boy and back to girl, is always in flight, whether from gods or mortals, the helpless victim of divine power and her own fear of shame.

When Ascanio meets her and realizes her transformed state, he shares her horror of loving his own "kind," activating the audience's awareness that both actors were boys. That awareness is also activated when Joculo advises his master to determine her gender: "take her aside and prove" (l. 73). Despite this raucous wag's knowing audacity, Joculo is unaware that such a test would reveal Eurymine to be a boy, for, as the audience already knew, (1) she has been metamorphosed rather than disguised into male form, and (2) the character's gender, whether or not transformed, is imaginatively projected onto the body of a male performer.

The only possible resolution to this impasse is a countermetamorphosis. Phoebus obliges—"I graunt your willes, she is a mayd againe" (V.ii.74)—and then presents her, in "cloathes according to her kinde" (V.ii.82), as a "woman, in her right shape instalde" (l. 122). Through a second divine intervention rather than through undisguising, the play-boy once again returns to the female character. Reliance on supernaturally authorized countermetamorphosis is reminiscent of Lyly's *Gallathea,* and the title suggests a conscious link to Lyly's *Love's Metamorphosis* (Paul's, 1590), which may also have been revived by the one of the resuscitated chorister companies, hoping to stress its continuity with the children's troupes that had been suspended in the early 1590s.[3]

Cymbeline: Male Disguise With a Difference

Once Imogen dons male apparel, she is more like the hapless Eurymine in *The Maid's Metamorphosis* than such assertive female characters as Julia, Portia, Rosalind, or even Viola. The difference may be due to Shakespeare's decision to write tragicomic romances rather than romantic comedies. As many commentators have noted, this new type of play involved complexity of plot over complexity of character and highlighted the dramatist's dexterity rather than the play-boy's. In such a play, a cross-dressed heroine would have had to be more of a victim than an active intriguer. Nor could she be the only or principal victim, for romance usually involves the rupturing of familial and marital bonds and dramatizes the suffering of several characters until twists of dramaturgical ingenuity lead to complicated but satisfying reconciliations and reunions.

For Shakespeare as for most contemporary playwrights, the female page was evidently a comedic convention, even though narrative versions of the motif often evoke considerable pathos for the cross-dressed heroine. Earlier playwrights had also done so: Kyd's *Soliman and Perseda* (c. 1589) ends with the female squire's self-sacrificial death, while Greene's *James the Fourth,* as already noted, brings its disguised heroine Dorothea into considerable peril. Some later tragic and tragicomic treatments of the motif will be examined after a discussion of *Cymbeline.* As Peter Hyland has observed, tragedies and tragicomedies depict the disguised heroine's vulnerability to physical danger and evoke pathos for her plight, elements usually suppressed or lightly treated in comedies.[4] Shakespeare made limited use of the disguised heroine's vulnerability and pathos in *Twelfth Night* and even less in the other three romantic comedies.

He excluded the motif entirely from two problem comedies, *All's Well* and *Measure for Measure,* even though they are present in analogues and sources. In a fifteenth-century French version of the plot of *All's*

Well, Le Livre du tres chevalereux comte d'Artois et de sa femme, the heroine becomes her husband's *valet de chambre,* and, as is usual in such tales, shares his chamber, overhears his amorous plaints, and helps him pursue other women.[5] Whether or not Shakespeare knew this French chivalric romance, he was familiar enough with the genre and free enough in his treatment of sources to have had Helena disguise herself as a page rather than as a pilgrim had he so wished.

In *Measure for Measure* the absence of a heroine in male disguise is more clearly the result of Shakespeare's deviation from some of his known sources. The heroine of George Whetstone's unacted play, *Promos and Cassandra* (pub. 1578), keeps her assignation, as requested by Promos (Angelo), "Cloth'd like a Page."[6] As many critics have observed, the lovers in these two plays encounter external impediments to union more formidable than cross-gender disguise per se as well as internal obstacles too problematic to be overcome by a female page or even a female doctor of the law. The device he used to resolve the plots of these plays, the so-called bed-trick, is no more plausible than the female page, but evidently seemed consistent with the franker exploration of sexual relations one finds in *All's Well* and *Measure for Measure*.[7] Some years later Shakespeare returned to the female page in *Cymbeline,* not to parody the motif, like Chapman and others, but with a seemingly artless naïveté.

This illusion of artistic simplicity is all the more striking when one contrasts Imogen with the earlier heroines in male disguise. As argued in preceding chapters, each of these earlier works employs a different and increasingly ingenious way to use the reflexivity of cross-gender disguise as a theatrical means of amplifying the heroine's assertive power or to deepen the audience's sympathetic engagement in her plight. In *Cymbeline,* by contrast, aside from the disguise itself, Shakespeare uses no reflexive tactics to accentuate Imogen and seems to reverse his usual polarities by having an assertive female character become a shy and vulnerable boy. In original productions, this persona of a bashful boy or youth blended imperceptibly with the performer's male identity, creating an impression of depth by reminding the audience that it was watching a play-boy, as it "always knew" it was, playing a female character who had adopted male dress and a male identity. As the boy actor negotiated these layers of identity with skill and precision, he had opportunities to develop what I have been calling theatrical vibrancy in spite of the female character's increasing powerlessness. Such opportunities became restricted, however, as such characters became less central to the main plot or appeared only in subplots.

Unlike Julia, Portia, and Rosalind, who display or discover assertive strength only when they don male disguise, Imogen is a far more assertive presence before she puts on the page's costume. She stands up courageously to her father, stepmother, and Cloten; she bids a brief but passionate farewell to Posthumus; and she boldly counters Jachimo's initial gambits even if she fails to anticipate his winning moves. The most intense moment of theatricalized intimacy occurs before rather than after she dons male disguise, when Jachimo, poised over her sleeping body, describes what the audience could never see in a boy actor: "On her left breast / A mole cinque-spotted, like the crimson drops / I' th' bottom of a cowslip" (II.ii.37–39). As Fidele, however, she is closer to the powerless female pages and squires of pastoral and romance or to Greene's Dorothea than she is to the enterprising and resourceful heroines who put on male clothing in novelle and many earlier Italian and English plays.

Cymbeline and Shakespeare's Adaptation of Narrative Sources

Imogen has less power than the heroines of the two prose tales that Shakespeare drew on for the first part of the play—Boccaccio's *Decameron* II.9 and the anonymous *Frederyke of Jennen*.[8] Both tales include the story of the husband's wager, his belief in the slanderous lie of his wife's infidelity, the attempted assassination of the wife, and her escape in male disguise—all of which Shakespeare adapted to his use in the play. But he rejected what follows in both versions: the disguised heroine of the prose tales makes her way to a nearby port, where she is hired by a merchant about to embark with goods destined for the sultan; she wins the sultan's favor, advances in his service, and when the opportunity arises she contrives to make her slanderer confess and to be reconciled with her husband. The heroines of the prose tales resemble Portia more than Imogen, who remains a victim of events beyond her control.

Imogen's powerlessness was in part anticipated in *Twelfth Night*. Viola, in a comic rather than a tragicomic world, discovers that Time and not she herself will have to untangle the knot of her circumstances, and she resigns herself to patient waiting. In more dire circumstances, Imogen seems to wilt as, or just before, she becomes Fidele. Taken for dead at one point, she can only be rescued by a far more complex series of events in which dramaturgical invention represents benevolent Providence. Just before Sebastian's arrival, Viola alone stands accused of treachery by virtually everyone onstage, whereas Imogen is one of a procession of characters caught in and now about to be delivered from a web of events beyond their comprehension. Whereas a romantic comedy like *Twelfth Night* may require a deus ex machina or one or two strokes of Fortune to resolve its complications, *Cymbeline* and other tragicomedies multiply these complications in order to make deliverance the more wondrous. As Arthur Kirsch has argued, the playwright's ingenuity is inseparable from the play's cosmic vision:

> the dynamics of tragicomedy become a means of expressing the human creative process and the genesis of the play becomes wholly and marvelously indistinguishable from the evolution of the providential pattern which it represents.[9]

If Shakespeare intended to rework Viola's powerlessness when he began to experiment with the new tragicomic mode, then he could not completely model his heroine on the energetic and resourceful protagonists of the two prose tales from which he borrowed the story of the wager.

The scene in which Imogen becomes Fidele marks her deviation from the disguised heroines in Boccaccio's tale and in *Frederyke of Jennen*. She opens the scene with a barrage of impatient questions, but her husband's accusations of infidelity quickly dash her spirits, and her strength ebbs as she reads Posthumus's letter ordering her death. As Pisanio observes: "What shall I need to draw my sword, the paper / Hath cut her throat already!" (III.iv.32–33). Submissive to her husband's will, Imogen prepares for death, reluctant even to accept Pisanio's plan to fake her death:

> Why, good fellow,
> What shall I do the while? where bide? how live?
> Or in my life what comfort, when I am
> Dead to my husband?
>
> (III.iv.127–30)

Neither heroine in the prose tales accepts her husband's sentence so readily. Instead, they plead successfully for their lives and they themselves devise the schemes that will convince their husbands they are dead. The heroine of *Frederyke of Jennen,* known only as Ambrose's wife, is particularly resourceful: "I have a lambe here; we shall kyll it and take his tongue, and I wyll cut a locke of my here and with the bloud anoynt my clothes; and bere these tokens to your maister" (8:71). In *Cymbeline* it is Pisanio who proposes that Imogen adopt male disguise, but the heroines of both prose tales, like Julia, Portia, Rosalind, and Viola, conceive the plan themselves.[10] Indeed, Boccaccio's Ginevra formulates the plan as soon as she begins pleading with her would-be murderer: "Take my clothes, and give me only your jacket and a hood. Bring my things to your master and tell him you've killed me, and I swear by the life I'll owe to you, that I shall vanish to some place from which neither he nor you will ever hear of me again" (127).

Pisanio counsels Imogen to "tread a course / . . . near / The residence of Posthumus" (III.iv.146–48), near enough to hear of him even if she cannot watch him herself. The other two wives decide to seek their own fortunes elsewhere, and they rise to positions of responsibility, power, and independence in the service of the sultan. When chance or fate brings their husbands and slanderers within their reach, they choose to clear their names and restore their marriages.

Pisanio also urges her to adopt the familiar persona of the cheeky page, to affect "a waggish courage, / Ready in gibes, quick-answer'd, saucy, and / As quarrellous as the weasel" (III.iv.157–59).[11] Unlike Julia and Rosalind, who adopt just such a bearing when they present themselves as Sebastian and Ganymed, respectively, Imogen's Fidele retains the "fear and niceness" (l. 155) of a woman. Weakened from hunger when we first see her disguised as Fidele in III.vi, Imogen is thoroughly intimidated by Bellarius, Guiderius, and Arviragus when they discover her at their cave. Instead of "waggish courage," Fidele offers entreaties, apologies, denials, and compensation for the food she has eaten. At this point in the play, Imogen's circumstances differ from those of the heroines in the prose tales, and her characterization alters accordingly from the outspoken and defiant princess of the wager plot to the forlorn castaway of chivalric romance. Unlike the role of Eurymine in *The Maid's Metamorphosis,* which asked to be played as a frail waif in both genders, the role of Imogen demanded that the young male actor differentiate between the initially bold heroine and her disguised identity as a shy boy. This differentiation between an artificially constructed adult woman and an equally artificial bashful lad, I suggest, reinforced and was reinforced by the audience's awareness of the play-boy.

Cross-Gender Disguise and Myths of
Homosexual Desire

A note of rustic piety is struck in the opening speech of III.iii, when Bellarius enjoins his "sons" to religious humility. In III.vi, when the three men discover Fidele and observe the youth's angelic beauty, they begin to enact what Bruce Smith calls the Myth of the Shipwrecked Youth, one of six master narratives used in the period to structure male homosexual desire.[12] In classical versions of the myth, male travelers to an exotic place chance upon and fall in love with a beautiful male youth. In an intricate variant of the classic pattern, here an angelic youth (really a princess in disguise) wanders into the pastoral domain of three mountaineers (her two long-lost brothers, themselves not yet aware of their royal birth). As always, male disguise accentuates the presence of the play-boy and so raises the issue of homoeroticism at the metatheatrical level. Sexual overtones begin with Guiderius's speech of welcome, which acknowledges the "boy's" feminine beauty: "Were you a woman, youth, / I should woo hard but be your groom *in honesty*" (III.vi.68–69; emphasis added). Arviragus's "He is a man" raises the faint possibility of homoerotic attraction, as was the case when Orsino praised Cesario's feminine qualities. In short, Shakespeare uses male disguise to accentuate the presence of the play-boy to lend a dimension of authenticity to the Myth of the Shipwrecked Youth, which is an illusion in the minds of the three "mountain-men."

But the scene also undermines sexuality even as it hints at it. Fidele is incorporated into the family as an honorary sibling: "I'll love him as my brother" (III.vi.71), which in fact is the case, although only the spectators can be aware of that relationship, which might be thought to add a new set of anxieties over possibilities of incest. However, as Ruth Nevo argues, the Welsh scenes dramatize a "green world," a retreat from adult sexuality to a mode of "childlike nondifferentiation," so that while the prospect of incest is evoked, it blends inseparably with other feelings, "narcissistic . . . and familial," to establish a bond of kinship among the siblings before they actually discover their relationship.[13]

Sexuality is also defused by an emphasis on Imogen's weakened physical state. Unlike Shakespeare's earlier heroines in male attire, or the heroines in either of the two prose sources, Imogen's physical condition begins to deteriorate immediately after she adopts cross-gender disguise.

She does not play a saucy lackey, young lawyer, or court favorite, but a castaway whose vulnerability evokes tenderness and compassion in other characters. When she first appears as a page in III.vi, she reveals in soliloquy that she is sick and hungry, and in her next scene (IV.ii), her health has worsened to the point where her brothers are reluctant to leave her unattended. It is perhaps not only the potion but also the cumulative effects of emotional stress and physical deprivation that cause her to lose consciousness while the brothers are away, so that they mistake her for dead when they return. Instead of evoking spectators' erotic interest in the play-boy by emphasizing pert vivacity or feminine beauty, Shakespeare somewhat downplays any such sexual appeal of the play-boy by underscoring the character's physical frailty, a quality that would not become sexually alluring until the romantic age.[14]

Imogen's vulnerability as Fidele is also reinforced by dramatic irony on the dramaturgical level. Whereas Shakespeare's earlier heroines in male disguise have an edge over all other characters in that they (and perhaps a single confidante) possess the secret of their real identity, any such advantage Imogen might hold is neutralized by her being unaware of other facts that the audience knows full well, such as her mistaking the headless corpse lying beside her for Posthumus's, although the audience knows it to be Cloten's:

> I know the shape of's leg; this is his hand,
> His foot Mercurial, his Martial thigh,
> The brawns of Hercules.
>
> (IV.ii.309–11)

Deceived by her husband's garments, she thinks she identifies the lineaments of his body and even notes their mythological attributes. Viola, by contrast, is never the victim of so blatant a dramatic irony, and her soliloquies register her astute appraisals of her situation rather than her mistaken interpretations of what she sees.

Imogen's relationship with Lucius also seems like a version of the Myth of the Shipwrecked Youth. When the Roman general finds the boy, he too is strongly attracted to the page. Responding as much to the youth's loyalty to his "dead" master as to his physical beauty, he makes a kind of proposal: "Wilt take thy chance with me? I will not say / Thou shalt be so well master'd, but be sure / No less belov'd" (IV.ii.382–84).

Fidele accepts this offer, but must first see "his master" buried, pay his last respects with a pastoral tribute, "And leaving so his service, follow you, / So please you entertain me" (ll. 393–94). Like Arviragus, Lucius casts his affection in familial terms: "Ay, good youth, / And rather father thee than master thee" (ll. 394–95), and with no undercurrent of actual incest. At the end of the play, Lucius echoes Guiderius's emphasis on Fidele's feminine aspect. Requesting a boon, he appeals to Cymbeline to save the life of Fidele:

> A page so kind, so duteous, diligent,
> So tender over his occasions, true,
> So feat, so nurse-like.
>
> (V.v.86–88)

Even in his outrage when Fidele refuses to save *his* life, he equates Fidele's evident treachery not with sexual betrayal but with youthful duplicity found in both genders:

> The boy disdains me,
> He leaves me, scorns me. Briefly die their joys
> That place them on the truth of girls and boys.
>
> (V.v.105–7)

Again, ambiguity of gender interplays with the layers of the gender identity of the play-boy/female character/male disguise to suggest the danger of mature men involving themselves in romantic or sexual relationships with youths of either sex.

While Imogen's brothers and Lucius play out an illusory version of the Myth of the Shipwrecked Boy, the plot also develops the familiar myth of the wife who follows her husband in male disguise, serves him faithfully as squire or page, and reveals her identity to him, often as she is wounded or dying, in a final moment of revelation. From this point of view, Lucius is a surrogate for Posthumus: just as Cloten's sexual jealousy makes him a kind of debased double for Posthumus, as many critics have argued, so Lucius's passionate tenderness toward Fidele may suggest a parallel with Posthumus, just as the Roman general's angry denunciation of what he sees as the page's childish fickleness echoes Posthumus's mistaken belief in his wife's infidelity.

"Shall's Have a Play of This?"

During the time Ginevra and Ambrose's wife are in male disguise in the narrative sources, neither attaches herself to a man with the mutual devotion of Fidele and Lucius. Both heroines impress the sultan with their competence, and while they rise and prosper in his service, they develop no emotional ties with him. They retain their personal independence and draw on the sultan's authority to punish their slanderers and redeem their husbands. Imogen has no such worldly advantage, having lost both royal identity and female assertiveness even as she adopted male disguise, while even her attachment to the Roman general proves useless once he is captured.

She also loses the central position that she occupied in the first half of the play. Whereas the first two and a half acts develop the story of the wager, the movement to the Welsh mountains establishes another focus of interest—Cymbeline's lost heirs, who have not been mentioned since the opening dialogue between the two nameless gentlemen. At the same time, the focus is further divided by the dispersal of the central characters in the wager story (Posthumus, Imogen, Jachimo), now presented as lone individuals adrift in the war-torn world of the play. This shift from the tight focus of domestic comedy to the broader panorama of romance will make it totally impossible for the heroine in male disguise to unravel the events of the play merely by revealing her identity, or for any one character, for that matter, to do so merely by revealing a piece of information he or she happens to possess. Collectively, however, several such disclosures will all fit together in the final scene like pieces in a jigsaw puzzle, as if they were so intended by the power of Providence as manifested through the skill of the dramatist. The proliferation of obstacles to a harmonious conclusion is required by Jupiter's words of reassurance to the ghosts of Posthumus's family: "Whom best I love, I cross; to make my gift, / The more delay'd, delighted" (V.iv.101–2).

Much has been written about the series of revelations in the last scene that produce this harmony, each one set off by its predecessor and leading to the next. The effect is like that described by Granville-Barker as the kind of dramaturgy in which the playwright exposes rather than camouflages the artificiality of his contrivances, but does so without seeming to flaunt his skill:

The other plan is to show one's hand, saying in effect: "Ladies and gentlemen, this is an exhibition of tricks, and what I want you to enjoy among other things is the skill with which I hope to perform them." This art, which deliberately displays its art, is very suited to a tragi-comedy, to the telling of a serious story that must yet not be taken too seriously, lest its comedy be swamped by its tragedy and a happy ending become too incongruous. Illusion must by no means be given the go-by; if this does not have its due in the theater, our emotions will not be stirred. Nor should the audience be overwhelmed by the cleverness of the display; arrogance in an artist antagonizes us. This is where the seeming artlessness comes in; it puts us at our ease, it is the equivalent of "You see there is no deception."[15]

This chain of revelations uses elements of the disguised heroine motif but intertwines them with other strands of the plot.[16] Lucius tries to spare the page but is outraged after Fidele refuses to return the favor when given a boon by Cymbeline. The king is also drawn to this castaway boy, as strongly as Lucius had been: "Thou'rt my good youth— my page; / I'll be thy master. Walk with me" (ll. 118–19). Once more Fidele is cast as the Shipwrecked Youth until Pisanio recognizes him as Imogen; as he says, in an aside, of Fidele as Imogen: "It is my mistress" (l. 127).

Posthumus, in what must be an aside, is baffled by the page's interest in Jachimo's ring: "What's that to him?" (l. 136). He, like everyone else in the play, is confined by his own limited and inaccurate vision of events. Not only does he believe his wife to be dead, but he fails to recognize her even when she responds to his heartfelt self-mortification with the words "Peace, my lord, hear, hear." Mistaking "reality for illusion," as Anne Righter [Barton] puts it,[17] he repulses her in a speech whose reflexivity points up the ingenuity of the scene:

Shall's have a *play* of this? Thou scornful page,
There lies thy *part*.

(ll. 228–29; emphases added)

As the theatrical language suggests, Posthumus resents this apparent reduction of his situation to a dramatic contrivance that a female page can untangle simply by revealing her true identity. From the audience's point of view the reflexivity is particularly sharp, for what Posthumus cannot know is that this servant is his wife, whose undisguising, as in so many other dramatic and narrative versions of the motif, will indeed resolve at least some of the contrivances of the plot.

The play, however, seems to move away from that ending, for, as the ensuing dialogue makes clear, Posthumus knocks or pushes Imogen down, and she lies still, apparently dead for the third time in the play.[18] Just as Sebastian's fortuitous appearance rescues Viola from the entanglements caused by her disguise as Cesario, Pisanio now comes forward to tell Posthumus that he "ne'er kill'd Imogen til now" (l. 231), her true identity finally manifest to everyone present.

Her first words spoken as Imogen are a rebuke to Pisanio for giving her poison. They have enough bite to convince her father that this is indeed "The tune of Imogen!" (l. 237). Recovering her bodily strength as well as the energy of her restoration to herself, she rises (one assumes) to ask her husband the unanswerable question: "Why did you throw your wedded lady [from] you?" (l. 261). Perhaps after a slight pause to emphasize the impossibility of any adequate reply, she embraces Posthumus in a gesture of forgiveness and he reaffirms his love:

> *Imo.* Think that you are upon a rock, and now
> Throw me again.
>   *Post.*   Hang there like fruit, my soul,
> Till the tree die!
>
> (ll. 262–64)

Like Julia and Viola, Imogen remains in male disguise, but here there are no jokes or double entendres, as there are in the final moments of *The Merchant* and the epilogue of *As You Like It,* calling attention to the multiple layers of gender identity of the play-boy/female character/male disguise. Despite the presence of Fidele's apparel, the ending of the play stresses the image of the wife restored to her identities, blended rather than layered, as woman, daughter, princess, and wife.

The scene, still only half over, now begins to undo the tangle surrounding the king's sons. The chain of revelations just traced, culminating in the embrace of Imogen and Posthumus, is typical of the play's combination of deep feeling with self-conscious theatricality. The critical question is whether the emotional content of such scenes is undercut by their presentation in a mode of theatricality so patently contrived, even by Jacobean standards. Unless Shakespeare intended self-parody, which seems unlikely, he expected his spectators to become engaged in the characters' feelings in spite of theatricality, or perhaps even *because* of it. Norman Rabkin has argued that the seemingly artless but quite sophisticated exposure of artistry in *Cymbeline* is due to its being "a play as much about plays and play-making as it is about reconciliation."[19] But the self-conscious style may also have had a disarming effect, acknowledging the play's artificiality and stylization in order to free the spectators to empathize more directly with the characters.[20] Imogen's disguise as a boy, for example, underscores the presence of the male performer. Awareness of the play-boy gave substance to the illusory homoerotic attraction of adult men to this female page, while the disguised persona of boyish shyness also served as a metaphor for the heroine's vulnerability.

Fletcher's Arcadian Adaptation: *Cupid's Revenge*

It is not clear whether *Cymbeline* preceded or followed Fletcher's (and Beaumont's?) *Cupid's Revenge* (Queen's Revels, 1608?),[21] but the heroines in male disguise in these two plays are both in the frail-waif mode of tragicomedy. Unlike Imogen, who becomes a powerless castaway only after she dons male attire, Urania, like the self-sacrificing female pages and squires of romantic epic and pastoral romance, is powerless in either gender. Her essential innocence is underscored by her country-bred naïveté and contrasts with the duplicity and depravity of her mother, the widow Bacha. In the final act, she decides to serve the exiled prince in male disguise:

> When I have found my Brother, I will begge
> To serve him; but he shall never kno who I am;
> . . . Ile say I am a countrey Lad that want a service.
>
> (V.i.71–75)

The final scene of the play begins with an intimate exchange between Leucippus and this "poore boy" (V.iv.1), exhausted, hungry, and weeping, who has found the prince in the woods and now says he will die before he leaves his master's side. Troubled that the boy stares at him and sighs, Leucippus registers embarrassment at the intensity of the boy's attachment: "This is a love I never yet heard tell of" (l. 39), a line that can both activate and assuage anxieties over possibilities of a homo-erotic relationship, again with metatheatrical resonances. Urania's weak-ened condition, like Imogen's, diminishes rather than accentuates the character's female sexuality. Combined with the "boy's" selfless devo-tion to Leucippus, the scene evokes pity in the audience and paternalistic tenderness in the prince, producing *"a sort of innocent pathos."*[22]

This mood is shattered when Bacha's assassin enters to slay Leucip-pus. Urania "steppes before" (l. 69), as the stage direction puts it, to take the blow, enabling the prince to strike at the killer. With his last breath, the assassin tells the prince that his page, "your boy there" (l. 116), is a woman. Urania, now dying, reveals herself and in her last speech tells the prince why she came to him disguised as a boy:

> Feth for love,
> I would not let you know till I was dying;
> For you could not love mee, my Mother was
> So naught.

(ll. 136–39)

The prince responds with equal tenderness but cannot preserve her life. Whereas Shakespeare encouraged his play-boy to heighten the contrast between Imogen's defiant courage and Fidele's doleful fragility, Beaumont and Fletcher created Urania as a more monochromatic charac-ter whose female identity did not differ fundamentally from her disguise as a sad and delicate youth.

Adding Surprise to the Frail Waif: *Philaster*

James Savage argues persuasively that *Philaster* (King's, c. 1609) is a tragicomic reworking of the Arcadian materials Beaumont and Fletcher had previously used in a more purely tragic mode in *Cupid's Revenge*.[23] Euphrasia, the heroine of *Philaster,* is cut from the same cloth as Urania, but her identity is not revealed to the audience until the end of the play.[24] Spectators, however, may have suspected that Bellario was really a woman. Philaster's account of his discovery of the orphaned page, a kind of inset "mannerist elaboration" that suspends the forward movement of the plot,[25] emphasizes his pathos, tearfulness, and vulnerability:

I found him, sitting by a fountaines side,
Of which he borrowed some to quench his thirst,
And payd the Nymph againe as much in teares;
A Garland lay him by, made by himselfe,
Of many severall flowers, bred in the bay,
Stucke in that misticke order, that the rarenesse
Delighted me: but ever when he turnd
His tender eyes upon um, he would weepe,
As if he meant to make um grow againe.

(I.ii. 114–22)

The literary trappings of this vignette—the fountain, the statue of a nymph, the tears, and the floral garland—suggest the lovelorn maiden of pastoral tradition, the precise role Euphrasia claims for herself in a thirty-three-line speech at the end of the play. After Philaster's introduction, Bellario's frequent weeping and his clinging to his master would probably have aroused spectators' suspicions that this "little boy" (III.i.100) represented a disguised heroine in the world of the play. (Megra, an unreliable commentator, perhaps overestimates his age at "about eighteene" [II.iv.160].) Despite such hints, cross-gender casting and cross-gender disguise made it impossible for the audience to tell with certainty whether the young male actor was playing a shy boy or a young woman pretending to be a boy. Whatever the page's gender, the actor was male, so that anxieties of various kinds evoked by the intimate relationship between the adult male actor and the boy playing Bellario may have imbued the relation between the two male characters with "at least a whisper of homosexuality."[26] *Cymbeline* makes no secret of Fidele's real identity, but *Philaster* depends for many of its effects on the ambiguity of Bellario's gender.

Whereas *Cymbeline* insulates Fidele from suggestions of sexual intimacy, *Philaster* places Bellario, even though (or precisely because) his gender is uncertain, in situations that recall the page-master-mistress triangle in *Twelfth Night*, as Lee Bliss has argued.[27] Like Orsino, Philaster sends his page Bellario to his beloved Arethusa but does so not to woo her, for she has already astonished him by declaring her love for him, but rather "To waite on you, and beare our hidden love" (I.ii.140). Arethusa does not become infatuated with her wooer's emissary, as Olivia does, but instead is accused by a jealous rival of having slept with the page, whom she believes to be the source of the slander. Philaster, like Orsino, feels himself betrayed by both his beloved mistress and by "the trustiest, lovingst, and the gentlest boy, / That ever maister kept" (I.ii.138–39). But whereas Shakespeare makes fleeting use of Orsino's pain and confines his homicidal vengefulness to threats, Beaumont and Fletcher prolong Philaster's enraged agony through several confrontations with his two betrayers and allow him to wound them. Nor does Bellario have a twin brother, whose timely appearance can clear up the errors that have led to the charge of sexual infidelity leveled against Arethusa.

Distrusted by those he has served faithfully, Bellario plays alternating duet scenes with his master and his mistress. Whereas the intimacy of Viola's duet scenes with Orsino and Olivia stressed the unrequited love of all three characters, Bellario's intimate relations with Philaster and Arethusa cast him as an innocent victim despised by those he loves. In one of the intimate duet scenes, for example, Philaster's interrogation of his page takes a lurid turn, as he tries to induce Bellario to confess. First he tells the boy that he had ordered Arethusa to sleep with the page, then recreates the scene in vivid physical detail heightened by richly sensuous metaphors. When Bellario protests his innocence and suspects slander, Philaster tries another tack: he claims that he wanted his page to spy on Arethusa, perhaps even to seduce her, in order to test her fidelity. Bellario counters by insisting on Arethusa's innocence as well as his own, Philaster threatens to "rip thy heart" (l. 227), "drawes his sword" (stage direction, l. 242), and Bellario kneels and asks him to "kill me" (l. 265). Philaster is torn between doubt and belief—"A love from me to thee / Is firme, what e're thou doest" (ll. 275–76). Instead of taking "revenge upon / Thy tender youth" (ll. 274–75), he merely banishes his page: "if thou tenderst me, / Let me not see thee" (ll. 281– 82).

Beaumont and Fletcher repeat this scene by contriving subsequent accidental meetings between Philaster and Bellario, one ending in banishment and the other in the enactment of the threatened revenge. Several scenes in *Philaster* expand the moment in *Twelfth Night* when both Orsino and Olivia believe themselves betrayed by Cesario. In IV.v, the play's most sensational scene, Philaster sees Bellario comforting the sick and exhausted Arethusa after she has fainted. Taking this tableau as the ocular proof of their liaison, he banishes Bellario once more and wounds Arethusa, who has asked him to kill her. Whereas the intimate scenes in *Twelfth Night* develop the exasperation and frustration of unrequited love, those in *Philaster* explore powerful emotional ambivalences capable of erupting into the kind of "savage jealousy / That sometimes savors nobly" (V.i.119–20) merely spoken of by Orsino.

But *Philaster* is a tragicomedy, not a tragedy. Eventually all three characters are reconciled, even before the charge of slander has been disproved. Bellario is revealed to be Dion's daughter, Euphrasia, said in the play's opening scene to have "undertooke a tedious pilgrimage" (I.i.322). Bellario first reveals herself to her father just before she is ordered to be stripped for torture. Beaumont and Fletcher stretch this moment out in twenty lines of question and answer, reminiscent of the reconciliation of Sebastian and Viola: "Know you this face my Lord" (V.v.92), "where wert thou borne?" (l. 111), "What's thy name?" (l. 112). Dion's surprise is nothing compared to Philaster's, whose "joyful hysteria," as Andrew Gurr points out, produces "a moment of superbly serio-comic relief."[28] Then, echoing Orsino, Philaster asks Euphrasia to explain herself:

> But *Bellario*,
> (For I must call thee still so) tell me why
> Thou didst conceale thy sex.

(V.v.145–47)

Euphrasia's reply is as self-consciously literary as Philaster's account of first meeting the page. She describes how she fell in love with Philaster— "you left a kisse / Upon these Lippes" (ll. 164–65)—but understood that his social superiority would prevent their union, and so vowed "to hide me from mens eyes / For other then I seem'd; that I might ever / Abide with you" (V.v.181–83). The discovery of her true identity refutes the slanderous charge against the female page and acquits the play's romantic heroine once and for all.

Euphrasia's narrative disrupts the general rejoicing of the final scene with its doleful imagery and tone. The quarto modulates back to festive celebration by arranging a match for Euphrasia, but the folio prolongs her melancholy by having her reject marriage so that she can continue "to serve the Princesse, / To see the vertues of her Lord and her" (V.v.189–90) in a chaste ménage à trois, an offer Arethusa graciously accepts.[29]

Whether or not spectators initially identified Bellario as a disguised heroine, by the end of the play the character is revealed as the forlorn maiden of romantic epic, of pastoral romance, and more recently of dramatized tragicomic romances such as *Cymbeline*. *Philaster* is not so much an imitation of life as it is an imitation of art, or better, the self-conscious adaptation of familiar features of the romance tradition to the medium of the stage. It was once thought to have been Shakespeare's model for *Cymbeline* when the King's Men took over the Blackfriars theater, but scholarly opinion now holds that Shakespeare wrote *Cymbeline* about the same time that Beaumont and Fletcher were writing *Philaster*.[30] Both works adapt the romance tradition to the commercial stage in a self-conscious style, but they selected different aspects from that tradition and developed them in different ways for different purposes, as Harold Wilson noted:

> *Philaster* is a lively series of incidents contrived with great ingenuity to provide constant excitement and surprise and to issue agreeably with the recognition and reward of virtue, the dismissal of the wicked in disgrace. And it is nothing more. *Cymbeline* is, by comparison, more old-fashioned in method, more complicated and altogether more ambitious. At least as ingeniously plotted, it employs an utterly different method in the conduct of the action: preparation of the audience to perceive the dramatic ironies of situation, the joys and sorrows of reunion; it aims at effecting the gratification of expectancy rather than the shock of surprise.[31]

Both plays also call attention to their literariness, to their theatricality, and to their own self-conscious artistry. *Philaster* features contrived moments of impassioned rhetoric, what Lee Bliss calls "the long, frequently lovely arias of bewilderment and desertion [that] ... float free of any naturalistic moorings in character or situation."[32] *Cymbeline* highlights ingenious turns of plot and multiple dramatic ironies. Neither play contains low-comic characters or episodes, an uncharacteristic practice for Shakespeare even in the romances.[33] The political overplot of *Cymbeline* is inflected toward folktale by such elements as the heroine's mock death, her wicked stepmother, and her lost brothers, whereas the anticourt politics of *Philaster* have a satiric flavor that sometimes clashes with romance conventions.[34]

Whereas the self-conscious artistry in *Cymbeline* finally induces fuller empathy with the characters' situations, *Philaster* focuses attention on their passionate rhetoric. Seventeenth-century spectators apparently found that rhetoric to be theatrically compelling and psychologically illuminating, even though the ambiguity surrounding Bellario's true gender implies but does not insure that Philaster's accusations may be unfounded and Arethusa's self-defense unnecessary. Modern critics object to such verbal and theatrical artistry as a sensationalistic display at the expense of consistency or continuity of character. Kirsch, restating the condemnation of Coleridge and Eliot, deems the play "parasitic and without inner meaning" because the characters "are all primarily elements in a spatial design . . . [who] follow completely from the design, not the design from them."[35] But those critics who have admired Fletcher's self-conscious use of artifice in *Philaster* recognize it as a distancing strategy designed to replace the spectators' empathy with more analytical responses. Such responses include the perception of the play's rhetoric as "a projection of the characters' psychological condition," as evoking a celebration of and a skeptical interrogation of romantic idealism, and as outlining a Sidneyan testing of the characters' mettle through various contrived but balanced situations.[36] The critical problem is whether the ambiguity over Bellario's gender would have provided the requisite detachment for such analytic responses or whether it would have heightened the sensationalism still further or both.

No such ambiguity exists in *Cymbeline,* where Imogen's true identity is submerged but always known beneath her male disguise. Whereas Euphrasia shuttles between master and mistress until the time has come to reveal her identity, Imogen recedes from the center of the play to become a part of a vast pattern of guilt and repentance, doubt and faith, loss and redemption—all played out under the watchful and benevolent eye of Eternity as represented by the cunning hand of the dramatist and embodied in the play through the appearance of Jupiter. As different as Imogen and Euphrasia are from one another, they are both supporting roles and so instead of controlling the plays in which they occur, as female pages of the 1590s often did, they conform to the playwrights' patterns and purposes, variously derived from the romance tradition.

Marginalizing the Frail Waif: Three Variations

The new mode of tragedy and tragicomedy based on the romance tradition was extremely influential throughout the remainder of the early Stuart period right up until the closing of theaters in 1642. A number of such plays include heroines in male disguise in peripheral roles, in subplots, and in tacked-on endings, often in combination with several of the techniques developed by Shakespeare and discussed in preceding chapters. With the notable exception of Ford's *The Lover's Melancholy*, most of the plays that seem to derive from *Cymbeline*, especially those written in the Caroline period, illustrate the exhaustion and cheapening of a once powerful artistic innovation.

The Hogge Hath Lost His Pearl

Robert Tailor's *The Hogge Hath Lost His Pearl* (c. 1613), acted by a mysterious group of apprentices at Whitefriars,[37] was one of the earliest imitations of *Cymbeline* and other Shakespearean romances. Its subplot revolves around a betrayal of male friendship, in which one man impersonates a bridegroom and seduces his friend's bride, Maria, just before their elopement. When the deception is discovered, the bride swoons and is taken for dead but reappears "in Pages apparrell," as the stage direction indicates (l. 980), and becomes a melancholic youth hovering about the periphery of the play. Eventually all three characters meet in the forest. The seducer, having become deeply penitent and now disguised as a hermit, nurses the sickly page back to health. The two men meet, and the groom forgives the seducer, prompting Maria to "discover himselfe" (ll. 1538–39), as the stage direction puts it.

Like Imogen and Euphrasia, Maria loses rather than gains in assertive power by donning male disguise, which she cannot use to resolve the complications of the play. Tailor grants that power to his other disguised character, the villain who seduces her. In *Cymbeline*, the equivalent of Tailor's strategy would be allowing a disguised Jachimo to work out his own repentance and then to arrange for Posthumus and Imogen to forgive him. Tailor is clearly closer to the sudden reversals of *Philaster* than to the interlocking revelations engineered by the skilled dramatist and benevolent Providence of *Cymbeline*. Like both Fletcher and Shakespeare in these two plays, Tailor imagines the heroine in male disguise as a victim rather than an agent, as a powerless and relatively flat figure confined not only to the subplot but to ironic patterns generated by other characters or by Providence. But Tailor fails to develop compensating strategies like those in *Philaster* and *Cymbeline;* Maria, unlike Euphrasia, is known as a female page from the outset, and unlike Imogen, she is as fragile as a woman as she is as a boy. Because she has no assertiveness to dissolve in her assumed male identity, the cross-gender disguise loses the capacity, which Imogen's had, to express her vulnerability.

The Pilgrim

Fletcher's *The Pilgrim* (King's, c. 1621),[38] combines the motif of the frail waif with nearly all of the others we have encountered in this study but does so with more exuberance than subtlety. The play's heroine in male disguise, Alinda, starts out with considerable resourcefulness and wit, but like Imogen she soon finds herself blown about by the winds of unfortunate circumstance. At the beginning of the play, she avoids marrying the man her father has chosen by running off in male attire to find her beloved, Pedro. Fletcher does not dramatize her decision to flee in male attire, but we hear of her disappearance and soon learn that Roderigo, the outlaw chief, is infatuated with a "pretty lad" he has recently acquired. When Roderigo asks the boy to kill a captive, none other than Pedro disguised as a pilgrim, one quickly infers from the boy's asides that the lad is Alinda. When Alinda and Pedro later meet in a madhouse (III.vii), they see through each other's disguises. Teasing the audience with a moment of physical intimacy, Fletcher allows them a passionate embrace and then makes the shocked keepers separate them once again, for they do not know that the boy they see is really a female character, although their reaction might well have been shared by some spectators, for everyone in the playhouse knew that this character was portrayed by a play-boy.

Like Imogen, Alinda's disguise merely intensifies her role as a pathetic victim of her circumstances, and her helplessness is highlighted by the contrast with a second female page, her cheeky servant Julietta, who takes over the intrigue, adopts several disguises, and so brings about the joyful reconciliations that end the play. This high-spirited potpourri of theatrical conventions appropriated several of Shakespeare's innovations in the handling of the cross-dressed heroine—layers of disguise, more than one character in cross-gender disguise, and playful exploitation of anxieties over scenes of sexual intimacy—all piled on in casual profusion.

The Maid's Revenge

Shirley's *The Maid's Revenge* (Queen Henrietta's, c. 1626) tacks on a female page as a kind of ornament. Castabella, the disguised heroine, does not appear until IV.ii. She is the sister of Antonio, one of two friends, Sebastiano being the other, who wish to cement their friendship by marrying each other's sister. When Sebastiano, whom Castabella loves, kills her brother Antonio in a fight, Castabella goes to Sebastiano "dressed like a Page" (175) in the doleful style of Fidele and Bellario. He, of course, does not recognize her, nor ostensibly does the audience. She presents herself as Antonio's page and claims that Antonio's dying wish was that this page should serve his friend, Sebastiano, who is stricken with remorse. When Sebastiano is murdered, Castabella reveals herself: "I am no boy, / But hapless Castabella" (184). She spurns the attentions of a surviving nobleman and truly becomes the sad castaway she had half pretended to be, resolved "To spend the poor remainder of my days / In some religious house" (185).

Castabella wears male disguise for only two scenes, but when she does so, she quickly establishes herself in the frail-waif mode, a mode to which Shirley gives a novel tragic twist. He does so by contriving an ending in which the events of the play sweep her not to deliverance, as in other plays, but to a deeper level of tragic suffering.

Revising *Philaster:* Ford's *The Lover's Melancholy*

In *The Lover's Melancholy* (King's, 1628), Ford forged a coherent design by making his female page into a frail waif and, like Fletcher and Shirley, surrounding her with a number of other motifs used in plays with heroines in male disguise. But whereas Fletcher and Shirley seem to have adapted those conventions somewhat meretriciously, Ford blended familiar motifs into a Caroline romance of regeneration.

Dorothy Farr has noted Ford's extensive borrowing and reshaping of material from *Philaster*.[39] Whereas Philaster discovered Bellario weeping at a fountain, Menaphon has a similarly elaborate set-piece account of his discovery of "this fair-faced youth" (I.i.115), appropriately named Parthenophill, playing his lute in competition with a nightingale. When a courtier named Rhetias tells Prince Palador the story of a "lovely beauty" (II.i.167) named Eroclea who disappeared from court to preserve her honor when "a rape by some bad agents was attempted" (ll. 174–75), only a very dull spectator would have failed in 1628 to suspect that she had returned as Parthenophill. Rhetias also tells a supposedly fictitious story about a similar lady who "was conveyed like a ship-boy" (l. 195) and "lived like a youth almost two years" (ll. 197–98). In the next scene, Parthenophill starts and then weeps at the sight of her sister and her still-grieving father, but her gender and identity are not definitively revealed until the following act.

That revelation grows out of a situation already encountered in *Twelfth Night* and *Philaster,* when an imperious court lady, Thomasta, mistakenly woos the female page. Ford doubles the possibilities of anxiety by having Kala, Thomasta's bawdy servant, attempt to seduce Parthenophill as well. The boy deflects Kala's advances but finds no other way to parry Thomasta's ardent wooing than to confess, "I am as you are—in a lower rank / Else of the self-same sex—a maid, a virgin" (III.ii.161–62).

This gradual and limited disclosure of Eroclea's identity is part of Ford's strategy, for her reappearance is the climax of a therapeutic plan to bring Prince Palador out of his melancholy, and to restore Eroclea's father to sanity. Palador has, not surprisingly, found himself inexplicably attracted to Parthenophill, who has now disappeared, "For he is like to something I remember / A great while since, a long, long time ago" (IV.iii.29–30). Ford even adds a sort of retro-disguise: Rhetias claims to "have apprehended a fair wench in an odd private lodging in the city, as like the youth in face as can by possibility be discerned" (ll. 35–37) and, at the prince's urging, has "Eroclea [enter] in woman's attire" (l. 44). Unlike the hero of Heywood's *The Four Prentices,* the prince mistakes reality for illusion by seeing not the true Eroclea but her disguised persona, Parthenophill. Tempted though he is by what he believes is a mirage, he several times angrily rejects this "cunning imposter" (l. 80), this "disdainful boy" (l. 96), this "seducing counterfeit" (l. 107). His confusion is finally cleared up, when, in answer to his demand "Give me thy name," Eroclea for the first time in the play explicitly reveals herself: "if I offend, / Know when he dooms me, that he dooms Eroclea. / I am that woeful maid" (ll. 117–19).

Ford handles Eroclea's reunion with her father with similar dexterity. Before she enters, the prince sends the old man her picture, turning his thoughts toward her so that he will recognize her when she appears. Much of this scene echoes similar moments in *Lear* and *Pericles,* but Ford also has the female page provide a narrative account of her escape and survival:

> I, by my uncle's care,
> Sophronos, my good uncle, suddenly

Was like a sailor's boy conveyed a-shipboard
That very night. . . .
The ship was bound for Corinth;
. . . From thence, in habit of a youth, we journeyed
To Athens, where till our return of late
Have we lived safe.

(V.ii.159–68)

Menaphon's Fletcheresque discovery of the lutenist in the woods, Rhetias's recollection of Eroclea and his fictionalizing of her escape, the "boy's" ability to insinuate himself into the prince's favor, his disappearance and subsequent return in female attire, the quasi-surprise of Eroclea's self-revelation—all of these familiar plot devices of Fletcherian tragicomedy were part of a "theatrical cure" devised by the good courtiers to cure Palador, their head of state, of his lover's melancholy.[40]

To further enrich this self-consciously derivative but ingenious handling of the female page, Ford added two additional devices often used in plays with heroines in male disguise. One, already discussed, the potentially volatile motif of a lady wooing a female page, was underscored and further varied when the lady's servant also decided to woo the page. The second device is the presence of a boy bride. Grilla, a boy dressed as a girl, is presented as a practical joke to Cuculus, a foolish courtier whose humor it is to have a female page:

Instead of a fine guarded page we have got him
A boy, tricked up in neat and handsome fashion,
Persuaded him that 'tis indeed a wench,
And he has entertained him.

(I.ii.27–30)

Master and "female page" reappear several times to provide low-comic relief, particularly between Eroclea's two climactic reunions with the prince and then with her father. Ford's farcical use of cross-gender disguise here seems designed to protect the female page of the main plot from a sense that she might be a parody of what was by 1628 a heavily used motif.

In a way quite unlike *Cymbeline, The Lover's Melancholy* treats the female page as a frail waif irrespective of gender and even adds a number of other motifs associated with heroines in male disguise. The page's identity, like Bellario's, is withheld for a time from the audience, not to produce the kind of ambiguities noticed in *Philaster* but for successive disclosure to different characters as part of a collective scheme of psychological and political renewal, compassionately engineered by several characters and deftly crafted by the playwright.

The marginalized frail waif, as we have been calling the type of cross-dressed heroine in plays derived from the romance tradition, appears in only one of Shakespeare's late romances. Loss and recovery of sexual identity through the donning and doffing of cross-gender disguise is only one way of developing the theme of symbolic death and rebirth of the heroine. Shakespeare found even more powerful ways in *Pericles* and *The Winter's Tale,* where mothers are magically and miraculously restored to life, while daughters lost since infancy are reunited with the parents. Nevertheless, the experiment of *Cymbeline* was noticed and emulated by other dramatists, some of whom, like Ford in *Love's Melancholy* and Jonson in *The New Inn,* consciously hoped to recapture something of the tone and atmosphere of Shakespearean romance in the 1630s. During the preceding decades, the frail waif, like the other Shakespearean variations on the cross-dressed heroine—the saucy lackey, the use of multiple cross-dressed heroines, and the eroticized page—were used relentlessly on the English stage—with both mechanical ineptitude and sprightly ingenuity.

Epilogue

As we have noticed throughout this study, other playwrights of the English Renaissance took up many of Shakespeare's innovations regarding heroines in male disguise. Some, like Shirley and Brome, used them in facile combination with other motifs rather than exploring them as fully as Shakespeare had or developing them in original ways. Others introduced inventive variants of their own: Middleton pushed the heroine in male disguise toward broad satiric comedy; Chapman and Heywood devised ingenious reflexive effects around her; Fletcher, with or without Beaumont, subjected her to ceaseless experimentation; while Ford and Jonson blended a number of related motifs yet treated the cross-dressed heroine with playful gravity in an effort to create a Caroline equivalent of Shakespeare's late romances. Whatever one's own individual preferences, the plays studied in this book reveal how powerfully the dramatists of the English Renaissance were drawn to the heroine in male disguise. Some dramatists, Middleton most prominently, exploited the social resonances created by cross-dressed heroines at moments in the period when the role and status of women were under active debate. But the primary cause of their attraction to the figure of the boy actor/ female character/male persona was their sense of the excitement of watching a young performer project the illusion of multiple identities and deftly maneuver among them.

Shakespeare's role in developing this motif was pivotal. Not the very first, he was nonetheless one of the earliest to discover how the theatrical combination of cross-gender casting and cross-gender disguise could release potentialities in the heroine in male disguise quite different from what was possible in the numerous narrative treatments of the motif. Yet in each one of his five plays discussed in this book, Shakespeare treated the heroine in male disguise in a radically different way, and those differences become magnified when one notices how other dramatists not only followed his lead but sometimes elaborated a particular variation even further.

The key to Shakespeare's success and influence in developing this device, I believe, was his discovery that when a boy actor played a woman, the character's assumption of male identity made the spectators acutely conscious of knowing what they always knew—that the disguised identity, whether a saucy lackey or a shy victim, blended imperceptibly with the stage personality if not the actual identity of the male performer. This reflexive principle must have operated independently of any particular performer(s), for in original productions and revivals before 1642, the disguised heroines' roles were taken by a succession of play-boys. Each time Shakespeare created a cross-dressed heroine, he devised new strategies to reinforce this simple form of reflexivity and enable the performer to generate theatrical vibrancy.

Whether or not such strategies had been exhausted by 1642, the English commercial stage was never again to see, at least on a regular basis, the particular combination of male actors playing women pretending to be men. The training of young male actors as female impersonators ended when the theaters were shut down, and no such specialists were available when the playhouses reopened in June of 1660. The first productions evidently used adult men to play women, but in late August Charles II ordered the two newly chartered theatrical companies, Thomas Killegrew's King's Players and William Davenant's Duke of York's Servants, to use only women in female roles, ostensibly to protect the stage from moral objections to cross-gender casting, but also to replicate the lively theatrical life he had enjoyed during his Parisian exile. Thomas Jordan welcomed the change in "A prologue to introduce the first Woman that came to act on the Stage, in the tragedy called The Moor of Venice":

Our women are defective, and so siz'd,
You'd think they were some of the guard disguis'd;
For to speak truth, men act that are between
Forty and Fifty, wenches of fifteen;
With bone so large and nerve so incompliant,
When you call *Desdemona*, enter *Giant*.[1]

In contrast to such "giants," Edward Kynaston (b. 1643) was so effective as a female impersonator that he continued to play women for a short time even after the introduction of actresses. After seeing a production of Fletcher's *The Loyal Subject,* probably on August 18, 1660, Samuel Pepys declared that "one Kinaston, a boy, acted the Dukes sister but made the loveliest lady that ever I saw in my life—only, her voice not very good."[2]

Most male spectators, including Pepys, found the presence of real women on the stage to be even more exciting than Kynaston's represen- tation of a woman. For many, the primary theatrical attractions were well-known female performers, whose physical charms, personalities, and reputations were rarely submerged in the roles they assumed. Al- though actresses' costumes became noted for their extreme décolletage, breeches and doublets afforded ampler views of legs and thighs than did skirts and petticoats. Thirty years after the introduction of actresses, Thomas Southerne could still tease his audience for leering at Susannah Mountfort in male attire in his epilogue to *Sir Antony Love, or, The Rambling Lady* (1690):

You'll hear with Patience a dull Scene, to see,
In a contented lazy Waggery,
The Female *Mountford* bare above the Knee.[3]

The disguised heroine might be a lovelorn maiden, a virago, or a madcap swaggerer, but the male costume accentuated the actress's female sexual- ity. The moment of undisguising usually involved the fall of her hair as her periwig fell off in a duel or skirmish, or the exposing of her breasts when her doublet was loosened after a swoon. Because of such opportu- nities for display, plays with "breeches roles" for actresses accounted for nearly a quarter of the repertory between 1660 and 1700, although new works of this type were far more common than revivals of Shakespeare's disguised-heroine plays.[4]

During the revival of interest in Shakespearean comedy around the mid-eighteenth century, *The Merchant of Venice* and *As You Like It* were especially popular. Jeanne Addison Roberts suggests that these and other Shakespearean comedies whose heroines "combine goodness with ag- gressive intelligence and wit" allowed spectators of both genders to wit- ness "a sort of female emancipation acted out with applause in a public place."[5] Female characters in male attire or male disguise were closely identified with the talented and independent-minded "self-made women" who played the roles, and some actresses, such as Peg Woffington, frequently appeared in male roles.[6] By the late eighteenth century, however, the assertive actress/character in male disguise had fallen out of favor: Sarah Siddons played Rosalind in 1785 with her breeches covered with a short skirt.

Nineteenth-century audiences continued to prefer milder notions of femininity rather than the assertiveness of earlier cross-dressed heroines. In an age when very few actresses would consent to play women of less than exemplary virtue, Victorian productions of Shakespearean comedies, as Russell Jackson has observed, conformed to "a subtext in which virtuous, modest and loving women, endowed with uncommon resources of wit and tact, found happiness through marriage."[7] For Victorian actresses, male disguise was a source of embarrassment rather than an opportunity for self-display and led to the practice, attacked by Granville-Barker, of "reminding the audience that they are girls dressed up."[8] Disguise costumes helped preserve the actresses' modesty by concealing legs under cloaks, tunics, and high boots, and by hinting at underlying femininity with flared doublets, quasi-Greek skirts, and pillbox caps.

In our own day, the casting of women in female roles is taken for granted. As Kathleen McLuskie has argued, our theater presents Shakespeare's heroines in terms of its own changed and changing notions of femininity, that is, by modeling them on images of women produced by our culture—both in the social world and in literary, theatrical, and popular art forms.[9] But the prevailing naturalistic theatrical style, which she terms "critical-interpretive," strives to present these figures as if they were real people and uses women performers to do so, so that we fail to notice the degree to which both Shakespeare's texts and the productions we attend employ socially and theatrically constructed versions of femininity. Modern actresses, she implies, function as transparent signs through which we are invited to see the female character, even, or especially, when that character adopts a male identity. Freed from Restoration ogling and Victorian prudery, modern actresses interpret male disguise as a dimension of female character, as a way of revealing traits of personality that women have been trained to suppress or conceal. When cross-gender disguise is required, it provides insights into characters we have agreed to accept as real persons within the world of the play. Nevertheless, in spite of everything that generations of actresses have taught us about these roles, the particular reflexive effects I have traced in this book have eluded even the most talented performers, for those effects depended on the Renaissance audience being reminded of what it "always knew"—the sex of the male actor playing the heroine.

The casting of women as women altered the meaning and effect of cross-gender disguise. The introduction of actresses not only transformed the older disguised-heroine plays but also led to the creation of new "breeches parts" written to exploit the novelty of female sexuality on the public stage. For example, when Margery Pinchwife, the title character of Wycherley's *The Country Wife* (1675), goes abroad disguised as her brother, the audience is aware of the disguise and watches knowingly as Horner recognizes her and begins to kiss the "dear sweet little gentleman" because he lusts after her and also to torment her jealous husband, Pinchwife.[10] The comedy of that torment is based on (1) Pinchwife's uncertainty as to whether Horner has deciphered his wife's disguise or is making homosexual advances to a boy, and (2) Pinchwife's fear that his interference will either make him the jealous butt of Horner's jest or give away his wife's identity if it is not already known. Whatever kissing and fondling take place between Horner and the cross-dressed Margery, now played by a woman rather than a boy, is from the audience's point of view uncomplicated by any suggestions of homosexuality in the world of the playhouse.

From Wycherley to the present, many plays and films have exploited cross-gender disguise. Cross-gender casting, however, has disappeared as a regular practice from the Western European stage and screen, although it still flourishes in opera, where countertenors often sing female roles and mezzo-sopranos male roles, and has been used in such plays as Ronald Tavel's *Screen Test* (1966) or Caryl Churchill's *Cloud Nine* (1979), where casting a male actor in one of the female roles is designed to reveal or accentuate the constructedness of conventional notions of femininity.[11] Cross-gender disguise involving both genders has flourished in American films, such as *Some Like It Hot* (1959), *Victor/Victoria* (1982), *Tootsie* (1982), *Yentl* (1983), and *Mrs. Doubtfire* (1993). English Renaissance theater, however, combined female impersonation and sexual disguise, producing particular forms of reflexivity that shaped responses to dramatic texts, and hence the writing of those texts, in ways we have nearly forgotten. I have tried to recapture the vitality of the dramatic motif in early modern England by reconstructing something of its theatrical milieu and social context, both of which differ significantly from the practices of our own day and hence produced different meanings when male performers played women who donned male apparel to pass as men or boys.

Appendixes

Appendix A

Sources, Analogues, and Models

The heroine in male disguise did not originate on the English stage but has a long history in medieval and Renaissance literature. She occurs in the Italian prose tales that dramatists like Greene and Shakespeare quarried in search of material, as well as in earlier narrative forms, such as the saint's life, the chivalric romance, and the Renaissance epic and romance. All of these narrative forms were available to English Renaissance dramatists, while in Italy the *commedia erudita* not only borrowed from but contributed to prose narratives including heroines in male disguise.

The Saint's Life

The earliest body of disguised-heroine stories are a series of saints' lives originally developed in early Christian monasteries in the Egyptian desert and later elaborated in the West. By the sixth century, according to John Anson, there was a complete cycle of tales about women who entered monastic life in male disguise.[1] Five stories derived from this cycle of transvestite saints appear in Jacobus de Voragine's compilation of *vitae sanctorum*, entitled *The Golden Legend* and usually dated in the thirteenth century: Marina (June 18), Theodora and Eugenia (September 11), and Margaret and Pelagia (October 8). Such stories were known in England through Caxton's translation of this collection, published in 1483, while Thomas Heywood briefly retells several of them under the rubric of "Women that have dessembled [*sic*] their shape" in book 7 of his *Gunaikeion: or, Nine Bookes of Various History Concerning Women* (1624).

Anson outlines the basic form of the transvestite saint's life: (1) flight from the world, (2) disguise and seclusion, and (3) discovery and recognition. By passing as a man, the transvestite saint sacrifices her sexuality, so that instead of tempting monks to break their vows of celibacy, she embodies the community's ideals of fraternal harmony and alleviates the monastic readers' anxieties over sexual temptation. In the story of Anastasia, a female monk serves as her husband's closest companion for twelve years, until her death, at which time he discovers her true identity.

In some tales, the woman who sacrifices her sexuality is contrasted with her opposite—the lustful temptress who, like Potiphar's wife, accuses the disguised saint of the very sin she refuses to commit. Such tales often begin with the heroine's decision to renounce an impending marriage to preserve her virginity, but after entering monastic life disguised as a man, she is frequently accused by a pregnant woman of fathering her unborn child. In some stories the false accusation is cleared up immediately, but in another cluster, the slander is not disproved until the disguised heroine dies, often after enduring severe punishment and deprivation, and her body is prepared for burial. Anson argues that this last type of story allows the monastic readers to atone through the sacrifice of the saint for their own harboring of sexual desire: "after she has been punished for their desires, their guilt is compensated by turning her into a saint with universal remorse and sanctimonious worship."[2]

The redemptive sufferings of transvestite saints emerge in stark relief when contrasted with the legend of Pope Joan, a kind of antisaint, who first appeared in fourteenth-century chronicles. Boccaccio's treatment of the story in *De claris mulieribus* (1355–59) inverts the transvestite saint's life. Instead of donning male disguise to flee an unwanted marriage or repent for adultery, as other saints do, Joan takes on male identity to follow her lover. They go as clerics to England, where the lover dies. Rather than resume her female identity, Joan retains male garb and "refuse[s] to attach herself to anyone else or acknowledge that she [is] a woman." She moves to Rome, where her scholarly achievements earn her election to the papacy. But whereas other transvestite saints exemplify resistance to sexual temptation, Joan is "spurred by the devil" and falls "prey to the ardor of lust." Instead of being falsely accused of fathering someone else's child, Joan becomes pregnant, miscalculates the due date, and gives birth in public. (By contrast, the true sex of most transvestite saints is discovered when their bodies are prepared for burial.) She is imprisoned and dies in disgrace, and unlike saints who become redemptive models of chastity for the monastic readers, she serves as scapegoat for the libidinous impulses of both male and female readers. Thus, according to Boccaccio, the pope avoids the spot where Joan gave birth, "because of his hatred for that place."[3]

The transvestite saints' lives conceal their protagonists' female sexuality for the benefit of monastic readers by creating and canonizing asexual heroines. Although no longer writing for monastic or all-male audiences, Boccaccio's anti-saint's life nevertheless makes the disguised heroine seem like the embodiment of sexual temptation through women. The saint's life and its parodic inversion permit no other alternatives. In later medieval versions of such stories, presumably intended for secular readers of both genders, heroines employ the disguise not only to escape from an unwanted marriage but as a way of achieving their aims, which often means marrying on their own terms. While some heroines become extremely assertive in male disguise, others take subordinate male roles as pages and squires, and even those who achieve a desired union or reunion with a lover or husband eventually attain or resume the status of a wife.

For these later, secularized treatments of the heroine in male disguise, we must turn from the saints' lives to such narrative genres of the later Middle Ages and early Renaissance as the chivalric romance, the romantic epic, the prose romance, the pastoral romance, and the novella, as well as to the body of Italian stage comedy known as the *commedia erudita*. These forms cannot be placed in a simple lineal relationship to one another, for influences flow among them in all directions and older forms remain current and viable for centuries, affording Elizabethan playwrights a rich and varied body of disguised-heroine material from which to choose.

Chivalric Romance and Romantic Epic

Heroines in male disguise occur infrequently and late in medieval French romances. Some are viragos, or women warriors, perhaps inspired by figures in classical literature if not by some of a surprisingly large number of women who fought in actual combat between the tenth and thirteenth centuries, not necessarily disguised as men. Megan McLaughlin argues that women warriors, though rare, were more common before the thirteenth century, because "military organization [in Western Europe] was essentially domestic in character," which is to say that the "military unit . . . was the small group of warriors tied to a lord by bonds of personal loyalty or vassalage—which often reinforced the still deeper bonds of kinship." McLaughlin cites Christine de Pizan's *The Treasury of the City of Ladies,* in which wives of noblemen are advised to acquire "some practical knowledge of warfare."[4] By this time, however, warfare was often organized in a more professional fashion, either by the use of militias or mercenaries, and actual women warriors like Joan La Pucelle had become rarer in the historical chronicles but more common in romances and other imaginative literary forms. Folk literature also had its women warriors, such as Mary Ambree, Long Meg of Westminster, and other heroines of folk and broadside ballads.[5] Whether drawn from models in life or in earlier literature, warrior women appeared more frequently in Renaissance epics and romances than they had in late medieval chivalric romances.

Tristan de Nanteuil, a thirteenth-century chivalric romance, includes two women warriors who fight under men's names. The first, Aye d'Avignon, is the conventional virago, while the second is Blanchandine, Tristan's beloved, who is pressed to marry Clarinde, the daughter of the sultan of Babylon. She manages to delay the consummation of the marriage for four nights before fleeing to the woods, where she meets an angel who offers to transform her into a man. Believing that Tristan is dead, she accepts the offer and returns to Clarinde, only to discover that Tristan still lives.[6]

Ide in *Huon of Bourdeaux* also attracts the love of another woman and undergoes a miraculous transformation of sex, albeit with a happier outcome than for Blanchandin. After delaying the consummation of her marriage during more than a week of wedding festivities, Ide finally reveals her true identity to her bride, a revelation overheard and reported to the emperor, who sentences her to be burned at the stake. But Ide prays to the Virgin and is saved when an angel tells the emperor that God wishes the marriage to stand, and for that reason Ide has been "chaunged in nature, and become a parfeyght man as all other be with out any difference."[7]

A few chivalric romances contain a third type of heroine in male disguise, the fiancée or wife who passes for a page or squire in order to follow husband or lover to battle. Jehane, the heroine of a thirteenth-century work, *Du Roi Flore et de la belle Jehane,* is her husband's squire for seven years before her identity is revealed.[8] Nerones, the heroine of a fourteenth-century work, *Perceforest* (pub. 1528), which is also the source of the English play *Clyomon and Clamydes*, serves her beloved disguised as a page, whose name of Coeur Dacier testifies to his faithfulness.

All three types of heroine in male disguise—the warrior woman, the female bridegroom, and the female page—are more common in Renaissance romantic epics than in chivalric romance. The virtuous virago is often derived from such classical models as Virgil's Camilla in book XI of *The Aeneid*. Two others, Semiramis or Penthesilea, the queen of the Amazons, are mentioned in such catalogs of noble women as Boccaccio's *De claris mulieribus* and Christine de Pizan's *The Book of the City of Ladies*. Both Boccaccio and de Pizan supplement the list of classical figures with such women as Hypsicratea, queen of Pontus, who followed her husband onto the battlefield, as she was "burning with her great love" and "did everything so well that she seemed to have changed from a delicate queen to a veteran soldier."[9]

Although Hypsicratea does not actually engage in battle, the viragos of Renaissance epics, such as Ariosto's Bradamante and Spenser's Britomart, usually fight as bravely and effectively as their classical counterparts and do so on behalf of the established social and political order in the service of a king or feudal lord. Their female adversaries, such as Marfisa and Radigund, reject marriage and refuse to submit to patriarchal power.[10] Like the classical models, the viragos of Renaissance epics do not actually adopt cross-gender disguise, but when they are dressed for battle, they are sometimes mistaken for men.

Just such an experience befalls Bradamante, a virtuous virago, in canto 25 of *Orlando Furioso* (1516–32). Richardetto tells Rogero how his sister Bradamante, disguised as a knight and having had her hair cut short to cure a head wound, arouses the passion of Fiordispina, princess of Spain. Bradamante reveals her sex, but the princess feels no less passion and prays for a "mightie myracle" to change the woman warrior "[in]to a better sex."[11] Whereas the chivalric romances mentioned above actually provide such miraculous transformations, Ariosto, by contrast, has the princess's prayers answered by the sudden appearance of Bradamante's twin brother, Richardetto. He reveals himself only to her and they sleep together for months. This episode from *Orlando Furioso*, possibly in conjunction with Ovid's story of Iphis and Ianthe in book IX of *The Metamorphoses*, is probably the source for most of the

subsequent narratives in which the disguised heroine is loved by another woman.

Another influential passage in *Orlando Furioso* is the moment when
Bradamante's sex is revealed as she removes her helmet:

> Now when the Ladie did disarme her hed,
> Off with her helmet came her little call,
> And all her haire her shoulders over spred,
> And both her sex and name was knowne withall.
>
> (32:74 [32:79])[12]

As a way of (re)establishing femininity, "the sudden outpouring of
hair which flows down the armoured body" was evidently derived from
classical sources and achieved wide currency in the Renaissance.[13] For
example, in the third book of Tasso's *Jerusalem Delivered* (1581),
Clorinda, "the fierce virago" attired as a knight, meets her beloved
Tancred in battle. He does not recognize her until he knocks her helmet
off and sees her hair: "About her shoulders shone her golden locks, /
Like sunny beams on alabaster rocks."[14]

Spenser employs both motifs—a woman attracted to the heroine in
male disguise and the cascade of hair—at the opening of book IV of *The
Faerie Queene*. Amoret takes her rescuer Britomart, "the warlike virgine," to be a man, a deception Britomart encourages for her own reasons.[15] But Spenser makes Amoret far more chaste than Ariosto's Fiordispina, and, instead of falling in love with her rescuer, she fears that he
will take unfair sexual advantage of her. A few stanzas later, Britomart
overthrows a young knight and then reveals her identity:

> With that her glistring helmet she unlaced;
> Which doft, her golden lockes, that were up bound
> Still in a knot, unto her heeles downe traced,
> And like a silken veile in compasse round
> About her backe and all her bodie wound.
>
> (IV.i.13)[16]

Spenser probably had Ariosto in mind, but he also follows Tasso, when
Britomart's helmet, like Clorinda's, is knocked off by Arthegall:

The wicked stroke upon her helmet chaunst,
And with the force, which in it selfe it bore,
Her ventayle shard away, . . .
And round about the same, her yellow heare
Having through stirring loosd their wonted band,
Like to a golden border did appeare.

                                            (IV.vi.19–20)

If Spenser follows Arisoto when he makes Britomart decide where and when to reveal her identity, he imitates Tasso when he makes her disclosure involuntarily. For both male and female readers, the virtuous virago may have been a volatile figure, representing the empowerment of women but contained within a framework of male authority. Some readers may have lost sight of the line between the chaste and obedient woman warrior like Bradamante and the rebellious and misanthropic Amazon like Marfisa.[17]

As a less threatening alternative to either the martial virago like Bradamante or the untamed Amazon like Marfisa, not to mention the female bridegroom, the narrative literature of the period also developed the forlorn maiden or dutiful wife who follows her fiancé or husband disguised as a page or squire and whose devotion usually leads to a self-sacrificial end. In revising *The Countess of Pembroke's Arcadia*, for example, Sidney introduced both the warrior woman and the forlorn page. He added to book III the story of Parthenia, who disguises herself as the Knight of the Tomb and issues a challenge to Amphialus, who had slain her husband Argalus in battle. Parthenia is no Britomart, however, and actually seems to welcome death. She quickly receives a devastating blow from Amphialus, who "went to pull off his helmet" to dispatch his foe:

But the headpiece was no sooner off but that there fell about the shoulders of the overcome knight the treasure of fair golden hair which, with the face . . . witnessed that it was Parthenia.[18]

Whereas Tasso and Spenser contrast the femininity of the released hair with the warrior woman's martial bearing and physical prowess, Sidney uses it to reveal the hidden femininity that is the core of the character's being. Now that her true sex is known, Parthenia can evoke the pathos of a self-abnegating wife. With her last words, she thanks Amphialus for killing her—"the service which I desired"—and anticipates reunion with her husband—"I come, my Argalus, I come" (p. 529). Despite her aggressively martial demeanor, her motive is self-sacrifice rather than revenge. She is, as Jon Lawry claims, a "new Penelope."[19]

To book II, Sidney added the inserted narrative of Zelmane, who had disguised herself as a page and served her beloved, Pyrocles, under the name of Daiphantus even after contracting a mortal illness. Zelmane revealed her identity only in her dying moments:

> Know then my lords, and especially you, my lord and master, Pyrocles, that your page Daiphantus is the unfortunate Zelmane. . . . For your sake myself have become of a princess, a page, and for your sake have put off the apparel of a woman, and (if you judge not more mercifully) the modesty. (p. 365)

The inserted story of Zelmane is carefully and elaborately framed, which stresses it as a narrative artifice and enshrines the heroine exactly as Pyrocles sees her as "the emblem of a wholly undemanding ardor."[20] It is a tale-within-a-tale told by Pyrocles, who was himself disguised for much of the work as an Amazon named Zelmane.

Often framed in inserted narrative, heroines like Parthenia and Zelmane appear in prose romances well into and beyond the seventeenth century. Sidney's niece, Lady Mary Wroth, includes both assertive and forlorn women in male disguise in her long prose romance entitled, in imitation of her uncle's work, *The Countess of Montgomery's Urania* (pub. 1621). In a tale inserted into the main narrative, a knight tells how Isabella, the woman who loved him even though he spurned her affection, nevertheless followed him disguised as a squire. When they met in single combat, "the valiant youth," distinguished by "his vallour and worth," felled the knight by accusing him of killing Isabella by his refusal to return her love. Lying on the ground, the narrator repented and vowed that if she were alive he would not only marry her but "fall at her feet prostrate and beg her to accept me and command my service."[21] The youth, of course, was none other than Isabella herself, whose male disguise is an index of her resourcefulness and leads to romantic success. A conventional self-sacrificing heroine in male disguise had already appeared in an inserted narrative in the printed portion of the work: Amphilanthus learns how the youth who sustained a serious wound while helping him escape from prison revealed himself to be his scorned lover just before she died.[22]

Both assertive and pathetic women in male disguise probably appeared in many plays adapted from or influenced by chivalric romance, such as *Clyomon and Clamydes* (1570–83).[23] Although *Clyomon* was adapted from a French prose romance entitled *Perceforest* (pub. 1528), it shows the influence of later literary forms, such as novelle, for the heroine of the play is more resourceful than her counterpart in the narrative version, where she escapes her abductor by feigning death and assumes male disguise as a shepherd at the suggestion of a woman who has given her shelter. In the play, the idea for male disguise comes solely from the heroine herself: "painfull Pages show . . . is an honest shift, the which I have devised" (ll. 1261–64).[24]

The heroine of *Soliman and Perseda* (1589–92), attributed to Kyd, combines assertiveness and pathos in the manner of Sidney's Parthenia. She dresses as a knight in order to challenge her husband's murderer to single combat but is defeated by him, as she seems to have wished, and when she reveals her true identity in her dying moments, he is humiliated to discover he has killed a woman.

One of the most combative dramatic heroines to don male disguise is Bess Bridges, the title character of Heywood's *The Fair Maid of the West,* part 1 (c. 1602), who models herself on such woman warriors as Mary Ambree and Long Meg of Westminster, dresses as a page, and wears a sword.[25] Charlotte, in Chapman's *The Revenge of Bussy D'Ambois* (1610), and Eugenia, in Massinger's *The Duke of Milan* (c. 1622), are grimmer versions of the virago. At the climax of both plays, they enter in male attire and threaten to take over the role of avenger from their brothers. Although most of Fletcher's heroines in male disguise are cast in the pathetic mold, a significant exception is Clara, the heroine of *Love's Cure, or the Martial Maid,* who serves as her father's squire and is mistaken for her own brother, who appears in female attire. Like Sidney's Parthenia, Aspatia, the heroine of Fletcher's *The Maid's Tragedy* (King's, 1610), combines both assertive and pathetic modes; disguised as her own brother, she challenges her faithless lover Amintor to a duel and loses, revealing her identity at her death.

The Novella

Whatever its obscure origins in oral traditions of storytelling, the novella makes its formal appearance in the mid-fourteenth century. Influenced by chivalric romances and folk tales, its tone and content usually reflect a more bourgeois orientation. The novella not only shifts its setting from the court and the field of battle to the town and hence to such localities as the inn and the marketplace but undergoes a corresponding shift both in the social status of its central characters and in its thematic concerns. Self-sacrificing heroines in male disguise still turn up on occasion, but the typical heroine of the novella, whether or not she assumes a male identity, is more often "the clever wench," a bourgeois version of the virtuous virago, with wit and audacity substituting for the woman war-rior's courage and martial prowess. She uses her cleverness to arrange a satisfactory marriage on her own terms or to restore marital harmony, her vigor and energy finally serving rather than challenging a patriarchal social order.

The heroines of two well-known stories in Boccaccio's *Decameron* may suffer enough to evoke some pathos, but they also possess the intelligence and boldness to extricate themselves from their plights. One of these tales, II.9, is the source of *Cymbeline,* but its heroine, Ginevra, is far more resourceful than Imogen, who, as we have seen, is a throw-back to older narrative forms. The heroine of II.3, the princess of En-gland, like the heroine of many later Italian stage comedies, adopts male disguise to escape from a marriage her father is trying to arrange with "a very old gentleman," the king of Scotland. Dressed and attended as an abbot, she sets out for Rome, and en route meets the hero, Alessan-dro, the nephew and business partner of three Florentine brothers en-gaged in moneylending. The princess falls in love with Alessandro and one night in an overcrowded village inn reveals her true identity to him in a scene that treats the confusion of genders with considerable erotic explicitness and playfulness. The princess and Alessandro exchange mar-riage vows and make love all night long, "much to their mutual de-light."[26] When they reach Rome they reveal the truth to the pope, who blesses the union. The reader knows from the headnote that this "abbot" will turn out to be "the King of England's daughter in disguise" (p. 52) and so is free to admire the princess's audacity, to enjoy Alessandro's horror at the abbot's "homosexual" advances, and finally to savor the couple's frank sensuality.

Long after Boccaccio, novelle of the sixteenth and seventeenth cen-turies continue to place both assertive and pathetic heroines in male disguise. These tendencies can be illustrated by two of the tales in Giam-battista Basile's *Pentameron* (pub. 1634). In III.3, the heroine, Renza, is resourceful and brave enough to escape from her father's tower in order to be with her beloved, Cecio. They make love freely and vigorously until he is summoned home. Disappointed but not undaunted, Renza disguises herself as a lay brother and overtakes Cecio, who asks the boy to accompany him. Arriving home, Cecio finds that his family has arranged his marriage. Renza is overcome with anguish and sorrow, and overhearing Cecio about to make love with his bride in an adjoining room, she dies of a broken heart. Cecio discovers her identity and takes his own life.

Unlike Renza, who starts out as a clever wench but ends up martyred like a transvestite saint, Marchetta, the heroine of IV.6, avoids a similar fate by a combination of luck and pluck. A trickster in the mold of Jack the Giantkiller, Marchetta spends most of the story in the house of Ghula, a kind of ogress, from whom she finally leaves with a magic ring and "a sumptuous suit of man's clothes."[27] Disguised as a man, she enters the service of the king, whose queen plays Potiphar's wife to Marchetta's Joseph, and she avoids the execution only when she remembers on the gallows to use the magic ring, which causes a voice from the heavens to say three times, "Let her go, she is a woman" (p. 338). This miraculous rescue leads to a delightfully folkloric ending: appalled at his wife's conduct, the king orders her put to death and makes Marchetta his queen. In an earlier but more sophisticated version of the same story, IV.i of Giovanni Francesco Straparola's *Tredeci piacevolissime notti* (pub. 1550), the female attendants of the wicked queen turn out be her male paramours in female disguise.[28]

Heroines in male disguise continue to appear in novelle throughout Western Europe for the next four hundred years. As in nearly all narratives using the disguise motif, the female page or woman warrior shares her secret with the reader and perhaps a confidant(e) or two, so that her multilayered identity gives her a kind of narrative vibrancy independent of the character's own vitality or her ultimate fate as victim, bride, or restored wife. That is to say, the disguise adds an illusion of depth and complexity to the heroine whether she is a helpless and forlorn creature martyred for unrequited love or wifely devotion or whether she ingeniously, audaciously, and successfully pursues her lover or husband. In short, the writers of novelle, like authors of earlier narratives and later dramatic adaptations with female pages, used disguise to energize or empower the female character within a tale without placing her in direct conflict with patriarchal social norms.

Commedia Erudita

Novelle by Boccaccio and others supplied many of the plots for the earliest secular plays of the Italian Renaissance, the vernacular neoclassical comedies produced under scholastic or academic auspices. *Commedia erudita,* as this body of drama is called, preserved the framework of Latin comedy but drew heavily on novelle for additional plot materials, often involving romantic love, as well as for details of characterization and intrigue, such as the motif of the heroine in male disguise, which is virtually nonexistent in Roman drama. These academic plays also borrowed the bourgeois, urban settings of the novelle, a world in which the only women who went about in male attire were courtesans, so that heroines dressing as men were aware of the risk to their reputations. Unlike the commedia dell'arte, in which romantic (but not farcical) female roles were assigned to women in the latter half of the sixteenth century, *commedia erudita* used men or boys to play women's parts. The presence in these plays of the fanciful and playful spirit of carnival undoubtedly undermined such normative attitudes as the shamefulness of cross-dressing, both for the female characters in the world of the plays and for the male performers who played women in the world of the playhouse. Even more importantly, the balance between mimetic and presentational elements encouraged an awareness of male performers behind the female characters, an awareness probably highlighted by the characters' assumption (or resumption) of male identity.[29]

The first play to bring a heroine in male disguise to the Italian stage was Bibbiena's *Calandria,* originally performed in Urbino in 1513. Bibbiena combined details from several of Boccaccio's tales with the shipwrecked twins from Plautus's *Menaechmi* but added one major alteration: he made the twins of opposite sex and had them disguise themselves as one another. The play was very successful. Bibbiena's play was subsequently performed in Rome, Mantua, and Venice, as well as at the Bavarian and French courts, and had been published twenty times by 1600.[30]

Even more influential than *Calandria* was *Gl'Ingannati,* a play written by a member of a Sienese academy in 1531. The unknown author borrowed from Bibbiena's play the idea of reciprocal cross-gender disguises. One of the twins is a girl disguised as a boy, while the twin brother disguises himself as a girl and is taken for his sister. Like Ariosto's Rogero, he can thus sleep with the girl who has fallen in love with his sister's male persona. Lelia, the female twin, learns that Flamminio, the man she loves, wants to hire a page. Disguised as a boy, she leaves the convent where her father has placed her and enters his service. Lelia's first assignment is to woo Isabella on Flamminio's behalf, and as in chivalric romance and romantic epic, as well as in *Twelfth Night,* she finds that the lady has fallen in love with her, and she thus becomes the target of her master's fury. But Lelia's old nurse, who is aware of the deception, tells Flamminio a story of a woman who disguised herself as a page to serve the man she loves. Unlike the chivalric narratives, which often include embedded but self-contained stories of disguised heroines, the story told by the nurse in fact is that of Lelia, the heroine of the play. Flamminio is so moved by the tale that he wishes such a thing might happen to him and vows to marry a girl who would go to such lengths for her beloved. Lelia appears in her own identity, to Flamminio's delight, and they thank chance and fortune, along with patience and good counsel, for their union, although she might have praised her own courage and resourcefulness as well.

Gl'Ingannati was an extraordinarily influential play. Translated or adapted into Latin, French, and Spanish, it was performed throughout Western Europe, and widely imitated. Latin versions were known in England in 1547 and performed at Cambridge in the 1590s. In Italy, it served as a model for other writers of *commedia erudita,* specifically for two plays written by Niccolo Secchi in the 1540s. In one of them, *L'Interesse* (1540s), Secchi has Lelia, his heroine in male disguise, all but reveal her gender and her feelings to Fabio, the man she loves:

> *Fab.* Is she young?
> *Lel.* About your age.
> *Fab.* Is she beautiful?
> *Lel.* A charming face, and good-looking as yours is.[31]

In Secchi's other play, *Gl'Inganni* (1547), Secchi's disguised heroine refers cryptically to her real identity, telling her beloved that a mysterious woman loves him far more than the lady he is doting on, that she is "near you," that he knows her "as well as you know me," and that he sees her "as often as you see me."[32]

Shakespeare may or may not have known Secchi's work. Although John Manningham compared *Twelfth Night* with *Gl'Inganni* after seeing a performance of the former, heroines like Lelia could have come to

Shakespeare's attention in the 1590s in other ways. Several scenarios of the commedia dell'arte derive from *Gl'Ingannati* and may have been among those performed by the Italian troupes that occasionally toured in England.[33] But visits by Italian companies were rare, whereas Shakespeare had ample opportunities to encounter *Gl'Ingannati* indirectly through its numerous dramatic adaptations as well as its countless prose versions, many of which were themselves influenced by plays.

Reciprocal influences of narrative and theatrical treatments of the female-page motif became common in the second half of the sixteenth century. Bandello borrowed the Lelia story from *Gl'Ingannati* in his *Novelle* (1554), which were translated by Belleforest in his *Histoires tragiques* (1582, English trans. 1608). Barnaby Googe used the Lelia story in one of his *Eglogs* (1563). Barnabe Riche borrowed it twice in *Riche His Farewell to the Military Profession* (pub. 1581): in his eighth story, "Phylotus and Emilia," which is the source of the Scottish play, *Philotus* (pub. 1603), and also in his second story, "Apolonius and Silla," the principal narrative source of *Twelfth Night*. As we have seen, Montemayor used the Lelia story from *Gl'Ingannati* for the story of Felix and Felismena, which then became an embedded narrative in *Diana enamorada*.[34] In this embedded tale, as in *Gl'Ingannati*, the heroine who dresses as a page and woos a woman at the request of her master/beloved is herself loved by that woman, but Montemayor omits the twin brother who can answer the lady's prayers and makes her die of a broken heart. Despite these touches of chivalric romance, the basic plot of this inserted narrative in *Diana* is a simplified version of *Gl'Ingannati*.

Montemayor's embedded version of the Lelia story found its way back to the stage: it was probably the basis of a lost play entitled *The History of Felix & Philiomena*, which "her majesty's servants" performed in 1585. As was noted in chapter 4, Montemayor's work was the immediate source of Shakespeare's first play to use a heroine in male disguise, *The Two Gentlemen of Verona*, but English dramatists of the period had a wide selection of prose and dramatic treatments of the heroine in male disguise to use as sources, models, and analogues.

Appendix B

Chronological List of Plays with Heroines in Male Disguise

The first date given is that of performance, and the bracketed date is that of first publication. Blank spaces in the relevant columns indicate that the author or acting company are unknown.[1]

1570–83 [1599]	*Clyomon and Clamydes*		
1576–80? [1594]	*The Wars of Cyrus*	Farrant	Chapel?
c. 1578 [1578]	*Promos and Cassandra*	Whetstone	unacted?
1583–85 [1592]	*Gallathea*	Lyly	Paul's
c. 1589 [1592?]	*Soliman and Perseda*	Kyd?	
c. 1590 [1598]	*James the Fourth*	Greene	Queen's?
1592–94 [1615]	*The Four Prentices of London*	Heywood	Admiral's
c. 1593 [1623]	*The Two Gentlemen of Verona*	Shakespeare	Chamberlain's
1593–94 [1599]	*George a Greene*		Sussex's
1596–98 [1600]	*The Merchant of Venice*	Shakespeare	Chamberlain's
1598 [1616]	*Englishmen for My Money*	Haughton	Admiral's
1599–1600 [1602]	*Antonio and Mellida*	Marston	Paul's
c. 1600 [1601]	*Cynthia's Revels*	Jonson	Chapel
1600 [1623]	*As You Like It*	Shakespeare	Chamberlain's
c. 1600 [1600]	*The Maid's Metamorphosis*		Paul's
1601–2 [1623]	*Twelfth Night*	Shakespeare	Chamberlain's
1601–2 [1611]	*May Day*	Chapman	Chapel
c. 1602 [1602]	*How a Man May Choose a Good Wife from a Bad*		Worcester's
c. 1602 [1631]	*The Fair Maid of the West, I*	Heywood	
1603? [1603]	*Philotus*		unacted?
1603–5 [1638]	*The Wise Woman of Hogsden*	Heywood	Queen Anne's
1604 [1608]	*The Honest Whore, I*	Dekker and Middleton	Prince Henry's
1604 [1605]	*The Fair Maid of Bristow*		King's
1604–7 [1608?]	*Your Five Gallants*	Middleton	Chapel?

221

1605–13? [1647]	*Love's Cure*	Fletcher	King's
1605–6 [1607]	*The Fleire*	Sharpham	Queen's Revel
1607–8 [1611]	*Ram Alley*	Barry	King's Revels
1608 [1608]	*The Dumb Knight*	Markham	King's Revels
1608? [1615]	*Cupid's Revenge*	Beaumont and Fletcher	Queen's Revel
1608–09 [1647]	*Wit at Several Weapons*	Beaumont and Fletcher	
1608–9 [1623]	*Cymbeline*	Shakespeare	King's
c. 1609 [1620]	*Philaster*	Fletcher	King's
1610 [1613]	*The Revenge of Bussy D'Ambois*	Chapman	Queen's Revel
1610 [1619]	*The Maid's Tragedy*	Fletcher	King's
c. 1610 [1612]	*A Christian Turned Turk*	Daborne	
1611? [1640]	*The Night Walker*	Fletcher	Queen's Revels?
1611 [1611]	*The Roaring Girl*	Dekker and Middleton	Prince Henry's
c. 1611 [1618]	*Amends for Ladies*	Field	Queen's Revel
c. 1611 [1657]	*No Wit, No Help Like a Woman's*	Middleton	Lady Elizabeth's?
c. 1613 [1614]	*The Hogge Hath Lost His Pearl*	Tailor	"apprentices"
1613? [1647]	*The Honest Man's Fortune*	Fletcher	Lady Elizabeth's
1614 [MS]	*Hymen's Triumph*	Daniel	
c. 1616 [1647]	*Love's Pilgrimage*	Fletcher	King's
c. 1616 [1652]	*The Widow*	Middleton	King's
1619 [1662]	*Anything for a Quiet Life*	Middleton	King's
1619? [1657]	*More Dissemblers Besides Women*	Middleton	King's?
1620 [1622]	*The Heir*	May	Red Bull troupe
1620–30 [MS]	*The Partial Law*		
c. 1621 [1647]	*The Pilgrim*	Fletcher	King's
1621 [1621]	*The Witch of Edmonton*	Dekker, Ford and Rowley	King's
1621? [S.R.1660]	*The Faithful Friends*	Fletcher?	
c. 1622 [1623]	*The Duke of Milan*	Massinger	King's
1623 [1647]	*The Maid in the Mill*	Fletcher and Rowley	King's
1625 [1631]	*The School of Compliment, or Love Tricks*	Shirley	Lady Elizabeth's
1626 [1629]	*The Wedding*	Shirley	Queen Henrietta's
c. 1626 [1639]	*The Maid's Revenge*	Shirley	Queen Henrietta's
1628 [1629]	*The Lover's Melancholy*	Ford	King's
1629? [1629]	*The Deserving Favorite*	Carlell	King's

1629 [1631]	The New Inn	Jonson	King's
1629 [1630]	The Grateful Servant	Shirley	Queen Henrietta's
c. 1631 [1632]	The Rival Friends	Hausted	Cambridge
1631 [MS]	The Swisser	Wilson	King's
c. 1632 [1632]	The Changes, or Love in a Maze	Shirley	King's Revels
c. 1633 [1636]	The Challenge for Beauty	Heywood	King's
c. 1635 [1641]	The Antiquary	Marmion	Queen Henrietta's
1636 [1640]	Hollander	Glapthorne	Queen Henrietta's
1637? [1651]	The Lady Errant	Cartwright	privately
1636 [1655]	The Bashful Lover	Massinger	King's
1636? [1653]	A Mad Couple Well Matched	Brome	Beeston's Boys?
1637? [1658]	The English Moor	Brome	Queen Henrietta's
1637? [1653]	The Damoiselle	Brome	Beeston's Boys?
1637? [1640]	The Prisoners	Killegrew	Queen Henrietta's
1638? [1639]	Argalus and Parthenia	Glapthorne	Beeston's Boys
c. 1638 [1640]	Sicily and Naples	Harding	Oxford
c. 1638 [1652]	The Doubtful Heir	Shirley	King's
c. 1639 [1657]	The Obstinate Lady	Cockayne	
1639? [1673]	The Distresses, or the Spanish Lovers	Davenant	King's
1640 [1652]	The Imposture	Shirley	King's
1642 [1652]	The Sisters	Shirley	King's

Appendix C

Legal Records of Cross-Dressing

R. Mark Benbow and Alasdair D. K. Hawkyard

Actual instances of cross-dressing are recorded in the Repertories of the Aldermen's Court and in the surviving Minute Books of Bridewell Hospital. The Repertories are housed in the City of London Record Office; the Minute Books are available on microfilm in the Guildhall Library.

While the number of cases of cross-dressing is not large, the records that survive probably do not record all the instances. This is especially true for the Repertories because more pressing business tended to crowd out routine matters; and this was especially true after the 1570s. Moreover, an alderman's deputy or a constable may have often bypassed the Aldermen's Court by sending offenders directly to Bridewell Hospital, which served in the sixteenth century as a "police court." It should be noted that the minutes for the Aldermen's Court seem to have been copied well after the meetings and that the minutes seldom contain the descriptive particulars that characterize the Minute Books of Bridewell Hospital. It should also be noted that in the late 1570s the Bridewell Court conducted a campaign to restrain sexual misdemeanors within the City and that the records are thus more detailed than in other periods. By the 1590s the court was inundated with a flood of vagrants, and sexual misdemeanors were less threatening than the potential for instability arising from masterless men and women. Unfortunately, few records survive for the Wardmote Inquests, where some cases of cross-dressing may have first been presented.

In the following transcriptions, capitalization has been normalized and some punctuation added. Where appropriate, *is* have been silently emended to *js*, *vs* to *us*, and initial *ffs* to *fs*. Emendation or glossing is in square brackets.

I

July 27, 1554

Item: it was ordered that John Mordreyte yeoman whoe of late procured and intysed a certayne damesell to horedom and incontine[n]te lyf and to be concubyne to a merchaunt straunger and for the accomplishment of that devyllishe and wycked purpose caused her to notte her heade [cut short her hair] and weare a mans cape and cloke, wherin she was taken by the bedyll of Bishopsgate warde, and hade prepared further for her a peare of mens hose and a dublett to have afterward used and worne shall tomorrow at nine of the clok be tied naked at the newe post by the standard in Chepe and there so remayne till twelve of the clok and in the meane season be sundrye tymes whipped in terror and example of other lyke offenders having a paper fixed upon the said post declaringe his said offence and th'examanacon and ordering of the said damesell was holly referred to Mr Alderman Wodruf in whose ward she was apprehended. (Repertories, 13:69ᵛ)

2

July 23, 1556

Item: Robert Chetwyn commyttyd to warde for goynge abrode in the Cytye yesterdaye in a womans apparell and Richard Myles lykewise commytted to warde for goynge then before hyme, the saide Chetwyn, with a scarf on his necke were this day pardonyd of theire folye and dischardged of theire imprysonmente and the said Chetwyn commandyd to geat hyme a master before Lammas nexte or else to avoyde oute of the Cytye by that daye at this peryll. (Repertories, 13:416ᵛ)

3

December 15, 1569

Item: for asmuch as John Godman porter and Johan his wife wer this daye lawfullie convicted and attainted aswell by there owne confessions as also by verye good and substancyall witnesses here brought forthe for that [purpose], that she the saide Johan by and with the consent, procure-

ment, and agremente of her saide husband being first disgised and appar-
eled in all thinges like a souldier and in a souldiers garments with wepons
accordinglie and so went abroade and shewed her self in divers parts of
this City as lackey, it was this day ordered and adjudged by the Courte
here this day that they both shall tomorrowe at 9 of the clock be sett
upon the pillorye in Chepeside havinge papers affixed to the same pillory
declaringe there saide offence and so there to remayne till 11 of the clock
and then to be conveyed to Bridewell and there to be whipped naked to
the girdlestead [waist] and then there to be safelie kepte till my Lord
Mayors further pleasure shalbe knowne. (Repertories, 16:522)

4

April 19, 1575

Item: yt was orderyd and adjudged by this Corte that Magdalyn Gawyn,
a yong woman of th'age of 21 yeres, for that she contrary to all honestye
of womanhood apparelyd herselfe in manes clothinge and wente abroade
the streates of this Cytie dysguised in [that] sorte, shall to morrowe at
eighte of the clokk in the forenoone be sette on the pyllorie in Chepesyde
there to remayne untill 11 of the clokk having her heare hangynge over
her sholders and apparelyd in th'attyre wherewith she ys nowe clothyd
and afterwardes to be comytted to Bridewell. (Repertories, 18:372)

April 20, 1575

Mawdlin Gawen, sente by my Lorde Maiour and the Aldermen, his
Britheren, for goinge and puttinge hir selfe into mans apparell—she
being of the age of xxii yeres or there aboutes [and] borne in the parishe
of Thame in Oxforde sheire, sayeth that she was in service with one
Goodwife Oliver in the saide towne of Thame, an Inne keper, where she
dwelled two yeres. And from thence, she saide, she wente to Tuddington in Bedforde sheire to an unckell of hirs to which place she came
on Mondaie in Whitsonweeke laste. And by hir saide unkell was placed
with one Mr Chaunce, the Lorde Chenyes Stewarde, and there remay-
ened untill Michelmas laste and then came to one Smithe, a tanner
dwellinge in Tuddington aforesaide, and was hyered with him for one
yere. And that she then by the entycemente of one Thomas Ashewell,
also servante with the saide Smithe, did consente to ronne from hir saide

M[aster] with the same Thomas, and so they two came from thence to Stansted in Herforde sheir where they tarryed iii daies. And from thence they came to London to one Thomas Balles howse in Finche Lane—the saide Thomas Ashewell, by the waye, alwaies saide she was his kinsewoman. And beinge in Finche Lane she was broughte to one Mr Fluell where she was placed in service. The saide Ashewell, comynge to hir to the saide Mr Fluelles howse, the saide Mr Fluell askinge what contrywoman she was, she saide she was borne in Collyweston, which the saide Ashewell also affirmed; and in askinge them how farre it was from Stamforde because the truthe mighte be knowne, the saide Ashewell colde not tell. Nevertheless the saide Fluell received hir into service where she remayned aboute iii weekes. But the saide Gawen saithe she spake not with the saide Ashewell from the tyme she was there placed in service untill Thursdaie last, at which tyme he persuaded hir to meete him at Powles Wharfe the Tuesdaie next followinge in the mornynge by fower of the clocke. She answered him againe, she wolde not come in hir owne apparell; and he tolde hir, that what apparrell soever she came in, he wolde receave hir and put on hir owne. And the tyme appoynted she changed hir selfe into mans apparell which she had in her saide M[asters] howse beinge aboute two of the clocke after midnighte and came awaie and so came to Powles Wharfe, being the place appointed, but the saide Ashewell was not presente nor came accordinge to his appoyntmente. She, callinge there for a boate to go downe westwarde, a water man lookinge out of a windowe saide it was to earli; and she saide she wolde staye untill it were tyme and that he wolde go. Whereuppon the waterman came downe and opened his dore, and she wente in to his howse with hir fardell under hir arme which she caste downe uppon the grounde within the dore. And then she desyred the waterman him selfe to do so muche as to powle hir, and she saide she wolde geve hym a groate for his labour; and the waterman made hir beleve he wolde, but he sente his man for the constable when he perceved what she was and so made a skuse sayenge he lacked his syssors and so made as thoughe he sente his man for them as he tolde hir; and, his man tarrynge longe, [he] wente him selfe for the constable. And when the constable came, she was apprehended; and she saithe she tolde the constable that she dwelled in Philpott Lane with one goodwife Osborne. Also she saithe that the saide Thomas Ashewell beganne to leve wickedlie with hir from Shroftyde laste untill suche tyme as she was placed in service here in London, and that he had the use of her bodie carnallie divers and sondrie tymes as at Stansted aforesaid and other places more, for the whiche wickedness she had by order of the Lorde Maiour and the Benche correction. (Bridewell Court Minutes, 2:89^v-90^v)

5

October 15, 1575

Margaret Bolton saieth that she, sittinge with hir frute, the saide John Gallawaie lynge at one Rogers nere where she satte [came] to buie frute of hir often. And in the ende asked hir where she dwelled, and she saide at Quene Hithe wher uppon he asked hir whome she knewe, and she saide she knewe divers. And then he asked hir yf she knewe Mrs Luddington, and she saide yea. And then he desired hir to carrie a lettre to Mrs Luddington; but she saieth that she was willed that Mr Luddington sholde not knowe of it, nor to delivere it in his sighte. And then she saieth she asked him yf there wolde no harme come of it, and he answered no; and thereuppon she took the lettre and sente the same by hir mayde to Mrs Luddington, and Mrs Luddington received the same [and] was verie angrie. And then she saieth she wente to Mrs Luddington and asked hir of an answere of the lettre, or els the lettre backe againe. Whereuppon she tolde the saide Gallawaie that Mrs Luddington was angrie at it, whereuppon the saide Gallawaie saide he cared not for suche a banckrowte.

Elizabeth Tompson confesseth that the saide Gallawaie delivered a lettre to hir M[istress], and willed her to delivere it to Mrs Luddington. And so hir M[istress] wente in the mornynge, and then Mr Luddington was in the shoppe; and at none hir M[istress] delivered the lettre unto hir to go carrie the same to Mrs Luddington which she did, and Mrs Luddington tolde hir that hir husbande sholde make him an answere of it sone.

The saide John Gallawaie denieth all the saide matter against him alledged and saieth that he willed the said Margaret Bolton to delivere the lettre to one Mrs Longe, but the saide Gallawaie saieth that the saide Margaret tolde him amongest other talke that Mrs Luddington was easelie to be intreated whereuppon he sente the saide lettre to Mrs Luddington. Mr Luddington saieth that the saide Margaret was before the wardemoote enquest of Quene Hithe warde for that she and hir daughter went a broade in mans apparell.

Yt is ordered for that the saide John Gallawaie can make no accompte how he liveth that he shall be sente to the Compter upon Sir Alexander [Avenon]'s commaundemente and to be examyned in the after none. (Bridewell Court Minutes, 2:163ᵛ)

October 22, 1575

Margaret Bolton, the wife of Anthonie Bolton Cobler, sente backe from the warde moote enquest unto whome she was sente by the Governours of this house and they not [hearing] the accusacon made againste hir by John Gallowaye in that she at his request carryed a lettre to one Mrs Luddington thereby entisinge hir to follie, yf she wolde therunto have consented, and for that she also encoraged the saide Gallawaie in sendinge the lettre, sayenge Mrs Luddington is a woman easie to be intreated, for the which wicked facte she had correction. (Bridewell Court Minutes, 2:168ᵛ)

6

July 3, 1576

Item: yt was this daye orderyd adjudged and decreyed by this Corte that Dorothy Clayton spinster who of late, contrary to all honestye of womanhood, hath used commenly to goe aboute this Cytie and the libertyes of the same apparyled in mans attyre and also hathe abbusyd her bodye with sundry persons by reason of her incontynancy of Lyfe shall on Frydaye nexte insuinge be sett on the pullory in Chepeside there to remayne by the space of two hole howres apparyled in suche manner and sorte and in such kynde of mans apparell, as at the tyme of her apprehension did [wear], and afterwardes to be comytted to Bridewell there to remyne untyll further order shalbe taken for her delyverance. (Repertories, 19:93)

7

November 8, 1576.

Item: Alice Yonge of Muche Monden in the cownty of Hertford, a gyrle of th'age of 17 yeres, for that she very lewdly dysguysed her selfe in mannes apparrell and wente abroade therein in th'open streetes of this

Citie was by this Corte comytted unto Brydewell there to be examyned by the maisters and governors of the same hospytall and they to make reporte unto this Corte. (Repertories, 19:137)

November 8, 1576

Alice Young, whiche is brought in like a roge in a mans apparrell, is sette labour untill further order be taken. (Bridewell Court Minutes, 3:85ᵛ)

November 24, 1576

Alice Younge, which was taken in mans apparrell and came from Mych Monden, is this day corrected. (Bridewell Court Minutes, 3:89)

8

March 9, 1577

Jane Trosse, being taken in unsemely apparrell more manlyke then women lyke and folowed from taverne to taverne was brought into the house the ixth of Marche 1576. (Bridewell Court Minutes, 3:183ᵛ)

9

March 16, 1579

Gilbert Pereman, late servante with Oratio Plafaryne, beinge here ex[amined] sayeth that he hath served him [there] 2 yeres; and, beinge at his firste comminge innocent and unacquaynted, and not willinge but lothinge lewde whordome and lecherye, his M[aster] procured him to fetche him harlottes, which he loathed to doe, first about this tyme xii moneth. His M[aster] went for his recreacon, as he saide, and laye at the Grehonde in Barkinge and Christofer Demonte with him. And his M[as-ter] sent the maide of the house for 2 women which he woulde have abused, and he bid this ex[aminee] when they came that he shoulde call for wyne and good chere and give them because he woulde have abused them; but the women came not. He saieth that the first tyme he [did] knowe his M[aster] committe a whordome was about a yere and more sins with one Jenetta, a Venition woman which lyeth about Ludgate. She came to his house in St. Nicholas Lane, and ther he abused her. And often he did [after] abuse hir in his owne house in Mynsinge Lane; and at Christmas last she laye ther agayne 2 nightes, and this ex[aminee] went awaye and lefte hir ther. Also his M[aster] often would have had him gett some mayden to abuse which had not bene dealte with all before, but he colde gette none. Whereupon he gave him ones x^s and hired him a horse to ride to Gilforde wher he willed him to gett one and bringe him. He went but made noe motion to any and tolde him that he had attempted. About an yere sens this ex[aminee] had intelligens of a thicke man of one, Dibell, which is saied to be a mayde, which he broughte to this ex[aminee] to the Red Bull in Cheapstrete and ther he appoynted her to come to his masters house in Mynsinge Lane. She came accordinglye, and ther she tarried and lay with his M[aster] vii nightes in his owne bedde. Then he gave her money and put her awaye. Also he sayeth that about an yere sens one Antonye Boyer a paynter brought a wenche from a house at Westminster nere th'abby at ix a clocke at nighte unto this ex[aminee's] masters house in Mynsynge Lane wher he laye with her alnighte. Boyer had a Frenche crone for his labore, delivered by this ex[aminee]. The woman was put out in the morninge. Afterwardes Boyer mett this ex[aminee] and tolde him that he coulde bringe his M[aster] verye proper women yf he woulde, but ther was none after broghte thether by him. Also he sayeth that his M[aster] had a childe of v or vi yeres sens by one Robert Thomas wife of Mark Lane, nowe gone into Flanders. And ther he came acquaynted with Jane Ludloe; and [there, by] consent of Thomas daughter, his M[aster] laye ther one nighte with the said Jane about 8 monethes sens. Afterwardes his M[aster] wrytte lettres for Jane to come and lye with him at his house and sent this ex[aminee] for her to Mark Lane. She came in a manes gowne and a hatt and laye one night with him. Also he sayeth that as Angell, the daughter of Robert Thomas, told him his M[aster] was the first . . . that had abused her, the said Angell. Also he sayeth that one Bonifacio Fasio and his wife which are in Palafarynes house doe knowe of the harlottes that lie with his M[aster] in his house. Also he sayeth that Penyes wife, wher Jenetta lyeth, did bringe a lettre from Jenetta to his M[aster], but she came within the dores and delivered it with her owne hande and would not deliver it any but to him. (Bridewell Court Minutes, 3:377–77^v)

10

January 17, 1600

Margaret Wakeley, sent into this house by Mr Deputy Wyatt, confessed that she hath had a bastard and that she went in mans apparrell. Punished and delivered. (Bridewell Court Minutes, 4:206^v)

11

September 24, 1601

This day Hellen Balsen alias Hudson sent unto this hospitall by Justice Fowler, being apprehended by him in manes apparrell, being present in court and examined what the cause was that she went in mans apparrell sayed that there was one Mr Taylors sonne lying at Black Sewces who perswaded her to putt on mans apparrell and sayeth that that was the cause she went in mans apparrell and further sayeth that she lay at the Signe of the Exchequer in Islington two or three nightes where she was apprehended and beinge demaunded whether the sayde Taylors sonne have not th'use of her body denyeth the same and for that she is knowne to be a notorious whore and hath bene in this Hospitall three or foure tymes heretofore, having bene punished for her evill life, was ordered kept till the next Session[s]. (Bridewell Court Minutes, 4:262^v)

12

October 31, 1601

Eliz Griffyn alias Partridge sent in by Mr Deputy H[a]nger upon suspicon of ill and lewd liefe; and be that yt was evidentlie proved to this Courte that she hath used to goe in manes apparrell, yt ys ordered she shalbe ponished and kep[t]. (Bridewell Court Minutes, 4:270)

13

December 1, 1604

Elizabeth Mason, whoe was brought in boyes apparrell, ponished and kept. (Bridewell Court Minutes, 5:5)

Notes

I use the standard abbreviations for titles of scholarly journals listed in the Modern Language Association Bibliography for Literature, published annually. I also use the following abbreviations for frequently cited collections of essays:

E.P.
    Erotic Politics: Desire on the Renaissance Stage. Ed. Susan Zimmerman. London: Routledge, 1992.
Rough Magic
    Shakespeare's *"Rough Magic": Renaissance Essays in Honor of C. L. Barber.* Ed. Peter Erickson and Coppélia Kahn. Newark: University of Delaware Press, 1985.
Shakespeare to Sheridan
    Comedy from Shakespeare to Sheridan. Ed. A. R. Braunmuller and J. C. Bulman. Newark: University of Delaware Press, 1986.

Introduction

1. Andrew Gurr, *Playgoing in Shakespeare's London* (Cambridge: Cambridge University Press, 1987), 3–4, 49–79. Gurr's discussion of the demography of theater audiences in the period revises conclusions reached by Alfred Harbage, *Shakespeare's Audience* (New York: Columbia University Press, 1941), and *Shakespeare and the Rival Traditions* (New York: Macmillan, 1952); as well as by Ann J. Cook, *The Privileged Playgoers of Shakespeare's London, 1576–1642* (Princeton: Princeton University Press, 1981). On women in the audience, see Gurr, *Playgoing in Shakespeare's London,* 60–64; Richard Levin, "Women in the Renaissance Theatre Audience," *SQ* 40 (1989): 165–74; Kathleen McLuskie, *Renaissance Dramatists* (Atlantic Highlands NJ: Humanities Press International, 1989), 87–99; and Susan Zimmerman, "Disruptive Desire: Artifice and Indeterminacy in Jacobean Comedy," in *E.P.,* 58–59 n. 15.
2. Stephen Orgel, "Nobody's Perfect," *SAQ* 88 (1989): 7–29.
3. Lisa Jardine, *Still Harping on Daughters* (Sussex: Harvester Press, 1983), 9–36. See also Leslie Fiedler, *The Stranger in Shakespeare* (New York: Stein and

Day, 1972), 37, 47. For Barbara Bono, "Mixed Gender, Mixed Genre in Shakespeare's *As You Like It*," in *Renaissance Genres: Essays on Theory, History, and Interpretation*, ed. Barbara K. Lewalski, Harvard English Studies 14 (Cambridge, 1986), 201–2 n. 26, female characters were no more than pawns in "an essentially male drama of power in which women are even further objectified as mere roles." On the range of subject positions available to male and female spectators, see Valerie Traub, *Desire and Anxiety: Circulations of Sexuality in Shakespearean Drama* (London: Routledge, 1992), 100–101, 122.

4. Jean E. Howard, "Crossdressing, the Theatre, and Gender Struggle in Early Modern England," *SQ* 39 (1988): 418–40. In a more recent essay, "Sex and Social Conflict: The Erotics of *The Roaring Girl*," in *E.P.*, 170–90, Howard succinctly articulates a basic principle of this book: "While in performance the fact of the boy beneath the woman's clothes could usually have been ignored by playgoers, it could *also* at any time have been brought to consciousness by a self-reflexive gesture or comment" (175).

5. Phyllis Rackin, "Androgyny, Mimesis, and the Marriage of the Boy Heroine on the English Renaissance Stage," *PMLA* 102 (1987): 29–41. Despite my reservations, *PMLA* 102 (1987): 836–38, Rackin's essay is one of the few in the "androgynist" camp to take full account of the presence of the boy actor behind the female page, a dimension resisted by Robert Kimbrough, "Androgyny Seen through Shakespeare's Disguise," *SQ* 33 (1982): 17. Kimbrough develops his argument at greater length in *Shakespeare and the Art of Humankindness* (London: Humanities Press International, 1990).

6. Joel Fineman, "Fratricide and Cuckoldry: Shakespeare's Doubles," in *Representing Shakespeare*, ed. Murray Schwartz and Coppélia Kahn (Baltimore: Johns Hopkins University Press, 1980), 92. See also Janet Adelman, "Male Bonding in Shakespeare's Comedies," in *Rough Magic*, 73–103.

7. William Slights, "'Maid and Man' in *Twelfth Night*," *JEGP* 80 (1981): 330, 338. See also Steve Brown, "The Boyhood of Shakespeare's Heroines: Notes on Gender Ambiguity in the Sixteenth Century," *SEL* 30 (1990): 259–60n. The author of *Hic Mulier, or, The Man-Woman*, (London, 1620), quoted in *Half Humankind: Contexts and Texts of the Controversy about Women in England, 1540–1640*, ed. Katherine Usher Henderson and Barbara F. McManus (Urbana: University of Illinois Press, 1985), 275, equates crossdressing, hermaphroditism, and depravity. On the pejorative use of the term *hermaphrodite*, along with the name of a person believed to be hermaphroditic, see Susan C. Shapiro, "A Seventeenth-Century Hermaphrodite," *SCN* 45, nos. 1–2 (Spring–Summer 1987): 12–13.

For a theory of "serial" developmental hermaphroditism, see Stephen Greenblatt, "Fiction and Friction," in *Shakespearean Negotiations: The Circulation of Social Energy in Renaissance England* (Berkeley and Los Angeles: University of California Press, 1988), 66–93. Greenblatt summarizes French medical treatises of the period, which, following Galen, maintain that while all embryos are male they pass through a female stage, where some are arrested, before achieving final male status. Greenblatt ends his essay by suggesting that the dramatic heroines who adopt male disguise represent "mirror images of masculine self-differentiation" as they "pass through the state of being men in order to become women" (92). Greenblatt's ingenuity here strikes me as overly dependent on the use of a "trick mirror," in which the notion of male-female-male progression of the human embryo is inverted to serve as a model for the female-male-female progression of heroines who temporarily adopt male disguise. The suggestion is weakened by the failure of Greenblatt's mirror to reflect the image of the boy actor playing the heroine, which he labels as "a different sexual reality, . . . presented but not represented" (93). While the difference is real, denying any interplay or tension between these "realities" seems to me an arbitrary compartmentalization of human consciousness.

8. Jonathan Dollimore, "Subjectivity, Sexuality, and Transgression: The Jacobean Connection," *RenD,* n.s., 17 (1986): 69.

9. Marjorie Garber, *Vested Interests: Cross-Dressing & Cultural Anxiety* (London: Routledge, 1991). See reviews by Liam Hudson, *TLS,* May 28, 1993, 10; and Adam Phillips, *LRB,* November 5, 1992, 25–26.

10. Catherine Belsey, "Disrupting Sexual Differences: Meaning and Gender in the Comedies," in *Alternative Shakespeares,* ed. John Drakakis (London: Methuen, 1985), 190. As put by Judith Butler, *Gender Trouble: Feminism and the Subversion of Identity* (Routledge: London, 1990), 146, who argues that all gender attributes are performative, "the parodic repetition of gender exposes as well the illusion of gender identity as an intractable depth and inner substance." See also Zimmerman, "Disruptive Desire," 55–56.

11. Linda Woodbridge, *Women and the English Renaissance* (Urbana: University of Illinois Press, 1984), 154.

12. Albert Tricomi, *Anti-court Drama in England* (Charlottesville: University Press of Virginia, 1989); and Margot Heinemann, "Political Drama," in *The Cambridge Companion to English Renaissance Drama,* ed. A. R. Braunmuller and Michael Hattaway (Cambridge: Cambridge University Press, 1990), 161–205; and Gurr, *Playgoing in Shakespeare's London,* 115–90. David Bevington, *Tudor Drama and Politics: A Critical Approach to Topical Meaning* (Cambridge: Harvard University Press, 1968), avoids the errors of earlier "lockpicking" critics and therefore emphasizes the treatment of political issues without linking it to personal satire.

13. Stephen Mullaney, *The Place of the Stage: License, Play, and Power in Renaissance England* (Chicago: University of Chicago Press, 1988), 26–59. Mullaney's sense of the ambience of the London theaters, even if it was somewhat contrived, seems plausible to me, although his work has recently been criticized for neglecting the importance of the acting companies' involvement in patronage, political, and commercial networks. On the difference between festive rituals in primitive or agrarian cultures and commercialized festivals in early modern and industrialized cultures, see Victor Turner's distinction between liminal and liminoid in *From Ritual to Theatre* (New York: Performing Arts Press, 1982), 53–54. See also Louis Montrose, "The Purpose of Playing: Reflections on a Shakespearean Anthropology," *Helios,*

n.s., 7, no. 2 (1979–80): 51–74. McLuskie, *Renaissance Dramatists*, 224–30, suggests that artistic and commercial considerations regularly disrupt or supersede ideological consistency in the plays of the period.

14. The phrase is the subtitle of *From Ritual to Theatre* (New York: Performing Arts Journal Publications, 1982).

15. Stephen Greenblatt, "Invisible Bullets: Renaissance Authority and Its Subversion, *Henry IV* and *Henry V*," in *Political Shakespeare*, ed. Jonathan Dollimore and Alan Sinfield (Manchester: Manchester University Press, 1985), 18–47 (reprinted in *Shakespearean Negotiations*, 21–65). Some (new) historicists, including Greenblatt himself, have recently become skeptical of the presence in early modern England of a monolithic power structure assumed to underlie the subversion-containment model.

16. Maynard Mack, "Engagement and Detachment in Shakespeare's Plays," in *Essays on Shakespeare and Elizabethan Drama in Honor of Hardin Craig*, ed. Richard Hosley (Columbia: University of Missouri Press, 1961), 175–96. From a psychoanalytic perspective, Peter Stallybrass, "Transvestism and the 'Body Beneath': Speculating on the Boy Actor," in *E.P.*, explains *theatrical vibrancy* or engagement on different planes of reality as "the play between indeterminacy and fixation" (80). He argues that such fictive details as the mole on Imogen's breast in *Cymbeline* placed obsessive emphasis on the heroine's unseen female body and thus heightened spectators' awareness of boy actor to produce "a radical oscillation between a sense of the absolute difference of the boy from his role and the total absorption of the boy into the role" (74).

17. Robert Weimann, *Shakespeare and the Popular Tradition in the Theater*, trans. Robert Schwartz (Baltimore: Johns Hopkins University Press, 1978), 73–85. As Stanton B. Garner, Jr., "Theatricality in *Mankind* and *Everyman*," *SP* (1987): 274, writes: "Theatricality . . . is an essential component of that tension, inherent in all drama, between the material reality of performance and the fictional realm which it is made to represent."

18. Bruce R. Smith, "Making a Difference: Male/Male 'Desire' in Tragedy, Comedy, and Tragi-comedy," in *E.P.*, 140, proposes that the boy heroine in male disguise was used romantically by Shakespeare and Fletcher writing for the King's Men but satirically by dramatists (including Fletcher) writing city comedies for other companies.

19. Bert O. States, *Great Reckonings in Little Rooms* (Berkeley and Los Angeles: University of California Press, 1985), 19–47, sees the tension between these two modes of looking at theater as an interplay between semiotic and phenomenological approaches. Semiotic theories about theater are surveyed by Marvin Carlson, *Theories of the Theatre: A Historical and Critical Survey, from the Greeks to the Present* (Ithaca: Cornell University Press, 1984), 492–512. The phenomenological position is stated by Michael Goldman, *The Actor's Freedom: Toward a Theory of Drama* (New York: Viking, 1974), 1–51. James Shirley described the interplay between the two approaches in his epistle to the 1647 folio of Beaumont's and Fletcher's plays, praising the dramatists

for moving the spectators while allowing them to see how they came to be moved. Their plays, Shirley writes, present

passions raised to that excellent pitch and by such insinuating degrees that you shall not chuse but consent, & go along with them, finding your self at last grown insensibly the very same person you read, and then stand admiring the subtile Trackes of your engagement.

The Works of Francis Beaumont and John Fletcher, ed. Arnold Glover and A. R. Waller, 10 vols. (Cambridge: Cambridge University Press, 1905–12), 1:xii. I am indebted to Eugene Waith for the reference.

Chapter 1

1. Quoted by G. P. V. Akrigg, *Jacobean Pageant* (Cambridge: Harvard University Press, 1963), 120–21. For a similar story involving Robert Dudley, see Anthony à Wood, *Athenae Oxonienses*, 2d ed., ed. Philip Bliss, 5 vols. (London: Rivington, 1813–20), 3:261. Both cases are summarized by Stephen Orgel, "The Subtexts of *The Roaring Girl*," in *E.P.*, 19–20. Cf. James Howell, *Familiar Letters*, ed. Joseph Jacobs, 2 vols. (London: David Nutt, 1890), 1:317. Even Queen Elizabeth fantasized disguising herself as a page, according to Sir James Melville, *Memoirs*, ed. A Francis Steuart (New York: Dutton, 1930), 97.

2. R. Mark Benbow, "Sexual Misdemeanors in Elizabethan London," unpublished essay, 19. G. R. Quaife, *Wanton Wenches and Wayward Wives* (London: Croom Helm, 1979), examines evidence from rural church courts, as does Martin Ingram, *Church Courts, Sex, and Marriage in England, 1570–1640* (Cambridge: Cambridge University Press, 1987).

3. Fernando Henriques, *Prostitution in Europe and America*, vol. 2 of *Prostitution and Society*, 2 vols. (New York: Citadel Press, 1965), 61.

4. John Stow, *The Survey of London* (London: J. M. Dent, 1912), 362; Wallace Shugg, "Prostitution in Shakespeare's London," *ShakS* 10 (1977): 291–313; Ann Jennalie Cook, "'Bargaines of Incontinencie': Bawdy Behavior in the Playhouses," *ShakS* 10 (1977): 271–90; and Ian W. Archer, *The Pursuit of Stability* (Cambridge: Cambridge University Press, 1991), 211–54.

5. Bridewell Minute Books, 3:424, and 3:404^v, quoted by Benbow, "Sexual Misdemeanors," 18.

6. Shugg, "Prostitution," 303–5. Part 2 of *The Honest Whore* was not published until 1630 but was probably produced shortly after part 1, usually dated 1604, on the basis of an entry in Henslowe's diary for that year. See E. K. Chambers, *The Elizabethan Stage*, 4 vols. (Oxford: Clarendon Press, 1923), 3:294–95; and Rosalind Knutson (Fayetteville: University of Arkansas Press, 1991), 174, who gives 1604–6 as the date of part 2. For a description of treatment of inmates of Bridewell Hospital, see A. L. Beier, *Masterless Men: The Vagrancy Problem in England, 1560–1640* (London: Methuen, 1985), 164–69.

7. Rudolf M. Dekker and Lotte C. van de Pol, *The Tradition of Female Transvestism in Early Modern Europe* (New York: St. Martin's, 1989). Subsequent references appear in the text.

8. Natalie Zemon Davis, "Women on Top: Symbolic Sexual Inversion and Political Disorder in Early Modern Europe," in *The Reversible World: Symbolic Inversion in Art and Society*, ed. Barbara A. Babcock (Ithaca: Cornell University Press, 1978), 163–71, 178–82. Much of Dekker's and van de Pol's material is somewhat later than the period I survey in this book, but a significant number of cases date from the first half of the seventeenth century. The greater leniency of Dutch justices toward female cross-dressing may be a result of their differing from Elizabethan alderman and magistrates in social origins, religious affiliations, and educational backgrounds.

9. Sandra Clark, *"Hic Mulier, Haec Vir,* and the Controversy over Masculine Women," *SP* 82 (1985): 169. Kathleen McLuskie, "'Lawless desires well-tempered,'" in *E.P.*, 116, succinctly explains the differences in attitude between juridical and theatrical representations of female cross-dressing: "The figures of women (played on stage by boys) were both the signs of sexuality, observed and constructed as such by men, and exemplars of the consequences of deviant behaviour. In the church courts, these signs had social consequences in shame and punishment, but on the stage the sexual narratives existed only in order to elicit emotional responses which subsumed morality within pathos and suspense."

10. Woodbridge, *Women and the English Renaissance*, 139–51. See also Mary Beth Rose, *The Expense of Spirit: Love and Sexuality in English Renaissance Drama* (Ithaca: Cornell University Press, 1988), 69–77. A few cases of defiant women in male attire before the *Hic Mulier* movement are cited by Valerie Lucas, *"Hic Mulier:* The Female Transvestite in Early Modern England," *Ren&R* 12 (1988): 66–68.

11. *Hic Mulier*, 267–68. Subsequent references follow quotations in the text.

12. John Chamberlain, *The Chamberlain Letters*, ed. Elizabeth McClure Thomson (New York: G. P. Putnam's Sons, 1965), 271. James would not have approved of Elizabeth's alleged appearance in armor before her troops at Tilbury, discussed by Leah Marcus, "Shakespeare's Comic Heroines, Elizabeth I, and the Political Uses of Androgyny," in *Women in the Middle Ages and the Renaissance*, ed. Mary Beth Rose (Syracuse: University of Syracuse Press, 1986), 135–53. Orgel, "The Subtexts of *The Roaring Girl*," 15–16, questions the authenticity of the incident.

13. William Harrison, *Description of England*, ed. Georges Edelen (Ithaca: Cornell University Press, 1968), 147. For other early allusions, see Rose, *Expense of Spirit*, 67–68; and Clark, *"Hic Mulier*," 161.

14. Bradamante and Marfisa appear in Ariosto's *Orlando Furioso*, translated by John Harington in 1591, while Claridiana, to whom Face compares Doll Common in the opening scene of *The Alchemist*, is the heroine of *The Mirror of Knighthood*, a translation of a work by Diego Ortunez de Calahorra, which went through thirteen printings between 1578 and 1601; see F. H. Mares, ed., Ben Jonson, *The Alchemist* (London: Methuen, 1967), 24n.

15. Woodbridge, *Women and the English Renaissance,* 179.
16. Fitzgeffrey and Williams are quoted by Woodbridge, *Women and the English Renaissance,* 142–43, 252.
17. William Shakespeare, *The Two Gentlemen of Verona,* in *The Riverside Shakespeare* (Boston: Houghton Mifflin, 1974), II.vii.41. Unless otherwise noted, all quotations are from this edition.
18. None are cited by Anne M. Haselkorn, *Prostitution in Elizabethan and Jacobean Comedy* (Troy, NY: Whitson, 1983). Nor is cross-dressing associated with the harlots of popular ballads, according to Joy Wiltenburg, *Disorderly Women and Female Power in the Street Literature of Early Modern England and Germany* (Charlottesville: University Press of Virgina, 1992), 165–73; Wiltenburg discusses romanticized heroines' cross-gender disguise on 63–64. For an allusion to cross-dressed prostitutes in Venice, see Ben Jonson, *Volpone,* in *Ben Jonson,* ed. C. H. Herford and Percy Simpson, 11 vols. (Oxford: Clarendon Press, 1925–52), vol. 5, IV.ii.48–55. Unless otherwise noted, all quotations from Jonson's work are from this edition and are hereafter cited in the text. Whether or not any prostitutes in Venice wore male apparel at the time is moot. Henriques, *Prostitution in Europe and America,* 88, cites a Venetian regulation of 1480 "which forbids prostitutes to dress up as men in public"; see also Guido Ruggiero, *The Boundaries of Eros: Sex Crime and Sexuality in Renaissance Venice* (Oxford: Oxford University Press, 1985), 119. For attitudes toward female cross-dressing elsewhere in Italy, see *Gl'Ingannati,* in *Narrative and Dramatic Sources of Shakespeare,* ed. Geoffrey Bullough, 8 vols. (London: Routledge and Kegan Paul, 1957–75), 2:294.
19. John Webster, *The White Devil,* ed. John Russell Brown, 2d ed. (London: Methuen, 1966), IV.ii.210–15.
20. Gunnar Boklund, "The Sources of *The White Devil,*" *Essays and Studies on English Language and Literature,* 17 (Uppsala: English Institute, Uppsala University, 1957), 42, 133–35, 166–67.
21. Paul A. Mulholland, "The Date of *The Roaring Girl,*" *RES,* n.s., 28 (1977): 18–31.
22. Thomas Middleton and Thomas Dekker, *The Roaring Girl,* ed. Paul A. Mulholland (Manchester: Manchester University Press, 1987), II.i.174. The editor notes that Moll's dress combines the short coat with a collar worn by men with an outer skirt worn "to protect the lady's costume from dust and soiling by the horse." Subsequent references to this edition will appear in the text.
23. Mulholland, ed., *The Roaring Girl,* 262; see also 12–13. For her "police" work, see 14. Cf. Simon Shepherd's account of her life, *Amazons and Warrior Women* (New York: St. Martin's, 1981), 74–92.
24. Howard, "Crossdressing," 436–38; Dollimore, "Subjectivity," 65–67. See also Lorraine Helms, "Roaring Girls and Silent Women: The Politics of Androgyny on the Jacobean Stage," in *Women in Theatre,* ed. James Redmond (Cambridge: Cambridge University Press, 1989), 63–67. In "Sex and Social Conflict," 179–80, Howard stresses the subversiveness of Moll's

autoeroticism in a world where women are either subordinated or exploited by men. Orgel, "The Subtexts of *The Roaring Girl*," 22–25, sees Moll as an essentially benevolent figure but one who raises questions about the manliness of the men in the world of the play and hence about gender boundaries.

25. Viviana Comensoli, "Play-making, Domestic Conduct, and the Multiple Plot in *The Roaring Girl*," *SEL* 27 (1987): 259–63.

26. Theodore Leinwand, *The City Staged: Jacobean Comedy*, 1603–13 (Madison: University of Wisconsin Press, 1986), 158. See also Andor Gomme, ed., *The Roaring Girl* (New York: W. W. Norton, 1976), xxiii; and Rose, *Expense of Spirit*, 77–92.

27. Mary Beth Rose, "Women in Men's Clothing: Apparel and Social Stability in *The Roaring Girl*," *ELR* 14 (1984): 387–89.

28. Anthony B. Dawson, "Mistris Hic & Haec: Representations of Moll Frith," *SEL* 33 (1993): 391, 399.

Chapter 2

1. Jardine, *Still Harping*, 10. Her argument that the "maide" is a play-boy rests on the fact that Somerset House had sometimes been a site for theatrical performance. Male cross-dressing, rare in medieval literature, appears in Renaissance prose romances; see Winfried Schleiner, "Male Cross-Dressing and Transvestism in Renaissance Romances," *SCJ* 19 (1988): 605–19.

2. Andrew Battell, as quoted by Winthrop R. Jordan, *White Over Black: American Attitudes toward the Negro*, 1550–1812 (Chapel Hill: University of North Carolina Press, 1968), 33.

3. E. K. Chambers, *The Medieval Stage*, 2 vols. (Oxford: Oxford University Press, 1903), 1:192–218; Alan Brody, *The English Mummers and Their Plays* (Philadelphia: University of Pennsylvania Press, 1969), 17, 21, 61, 99; D. E. Underdown, "The Taming of the Scold: The Enforcement of Patriarchal Authority in Early Modern England," in *Order and Disorder in Early Modern England*, ed. Anthony Fletcher and John Stevenson (Cambridge: Cambridge University Press, 1985), 129–32; Peter Clark, "The Alehouse and the Alternative Society," in *Puritans and Revolutionaries*, ed. Donald Pennington and Keith Thomas (Oxford: Clarendon Press, 1978), 63; Martin Ingram, "Ridings, Rough Music, and Mocking Rhymes in Early Modern England," in *Popular Culture in Seventeenth-Century England*, ed. Barry Reay (London: Croom Helm, 1985), 166–97; and Francois Laroque, *Shakespeare's Festive World: Elizabethan Seasonal Entertainment and the Professional Stage* (Cambridge: Cambridge University Press, 1991), 100–101. Davis, "Women on Top," 164, notes that "festive inversion more often involved the male taking on the role or garb of the woman—that is, of the unruly woman."

4. Bruce R. Smith, *A Poetics of Homosexual Desire in Shakespeare and His Contemporaries* (Chicago: University Chicago Press, 1991), 123–25.

5. Alan H. Nelson, ed., *REED [Records of Early English Drama]: Cambridge*, 2 vols. (Toronto: University of Toronto Press, 1989), 1:543, 544, 721. Ambivalence over female impersonation evidently prevailed at Oxford as well,

as is clear from the controversy between Rainoldes and Gager in 1592, discussed in chapter 7. Rainoldes, who objected to students playing female roles, had himself played Hippolyta in Richard Edward's *Palamon and Arcite* when Elizabeth visited the university in 1566.

6. Elissa Weaver, "Spiritual Fun: A Study of Sixteenth-Century Tuscan Convent Theater," in *Women in the Middle Ages and the Renaissance,* ed. Mary Beth Rose (Syracuse: Syracuse University Press, 1986), 173–205; and Meg Twycross, "'Transvestism' in the Mystery Plays," *Medieval English Theatre* 5 (1983): 133.

7. Kenneth Richards and Laura Richards, *The Commedia dell'Arte: A Documentary History* (London: Basil Blackwell, 1990), 39. See also Richard Andrews, *Scripts and Scenarios: The Performance of Comedy in Renaissance Italy* (Cambridge: Cambridge University Press, 1992), 224, 258 n. 65; Kathleen M. Lea, *Italian Popular Comedy,* 2 vols. (Oxford: Clarendon Press, 1934), 1:113–14; and Kathleen McGill, "Women and Performance: The Development of Improvisation by the Sixteenth-Century Commedia dell'Arte," *TJ* 43 (1991): 61.

8. On Spanish theater history, I have consulted Melveena McKendrick, *Theatre in Spain, 1490–1700* (Cambridge: Cambridge University Press, 1989), 48–49; and N. D. Shergold, *A History of the Spanish Stage* (Oxford: Clarendon Press, 1967), 143ff.; I have also been assisted by Ms. Luz Vega-Vega, who informs me that Medieval and Renaissance Spanish records sometimes refer to female instrumentalists, singers, and dancers under such terms as *juglaresa,* but it is not clear whether they can be considered actresses. Ursula K. Heise, "Transvestism and the Stage Controversy in Spain and England, 1580–1680," *TJ* 44 (1992): 357—74, argues that a *Pragmatica* of 1534, regulating performers' dress, refers to female as well as male *comediantes,* so that the Italian troupe was petitioning for a return to a previous practice. Such a request, however, would have been unnecessary had actresses still been employed in Spanish theaters. She further argues that the exclusion of playboys as female impersonators from the Spanish stage, except for a very brief period, was "in large part due to the long Spanish history of violent repression of homoerotic tendencies, intensified at precisely this historical juncture by increased inquisitorial prosecution" (366). She notes too that the Spanish authorities were also troubled by female characters adopting male disguise and tried to curtail if not forbid it in a series of edicts (359–60), fearful that male attire actually revealed more of the woman's body and thus accentuated rather than veiled femininity (367–68). For Heise, the Spanish anxieties about crossing gender lines in the theater add up to a fear of effeminization and thus cast an interesting light on the fear expressed by English antitheatrical writers that female impersonators would have a similar effeminizing effect on spectators. Despite her indebtedness to Orgel's work, Heise finally expresses doubt that English "cultural anxieties about the nature of male identity" were "due to the convention of *male* crossdressing in particular" and suggests that "the same dynamic would have asserted itself had women been admitted to the stage" (371), as happened in Spain.

9. For France, see W. L. Wiley, *The Early Public Theatre in France* (Cambridge: Harvard University Press, 1960), 20–25, 87–91; and Rosamond Gilder, *Enter the Actress: The First Women in the Theatre* (Boston: Houghton Mifflin, 1931), 46–99. For Holland, see Henk Gras, "All Is Semblative a Woman's Part?" (Ph.D. diss., University of Utrecht, 1991), 431; significant portions of this work are published in Henk Gras, *Studies in Elizabethan Audience Response to the Theatre*, 2 parts (Frankfurt: Peter Lang, 1993).

10. Appearances of the commedia dell'arte in England are recorded in Lea, *Italian Popular Comedy*, 2:352–58. For the French troupe at Blackfriars, see Gerald Eades Bentley, *The Jacobean and Caroline Stage*, 7 vols. (Oxford: Clarendon Press, 1941–68), 1:25 and 6:23. See also Gras, "All Is Semblative," 528.

11. Orgel, "Nobody's Perfect," 8. In "Call Me Ganymede: Shakespeare's Apprentices and the Representation of Women," an unpublished paper, Orgel argues that the apprenticeship system was not the cause of the exclusion of women from acting companies, as the craft guilds, through which play-boys were apprenticed even though their training was as actors, admitted some female apprentices. However, the numbers of female apprentices seem to decline rapidly in the late sixteenth and early seventeenth century as women's roles in the economy diminished. Whereas other sectors of the economy squeezed women out, acting troupes had never admitted them in the first place. The reasons for these trends are not clear but seem to me broader than the audience's fear of unmediated female sexuality, which Orgel believes explains the absence of women from the English Renaissance stage. A more practical explanation for the absence of actresses in theatrical troupes during the time when such companies were itinerant is the fear that pregnant women would give birth and abandon their infants to be supported by local parishes. See A. V. Judges, *Elizabethan Underworld* (London: George Routledge, 1930), xlvii; and Beier, *Masterless Men*, 53–54.

12. Doubling schemes are printed in David Bevington, *From "Mankind" to Marlowe* (Cambridge: Harvard University Press, 1962), 265–73. In more than half of the schemes, one or two actors play virtually all of the female and juvenile roles.

13. Anthony Munday et al., *Sir Thomas More*, ed. Vittorio Gabrieli and Georgio Melchiori (Manchester: Manchester University Press, 1990), III.ii.72–77. Bevington, *From "Mankind" to Marlowe*, 18, quotes and discusses this passage.

14. Colley Cibber, *An Apology for the Life of Mr. Colley Cibber*, 2 vols. (London: John C. Nimmo, 1889), 2:90. Gerald Eades Bentley, *The Profession of Player in Shakespeare's Time, 1590–1642* (Princeton: Princeton University Press, 1984), 113–46, challenges the evidence for the theory, originally put forward by T. W. Baldwin, *The Organization and Personnel of the Shakespearean Company* (Princeton: Princeton University Press, 1927), 113–14, that adult male actors played some female roles, as does J. B. Streett, "The Durability of Boy Actors," *N&Q* 218 (1973): 461–65. Baldwin, 204–7, argues that Field played female roles for the King's Men, apparently relying on Chapman's

allusion to "thy Acted woman" in a dedicatory epistle to Field's *A Woman Is a Weather-cocke, The Plays of Nathan Field,* ed. William Peery (Austin: University of Texas Press, 1950), 70, although Chapman may be referring to the play itself.

15. T. J. King, *Casting Shakespeare's Plays: London Actors and Their Roles* (Cambridge: Cambridge University Press, 1992), 48–49, 77. On Ezekiel Fenn, see Bentley, *Jacobean and Caroline Stage,* 2:433–34; Bentley reprints Henry Glapthorne's Poem, "For *Ezekial Fen* at his first Acting a Man's Part," from his 1639 quarto, *Poems.* Edward Kynaston (b. 1643) played female roles after the theaters reopened in 1660 but with the introduction of actresses soon switched to male roles. See epilogue. For Kynaston's date of birth and theatrical career, see Philip H. Highfill, Kalman A. Burnim, and Edward A. Langhans, *A Biographical Dictionary of Actors, Actresses, Musicians, Dancers, Managers, and Other Stage Personnel in London, 1660–1800,* 17 vols. (Carbondale: Southern Illinois University Press, 1984), 9:79. For evidence of late puberty in early modern Europe, see Richard Rastall, "Female Roles in All-Male Casts," *Medieval English Theatre* 7 (1985): 28–35.

16. Victor O. Freeburg, *Disguise Plots in Elizabethan Drama* (New York: Columbia University Press, 1915), 101–20.

17. P. K. Ayers, "Dreams of the City: The Urban and the Urbane in Jonson's *Epicoene,*" PQ 66 (1987): 83.

18. Anne Barton, *Ben Jonson, Dramatist* (Cambridge: Cambridge University Press, 1984), 228.

19. John Rainoldes, *Th'Overthrow of Stage-Playes* (Middleburgh, 1599), 102. For an extremely violent modern reaction to mistaken gender identity, see "Man Kills [male transvestite] Prostitute, Then Kills Himself," *New York Times,* February 9, 1992, 17.

20. Cibber, *An Apology,* 1:120–21.

21. See Michael Shapiro, "Framing the Taming: Metatheatrical Awareness of Female Impersonation in *The Taming of the Shrew,*" YES 23 (1993): 143–66; and "The Casting of Flute: *A Midsummer Night's Dream,*" *Elizabethan Theatre* 13 (Waterloo, 1989 [1994]): 1–29.

22. David Wiles, *Shakespeare's Clowns* (Cambridge: Cambridge University Press, 1987), 44–56.

23. William Prynne, *Histrio-Mastix* (London, 1633; photoreprint, New York: Garland, 1974), 208. William B. Worthen, *The Idea of the Actor: Drama and the Ethics of Performance* (Princeton: Princeton University Press, 1984), 25, argues that the virulence of such attacks arises from the perception of transvestism as a form of "social and cosmic subversiveness." See also Jonas Barish, *The Antitheatrical Prejudice* (Berkeley and Los Angeles: University of California Press, 1981), 80–131; Laura Levine, "Men in Women's Clothing: Anti-theatricality and Effeminization from 1579 to 1642," *Criticism* 28 (1986): 121–44; David Leverenz, "Why Did Puritans Hate Stage Plays?" in *The Language of Puritan Feeling: An Exploration in Literature, Psychology, and Social History* (New Brunswick: Rutgers University Press, 1980), 23–40; and Jean-Christophe Agnew, *Worlds Apart: The Market and the Theater in Anglo-*

American Thought, 1550–1750 (Cambridge: Cambridge University Press, 1986), 125–35. Colin MacCabe, "Abusing Self and Others: Puritan Accounts of the Shakespearian Stage," *CritQ* 30, no. 3 (1988): 5–17, draws an important distinction between Gosson's fear of effeminization and Prynne's homophobia.

24. Thomas Heywood, *An Apology for Actors* (London, 1612), sig. C3ᵛ. Heywood also claims that spectators of "our domesticke hystories" respond to "the person of any bold English man presented . . . as if the Personator were the man Personated" (sig. B4). Gras, "All Is Semblative," 43–46, prefers to believe Heywood on the history plays rather than on female impersonators.

25. Rainoldes, *Th'Overthrow of Stage Playes,* 11. See J. W. Binns, "Women or Transvestites on the Elizabethan Stage?: An Oxford Controversy," *SCJ* 5 (1974): 101–2. Alan Bray, *Homosexuality in Renaissance England* (London: Gay Men's Press, 1982), has studied both orthodox denunciations of male homo-erotic activity as well as evidence of such activity. Although some Elizabethans linked theatrical female impersonation to male homoeroticism, Bray finds little evidence of perceptual connections in the period between male transvestism and male homosexuality. He also finds no evidence of individuals forming a specifically homosexual identity nor of male homosexual subcultures before the later seventeenth century. For a challenge to this view, see Joseph Cady, "'Masculine Love,' Renaissance Writing, and the 'New Invention' of Homosexuality," *Journal of Homosexuality* 23 (1992): 9–40. Bray, "Homosexuality and the Signs of Male Friendship in Elizabethan England," *History Workshop* 29 (Spring 1990): 1–19, modifies some of his earlier conclusions.

26. Prynne, *Histrio-Mastix,* 211–12. For Gager's response to these allegations, see chapter 7. Thomas Nashe, *Pierce Pennilesse His Supplication to the Divill,* in *Works,* ed. R. B. McKerrow, 5 vols. (London: Sidgwick and Jackson, 1958), 1:215, contrasted the sexual innocence of English play-boys with their female counterparts on the continent: "Our Players are not as the players beyond sea, a sort of squirting baudie Comedians, that have whores and common Curtizens to playe womens partes, and forbeare no immodest speech or unchast action that may procure laughter." Given the controversy over cross-gender casting and the allegations of homoeroticism surrounding the play-boys, I read Nashe's statement ironically.

27. John Florio, *Queen Anna's New World of Words* (London, 1611), 88.

28. Thomas Middleton, *Father Hubburd's Tale,* in *Works,* ed. A. H. Bullen, 8 vols. (Boston: John C. Nimmo, 1885–86), 8:77. Unless otherwise noted, all references to Middleton's works are to this edition. Cf. Jonson, *Cynthia's Revels,* induction, ll. 165–66. Gras, "All Is Semblative," 120–251, 529–30, finds much evidence of a common belief in homoeroticism involving boy actors in both adult and children's troupes, as in J. Cooke's "A Common Player" (1615), printed by Chambers, *Elizabethan Stage,* 4:255–57, but notes the absence of legal or other documentary evidence.

29. Jardine, *Still Harping,* 9–36.

30. Thomas Laquer, *Making Sex: Body and Gender from the Greeks to Freud* (Cambridge: Harvard University Press, 1990), 63–113.
31. Philippe Ariès, *Centuries of Childhood*, trans. Robert Baldick (New York: Vintage Books, 1962), 50ff.
32. Woodbridge, *Women and the English Renaissance*, 154–55.
33. Belsey, "Disrupting Sexual Difference," 166–90; see also Montrose, "The Purpose of Playing," 51–74.
34. See Gras, "All Is Semblative," 106–8. But as Howard, "Sex and Social Conflict," 171, writes: "Boys and women were 'the same' in their hierarchical relationship to adult males, but they were also 'different,' if only in the crucial matter of their respective roles in reproduction."
35. Thomas Coryate, *Coryate's Crudities* (London, 1611), 247. In quoting from Coryate, I have emphasized a phrase that is often omitted when the passage is quoted, as in Michael Jamieson, "Shakespeare's Celibate Stage," in *The Seventeenth-Century Stage*, ed. Gerald Eades Bentley (Chicago: University of Chicago Press, 1968), 76; and Bentley, *Profession of Player*, 114. Richard Wynn was even more appreciative of the actresses he saw in Madrid: "The Players themselves consist of Men and Women. The Men are indifferent Actors, but the Women are very good, and become themselves far better than any that I ever saw act those Parts." See *Account of the Journey of Prince Charles's Servants into Spain in the Year 1623*, quoted by McKendrick, *Theatre in Spain*, 49.

    Other English travelers were less impressed. To Roger Ascham, the women he saw performing on the continent in 1551–52 "semide boies rather than Ladies excellent to have plaide in tragedies," quoted in Nelson, ed., *REED: Cambridge*, 2:845. George Sandys found the actresses he saw in Messina, Sicily, "were too naturally passionated," *A Relation of a Journey begun Anno Domini 1610*, 2d ed., 245–46, quoted by Smith, *Poetics of Homosexual Desire*, 149.
36. Chambers, *Elizabethan Stage*, 1:371 n. 4. Queen Henrietta-Maria and court ladies appeared in pastorals performed at court in 1625–26 and 1632; see Bentley, *Jacobean and Caroline Stage*, 4:549–50, 917. As pointed out by Suzanne Gossett, "'Man-Maid, begone!': Women in Masques," *ELR* 18 (1988): 96–113, court ladies occasionally performed in court masques alongside female impersonators. James Stokes has collected evidence of the involvement of women and girls in a variety of theatrical activities in "Women and Mimesis in Medieval and Renaissance Somerset (and Beyond)," *CompD* 27 (1993): 176–196; see also Stokes, "The Wells Cordwainers Show: New Evidence Concerning Guild Entertainments in Somerset," *CompD* 19 (1985–86): 336.
37. Jerzy Limon, *Gentlemen of a Company: English Players in Central and Eastern Europe*, 1590–1660 (Cambridge: Cambridge University Press, 1985), 140.
38. Translated by Andrew Gurr, *The Shakespearean Stage, 1574–1642*, 2d ed. (Cambridge: Cambridge University Press, 1980), 209, following Geoffrey Tillotson, "*Othello* and *The Alchemist* at Oxford in 1610," *TLS*, July 20, 1933, 494.

39. Lady Mary Wroath [sic], *The Countesse of Mountgomeries Urania* (London, 1621), 60.

40. Lady Mary Wroth, *The [first and] secound booke of the secound part of the Countess of Montgomery's Urania,* MS in the Newberry Library, [book I] fol. 30 [2ᵛ]. I wish to thank Gwynne Kennedy for her help in transcribing this passage. I am also grateful to her and to Mary Lamb for guiding me to these allusions. See Michael Shapiro, "Lady Mary Wroth Describes a 'Boy Actress,'" *MaRDiE* 4 (1987): 187–94.

41. For a concise summary of Lady Mary Wroth's involvement in court entertainment, see *The Poems of Lady Mary Wroth,* ed. Josephine Roberts (Baton Rouge: Louisiana State University Press, 1983), 12–13; and Shapiro, "Lady Mary Wroth," 188.

42. Peter Hyland, "'A Kind of Woman': The Elizabethan Boy-Actor and the Kabuki *Onnagata,*" *ThR* 12 (1985): 1–8, suggests that some Shakespearean female characters were played by adult male actors in a highly stylized fashion, analogous to that used in Kabuki. What appears to us as a formalized acting style, however, may have seemed quite natural in its own day. See Joseph Roach, *The Player's Passion: Studies in the Science of Acting* (Newark: University of Delaware Press, 1985), 23–57.

43. W. Robertson Davies, *Shakespeare's Boy Actors* (London: J. M. Dent, 1939), 136. Davies's position is restated by James L. Hill, "Tragic Women and Boy Actors," *SEL* 26 (1986): 235–48.

44. Samuel Johnson, "Preface [to Shakespeare], 1765," in *Johnson on Shakespeare,* ed. A. Sherbo, *The Yale Edition of the Works of Samuel Johnson,* ed. E. L. McAdam, Jr., 16 vols. (New Haven: Yale University Press, 1958–90), 7:77; and S. L. Bethell, *Shakespeare and the Popular Dramatic Tradition* (Durham NC: Duke University Press, 1944), 26ff., and "Shakespeare's Actors," *RES,* n.s., 1 (1950): 203. Bethell's position is restated by P. H. Parry, "The Boyhood of Shakespeare's Heroines," *ShS* 42 (1989): 99–109.

45. Michael Shapiro, "Boying Her Greatness: Shakespeare's Use of Coterie Drama in *Antony and Cleopatra,*" *MLR* 77 (1982): 1–15. See also Madelon Sprengnether, "The Boy Actor and Femininity in *Antony and Cleopatra,*" in *Shakespeare's Personality,* ed. Norman N. Holland, Sidney Homan, and Bernard J. Paris (Berkeley and Los Angeles: University of California Press, 1989), 191–205; Lorraine Helms, "'The High Roman Fashion': Sacrifice, Suicide, and the Shakespearean Stage," *PMLA* 107 (1992): 559–60; and Peter Stallybrass, "Transvestism and the 'Body Beneath,'" 71.

Chapter 3

1. Freeburg, *Disguise Plots,* 98–99.

2. John Marston, *Antonio and Mellida,* ed. G. K. Hunter (Lincoln: University of Nebraska Press, 1965), induction, ll. 68–72, 77–79.

3. Two recent films illustrate contrasting ways of performing layered gender identities. In *All of Me* (1984), Steve Martin appears in court as a male lawyer possessed by a female spirit and plays at various moments a man, the woman

in a man's body fighting its owner for control over it, and the woman (having won the fight) trying to (over)act as a man. The incident, played for broad comedy, is quite brief. In *Victor/Victoria* (1982), Julie Andrews plays an actress-singer who pretends to be a male performer billed as a female impersonator. When Victor is offstage, Andrews plays him as a slightly effeminate man, but she performs his nightclub routines not as a man imitating a woman but directly as a woman (even though in rehearsal she had been shown by a male choreographer how to use exaggerated body movements of a "drag queen"). As a result, Victor produces a flawless imitation of a woman.

4. Raymond J. Pentzell, "Actor, *Maschera,* and Role: An Approach to Irony in Performance," *CompD* 16 (1982): 206–7.

5. Wolfgang Clemen, "Appearance and Reality in Shakespeare's Plays," in *Shakespeare's Dramatic Art: Collected Essays* (London: Methuen, 1972), 169. Zimmerman, "Disruptive Desire," 47, lists a number of "strategies for interrupting and displacing dramatic fictions" involving cross-gender casting and cross-gender disguise: "references, implicit or explicit, to the body beneath that of the actor's impersonation (including scenes of broad, bawdy humour); excessive attention to the age, beauty and apparel of the cross-dressed boy, and especially to the complex sexual appeal of boy actors twice cross-dressed; ostentatious kissing and embracing; attenuated scenes of primarily sexual interest (such as bedroom scenes); and meta-theatric commentary on theatrical artifice, particularly 'send-ups' of the transvestite convention itself."

6. Female pages appear in the following plays performed by children's troupes: *The Wars of Cyrus;* Lyly, *Gallathea;* Marston, *Antonio and Mellida;* Chapman, *May Day;* Machin, *The Dumb Knight;* Barry, *Ram Alley;* Sharpham, *The Fleire;* and Fletcher, *Cupid's Revenge* and *Philaster.* The heroine of *The Maid's Metamorphosis,* discussed in chapter 8, is transformed into a boy. In Jonson's *Cynthia's Revels,* Anaides' "punquetto" Gelaia, described in the induction as "a wench in boyes attire" (ll. 60–61), dresses but does not disguise herself as a page. Barton, *Ben Jonson, Dramatist,* 74, sees this moment as a gibe at Dekker, a "patent travesty of . . . romantic disguising popular in comedies written for the public theatres."

7. Juliet Dusinberre, *Shakespeare and the Nature of Women* (New York: Macmillan, 1975), 263. See also Zimmerman, "Disruptive Desire," 46. Female and male pages rarely appear onstage at the same time in plays acted by children's troupes, although Marston's *What You Will* includes a boy bride surrounded by other pages, and Gelaia appears disguised as a page in act II of *Cynthia's Revels* with Cupid and Mercury (also disguised as pages).

8. D. J. Lake, "The Date of *More Dissemblers Besides Women,*" *N&Q* 221 (1976): 219–21. Frank Tolle Mason, "A Critical Edition of Thomas Middleton's *More Dissemblers Besides Women*" (Ph.D. diss., Michigan State University, 1974), 3–9, argues for 1611 or soon thereafter. Malone dated the play c. 1615, the year Middleton began to write for the King's Men. See Bentley, *Jacobean and Caroline Stage,* 4:888–89.

9. George E. Rowe, *Thomas Middleton and the New Comedy Tradition* (Lincoln: University of Nebraska Press, 1979), 164–73.
10. John F. McElroy, *Parody and Burlesque in the Tragicomedies of Thomas Middleton,* Jacobean Drama Studies, no. 19 (Salzburg: Institut für Englische Sprache und Literatur, 1972), 153. For discussion of *Philaster,* see chapter 7.
11. Rowe, *Thomas Middleton,* 173.
12. Mason, "A Critical Edition," 17–27.
13. Blurring of genders occurs frequently in the play: in Dondolo's reference to "a young gallant lying a-bed with his wench . . . being both in smocks they'd be taken for sisters" (I.iv.71–74) and other passages noted by Zimmerman, "Disruptive Desire," 53. If the cardinal were costumed in some type of clerical gown, he might well have appeared to be in transvestite garb, a frequent Puritan charge against Roman Catholic clergy.
14. The date is established by Lowell E. Johnson, ed., *No Wit, No Help Like a Woman's* (Lincoln: University of Nebraska Press, 1976), xi–xiii.
15. Woodbridge, *Women and the English Renaissance,* 258.

Chapter 4

1. Clifford Leech, ed., *The Two Gentlemen of Verona* (London: Methuen, 1969), xxxiv–xxxv, xii.
2. Michael Shapiro, *Children of the Revels* (New York: Columbia University Press, 1977), 105, 149, 239–42; T. W. Craik, *The Tudor Interlude* (Leicester: Leicester University Press, 1958), 42–45; and G. K. Hunter, *John Lyly: The Humanist as Courtier* (London: Routledge and Kegan Paul, 1962) 220–43.
3. Hunter, *John Lyly,* 314. See 311–17 for other Lylian features of *Two Gentlemen;* as well as Marco Mincoff, "Shakespeare and Lyly," *ShS* 14 (1961): 15–24.
4. *Clyomon and Clamydes: A Critical Edition,* ed. Betty J. Littleton, Studies in English Literature 25 (The Hague: Mouton, 1968), l. 1261. I quote throughout from this edition. See also Lee Ellison, *Early Romantic Drama at the English Court* (Chicago: University of Chicago Libraries, 1917), 117.
5. John Lyly, *Gallathea,* in *The Complete Works,* ed. R. Warwick Bond (Oxford: Clarendon Press, 1902), vol. 2, II.i.31. Quotations from Lyly's works are from this edition. *Gallathea* is discussed in chapter 5.
6. Norman Sanders, ed., *James the Fourth,* by Robert Greene (London: Methuen, 1970), xxv–xxix. I quote throughout from this edition. The play is discussed in chapter 7.
7. Weimann, *Shakespeare and the Popular Tradition,* 256–57. See also Leech, ed., *Two Gentlemen,* xxvi; Inga-Stina Ewbank, "'Were man but constant, he were perfect': Constancy and Consistency in *The Two Gentlemen of Verona,*" in *Shakespearian Comedy,* Stratford-upon-Avon-Studies 14 (London: Edward Arnold, 1972), 40; and Harold F. Brooks, "Two Clowns in a Comedy (to Say Nothing of the Dog): Speed, Launce (and Crab) in *The Two Gentlemen of Verona,*" English Association 16, n.s., *Essays and Studies* (London: John Murray, 1963), 91–100.

8. Alexander Leggatt, *Shakespeare's Comedy of Love* (London: Methuen, 1974), 36. Margaret Loftus Ranald, *Shakespeare and His Social Context* (New York: AMS Press, 1987), 57, notes Julia's resemblance to the play's other "comic commentator[s]." Dale G. Priest, "Subjunctivity in *The Two Gentlemen of Verona,*" in *Explorations in Renaissance Culture* 6 (1980): 41, observes that Julia has ten asides and three soliloquies in the play and thus "reinforces . . . the audience's sense of detachment.".

9. According to Judith M. Kennedy, ed., *A Critical Edition of Yong's Translation of George of Montemayor's "Diana" and Gil Polo's "Enamoured Diana"* (Oxford: Clarendon Press, 1968), xxxi–xxxii, Jorge Montemayor's *Diana,* published in 1559, was translated into English by Bartholomew Yong by 1583 but was not published until 1598. Thomas Wilson completed an unpublished translation by 1596. See also Dale B. J. Randall, *The Golden Tapestry* (Durham NC: Duke University Press, 1963), 71, 77–79; R. W. Bond, ed., *The Two Gentlemen of Verona* (London: Methuen, 1906), xvii–xviii; and Thomas Amherst Perry, "*The Two Gentlemen of Verona* and the Spanish *Diana,*" *MP* 87 (1989): 76. On the lost play *The History of Felix and Philiomena,* performed by the Queen's Men in 1584–85, see Kennedy, xlii–xliv, and Chambers, *Elizabethan Stage,* 4:160.

10. I quote here and throughout from the tale of Felix and Felismena in Yong's translation of Montemayor's *Diana,* reprinted in Bullough, *Sources,* 1:233. See 1:205–7 for discussion of Shakespeare's modifications.

11. Gras, "All Is Semblative," 90–93.

12. Muriel C. Bradbrook, *The Growth and Structure of Elizabethan Comedy* (London: Chatto and Windus, 1961), 88, describes the contrasts between heroine and page as "giving an effect like shot silk, as the boyish wit or the feminine sensibility predominates."

13. Anne Righter [Barton], *Shakespeare and the Idea of the Play* (Harmondsworth: Penguin, 1967), 94, comments aptly: "The passage sets up a series of illusions receding into depth of which the most remote, the tears wrung from Julia by the stage presentation of a lover's perfidy, in fact represents reality." For other valuable commentary, see Charles Brooks, "Shakespeare's Heroine-Actresses" *ShJW* 96 (1960): 137; Ruth Nevo, *Comic Transformations in Shakespeare* (London: Methuen, 1980), 65; and Priest, "Subjunctivity," 41–43.

14. In W. Holman Hunt's painting of the moment just before the swoon, *Valentine Rescuing Sylvia from Proteus* (1851), Julia, isolated from the other three characters, slouches against a tree as if about to collapse; for a reproduction and commentary, see Martin Meisel, *Realizations: Narrative, Pictorial, and Theatrical Arts in Nineteenth-Century England* (Princeton: Princeton University Press, 1983), no. 163 and pp. 360–63. Belsey, "Disrupting Sexual Difference," argues that the swoon "reaffirms her femininity" (179) but extricates herself from this Victorian response by reading Julia's movement in and out of disguise as an example of the discontinuity of identity used to disrupt sexual difference and hence question stereotypical gender roles (188–89). Such disruption may have occurred whether or not intended, but I

would argue that from the dramaturgical point of view the passage was primarily intended not so much to challenge patriarchal sexist assumptions as to endow the heroine with theatrical power.

15. Critics differ as to which if any of Julia's actions in this episode are meant to seem intentional. I agree with Leech, ed., *Two Gentlemen*, who notes that her confusion of rings, which "repeats the mistake with the letters," indicates that she "doubtless does it deliberately" (118n) and that her "well-timed swoon . . . is a deliberate one" (lxvii). The opposing view is argued by Kenneth C. Bennet, "Stage Action in *The Two Gentlemen of Verona*," *ShJW* 116 (1980), 99: "I feel that Julia must faint naturally because she has been established as the most romantic and sympathetic of the principals." Leggatt, *Shakespeare's Comedy of Love*, 37, feels "a final decision must rest with the performer." In Fletcher's *Love's Pilgrimage* (King's, c. 1616), a brother refers to his sister's swoon as part of "that seal'd religion / You women bear to swownings." The words that follow might well serve as a gloss on Julia's "swoon":

> you do pick
> Your times to faint, when some body is by,
> Bound or by nature, or by love, or service
> To raise you from that well dissembled death.

Love's Pilgrimage, ed. L. A. Beaurline, Beaumont and Fletcher, *The Dramatic Works in the Beaumont and Fletcher Canon*, gen. ed. Fredson Bowers, 7 vols., (Cambridge: Cambridge University Press, 1966–), vol. 2, IV.i.153–57. Unless otherwise stated, all references to the plays of Beaumont and Fletcher are to this edition.

16. Some critics argue that the play intends to criticize if not parody the cult of male friendship. See William Rossky, *"The Two Gentlemen of Verona* as Burlesque," *ELR* 12 (1982): 210–19; and Ralph Berry, *Shakespeare's Comedies: Explorations in Form* (Princeton: Princeton University Press, 1972), 40–53. Priest, "Subjunctivity," 32–36, challenges the parodic view. A production in 1983 at the University of Illinois carried the parodic approach to the limit: Silvia refused to become glue for a male bond and stalked off the stage in defiant rage.

17. Eve Kosofsky Sedgwick, *Between Men: English Literature and Male Homosocial Desire* (New York: Columbia University Press, 1985), 25–26. For readings of the play in the light of Renaissance theories of friendship, see Camille Wells Slights, *Shakespeare's Comic Commonwealths* (Toronto: University of Toronto Press, 1993), 57–74; Ruth Morse, *"Two Gentlemen* and the Cult of Friendship," *NM* 84 (1983): 214–24; and Ewbank, "Were man but constant." The climax of the BBC production is precisely this recementing of male friendship: Silvia is conveniently off camera while the viewer sees a close-up of the two men and then an even closer shot of their clasped hands.

18. The date of *The Night Walker* is uncertain. A quarto was published in 1640, probably based on Shirley's revision of 1633. William W. Appleton,

Beaumont and Fletcher: A Critical Study (London: George Allen and Unwin, 1956), 121, dates the play 1609–14. Chambers, *Elizabethan Stage*, 2:60, argues for performance by the Children of the Queen's Revels between 1610 and 1613, but he sounds much less convinced of so early a date at 3:230–31. Charles Squier, *John Fletcher* (Boston: Twayne, 1986), chronology and 121, gives both 1611 and 1611–14. See also Bentley, *Jacobean and Caroline Stage*, 1:176, 3:386. On the date of *Philaster*, see Andrew Gurr, ed. (London: Methuen, 1969), xxvi–xxix, who proposes 1609, while Dora Jean Ashe, ed. (Lincoln: University of Nebraska Press, 1974), xi, suggests 1608–10.

19. John Fletcher, *The Night Walker*, ed. Cyrus Hoy, *Beaumont and Fletcher Canon*, vol. 7, I.i.53–59.

20. Woodbridge, *Women and the English Renaissance*, 245–48, 287–94.

21. Muriel C. Bradbrook, "Shakespeare and the Use of Disguise in Elizabethan Drama," *EIC* 2 (1952): 167. See also Freeburg, *Disguise Plots*, 84–89, 95–96.

22. *The Honest Man's Fortune, Beaumont and Fletcher*, ed. A. R. Waller, 10 vols. (Cambridge: Cambridge University Press, 1905–12), 10:277. Unless otherwise indicated, subsequent references to the play are by page number and refer to this edition, which is based on the 1647 folio. The comma before "Lady" appears to be the functional equivalent of the indefinite article. It is present in the folios of 1647, 1679, and 1711 but was removed in subsequent editions by Weber (1812), Dyce (1843), Darley (1856), and Gerritsen (1952).

23. "*The Honest Mans Fortune:* A Critical Edition of MS Dyce 9 (1625)," ed. J. Gerritsen, *Groningen Studies in English* 3 (1952), V.iv.253. Subsequent references to this edition, by act, scene, and line number, appear in the text. Gerritsen believes that the folio prints the original ending and that the manuscript, on which his edition is based, provides a revised version. His argument hinges on imagined stage business that he maintains was too bawdy to be permitted and therefore had to be revised. He believes that the revised version, recorded in manuscript, represents the play as audiences actually saw it. It is useful to have the MS available, but hard to believe that it represents a more "acceptable" version than the folio text or even that such moral criteria applied.

24. Gurr, *Playgoing in Shakespeare's London*, 177–82.

25. Philip Massinger, *The Bashful Lover, The Plays and Poems*, ed. Philip Edwards and Colin Gibson, 5 vols. (Oxford: Clarendon Press, 1976), vol 4, I.i.70–71. Subsequent references to the play are to this edition.

Chapter 5

1. Hunter, *John Lyly*, 199.

2. Anne Begor Lancashire, ed., John Lyly, *Gallathea* and *Midas* (Lincoln: University of Nebraska Press, 1969), xxvi.

3. Ellen M. Caldwell, "John Lyly's *Gallathea:* A New Rhetoric of Love for the Virgin Queen," *ELR* 17 (1987): 22–40. Cf. Leah Scragg, *The Metamorphosis of "Gallathea": A Study in Creative Adaptation* (Washington: University Press of America, 1982).

4. Joel B. Altman, *The Tudor Play of Mind: Rhetorical Inquiry and the Development of Elizabethan Drama* (Berkeley and Los Angeles: University of California Press, 1978), 209, argues that Gallathea is the one who will be transformed to a boy, for she seems to him to be more "heroic" in act I than the more "feminine" Phillida. Caldwell, "John Lyly's *Gallathea*," 34 n. 17, however, justifies the indeterminacy because of the "arbitrary nature and relative unimportance of the physical transformation in a play which celebrates Platonic union."

5. Jessica Milner Davis, *Farce* (London: Methuen, 1978), 62–63, explains the frequent use of twins and doubles in farce: "The artificiality . . . signals both a distancing of the characters from the audience and a lessening of their humanity: they lack the flexibility and the individuality of life."

6. Believing Antonio's "wealthy Andrew" to refer to the ship captured by Essex at Cadiz in mid-1596 and renamed *The Andrew*, most scholars now think the play was probably written in the latter half of that year. See M. Mahood, ed., *The Merchant of Venice* (Cambridge: Cambridge University Press, 1987), 1–2.

7. Joan Hartwig, *Shakespeare's Analogical Scene* (Lincoln: University of Nebraska Press, 1983), 12. As Bradbrook, "Shakespeare and the Use of Disguise," 166, comments, Shakespeare observes "a scale of contrast between Jessica's purely formal disguise, Nerissa's imitative one, and the significant robing of Portia."

8. Kenneth Muir, *Shakespeare's Sources*, 2 vols. (London: Methuen, 1957), 1:51. See also Bullough, *Sources*, 1:457.

9. John Dover Wilson, "The Copy for *The Merchant of Venice*, 1600," in *The Merchant of Venice* (Cambridge: Cambridge University Press, 1926), 110–11, 179–80, proposed that a scene of feasting at Bassanio's house, including the disguised Jessica and Shylock, was cut during revision.

10. Jessica's disguising was very important in Mark Lamos's 1984 production in Stratford, Ontario, as described by Paul Gaudet, "Lorenzo's 'Infidel': The Staging of Difference in *The Merchant of Venice*," *TJ* 38 (1986): 275–90. Ellis Rabb's New York production (1973) also stressed Jessica's vulnerability in the elopement scene, whereas Irving invented stage business and devised elaborate pictorial effects to emphasize the pathos of Shylock; see James C. Bulman, *The Merchant of Venice* (Manchester: Manchester University Press, 1991), 36–38, 147.

11. Mahood, ed., *The Merchant of Venice*, 97–98nn. Unlike the first quarto, on which the Riverside text is based, the second quarto and the folio print "On, gentlemen, away," which may exclude or include Jessica.

12. For other parallels and contrasts between Lorenzo/Jessica and Portia/Bassanio, see Keith Geary, "The Nature of Portia's Victory: Turning to Men in *The Merchant of Venice*," *ShS* 37 (1984): 61–62; and Harry Berger, "Marriage and Mercifixion in *The Merchant of Venice*," *SQ* 32 (1981): 160. As Norman Rabkin notes, *Shakespeare and the Problem of Meaning* (Chicago: University of Chicago Press, 1981), 5, 17–19, readers differ as to whether Jessica and Lorenzo liberate or steal Shylock's money and jewels, whether

they are attractively or foolishly prodigal. Mahood, ed., *The Merchant of Venice*, 29–31, believes that discordant elements eliciting moral judgment are ignored by a theatrical audience, which always "loves a lover whatever his actions" (31). Paul Gaudet, in two conference papers (Shakespeare Association of America, 1985, 1989), sees ironies too trenchant to ignore in each of Jessica's appearances.

13. John Donne, "Elegie: On His Mistres," in *The Complete Poetry*, ed. John T. Shawcross (Garden City NY: Anchor Books, 1967), 62, l. 14. One manuscript version is entitled "On his mistres desire to be disguised, and to goe like a Page with him" (439). The speaker fears the scheme will not work, because "the rightest company / Of Players . . . / Will quickly know thee, / and no lesse, alas! / Th'indifferent Italian . . . / well content to thinke thee Page, / Will hunt thee with such lust, and hideous rage, / As *Lots* faire guests were vext" (ll. 35–41).

14. Belsey, "Disrupting Sexual Difference," 179.

15. Vera Jiji, "Portia Revisited: The Influence of Unconscious Factors upon Theme and Characterization in *The Merchant of Venice*," *L&P* 26 (1976): 8.

16. Diane Elizabeth Dreher, *Domination and Defiance: Fathers and Daughters in Shakespeare* (Lexington: University Press of Kentucky, 1986), 131; and Christopher Spencer, *The Genesis of Shakespeare's "Merchant of Venice"* (Lewiston NY: Edwin Mellen Press, 1988), 59–62.

17. Richard Wheeler, "'. . . And my loud crying still': The *Sonnets*, *The Merchant of Venice*, and *Othello*," in *Rough Magic*, 196–97.

18. Lynda E. Boose, "The Comic Contract and Portia's Golden Ring," *ShakS* 20 (1988): 247. Karen Newman, "Portia's Ring: Unruly Women and Structures of Exchange in *The Merchant of Venice*," *SQ* 38 (1987): 26, argues that "Portia gives more than Bassanio can ever reciprocate." See also Dreher, *Domination and Defiance*, 132–33, 135.

19. Coppélia Kahn, "The Cuckoo's Note: Male Friendship and Cuckoldry in *The Merchant of Venice*," in *Rough Magic*, 104–12. On the rivalry between Portia and Antonio, see also Geary, "The Nature of Portia's Victory"; Graham Midgley, *"The Merchant of Venice*: A Reconsideration," *EIC* 10 (1960): 119–33; John Hurrell, "Love and Friendship in *The Merchant of Venice*," *TSLL* 3 (1961): 328–41; Marc Shell, "The Wether and the Ewe: Verbal Usury in *The Merchant of Venice*," *KR*, n.s., 1, no. 4 (1979): 65–92; and Jan Lawson Hinely, "Bond Priorities in *The Merchant of Venice*," *SEL* 20 (1980): 217–39. In the opening scene, in what may be a trace of the source, Bassanio is referred to as Antonio's "most noble kinsman" (I.i.57).

20. Nevo, *Comic Transformations*, 132.

21. Boose, "Comic Contract," 248.

22. Katherine E. Kelly, "The Queen's Two Bodies: Shakespeare's Boy Actress in Breeches," *TJ* 42 (1990): 87, glosses the line to refer to "the professional vulnerability of the boy player . . . [with] his dangerously changeable voice."

23. Geary, "The Nature of Portia's Victory," 58. The stress on Balthazar's maleness is necessary, Geary argues, because "Portia's disguise allows her

to intervene directly to recover her husband, not, of course, from another woman, but from another man" (64). But he overstates the case, as in the following assertion, by ignoring the audience's mental retention of layers gender not visible at the moment: "the theatrical fact of the boy actor in the Elizabethan theatre makes Portia's sexual transformation complete" (58).

24. R. Chris Hassel, *Faith and Folly in Shakespeare's Romantic Comedies* (Athens: University of Georgia Press, 1980), 198.

25. Shylock's position in this duel is a Pauline distortion of Judaism; see John R. Cooper, "Shylock's Humanity," *SQ* 21 (1970): 117–24; Bernard Glassman, *Anti-Semitic Stereotypes without Jews: Images of the Jews in England, 1290–1700* (Detroit: Wayne State University Press, 1975), 14–83; and Michael Shapiro, "Shylock the Jew Onstage: Past and Present," *Shofar* 4, no. 2 (1986): 1–11. In a conference paper (Shakespeare Association of America, 1991), Randall Martin points out that once Shylock drops his claim to Antonio's flesh, Portia has freed Bassanio from any obligation and thus no longer has a clear motive for further action against Shylock other than generalized hostility toward an alien or personal revenge, much to the distress of the actresses he interviewed.

26. Mahood, ed., *The Merchant of Venice*, 40.

27. Mahood, ed., *The Merchant of Venice*, 151n. See also Marianne L. Novy, *Love's Argument: Gender Relations in Shakespeare* (Chapel Hill: University of North Carlina Press, 1984), 77.

28. I quote from the translation of *Il Pecorone* in Bullough, *Sources*, 1:474. Subsequent references to this translation will appear in the text.

29. John Russell Brown, ed., *The Merchant of Venice*, 121n.

30. Joan Landis, "'By Two-headed Janus': Double Discourse in *The Merchant of Venice*," conference paper (Shakespeare Association of America, 1990), 3, points out that the Latin word for ring is *ano* or *anulus*, and Howard Jacobson has referred me to a passage in one of Cicero's letters (*Epistulae ad Familiares* IX.xxii.2), that plays on *anulus* and *anus*. See also Frankie Rubinstein, *A Dictionary of Shakespeare's Sexual Puns and Their Significance* (London: Macmillan, 1984), 220–21.

31. Several critics have commented on Portia's retention of power and authority in the final act after she has dropped male disguise. See Richard Horwich, "Riddle and Dilemma in *The Merchant of Venice*," *SEL* 17 (1977): 191–200; Dusinberre, *Shakespeare and the Nature of Women*, 267; and Kirby Farrell, "Self-Effacement and Autonomy in Shakespeare," *ShakS* 16 (1983): 78. On her use of fear of cuckoldry, see Kahn, "The Cuckoo's Note," 109; and Anne Parten, "Re-establishing Sexual Order: The Ring Episode in *The Merchant of Venice*," *Selected Papers from the West Virginia Shakespeare and Renaissance Association* 6 (1981): 27–34. For negative views of Portia's tactics, see Frank Whigham, "Ideology and Class Conduct in *The Merchant of Venice*," *RenD*, n.s., 10 (1979): 110; Thomas Cartelli, "Ideology and Subversion in the Shakespearean Set Speech," *ELH* 53 (1986): 16–21; and Hassel, *Faith and Folly*, 207.

32. Benjamin Nelson, *The Idea of Usury*, 2d ed. (Chicago: University of Chicago Press, 1969), 141–42, describes Antonio's offer as the kind "denounced by Luther as a challenge to God's total authority [and] . . . an inexcusable effort to imitate Christ's inimitable goodness." *The Geneva Bible* (1560), Hebrews 7:22, refers to Jesus as "a surety of a better Testament." See also Harry Morris, "The Judgment Theme in *The Merchant of Venice*," *Renascence* 39 (1986): 310.

33. Monica J. Hamill, "Poetry, Law, and the Pursuit of Perfection: Portia's Role in *The Merchant of Venice*," *SEL* 18 (1978): 243. See also Berger, "Marriage and Mercifixion," 162. Portia's triumph over Antonio is often suggested in production by having him remain onstage alone for a moment.

34. Christopher Gordon Petter, ed., *A Critical Old Spelling Edition of the Works of Edward Sharpham* (New York: Garland, 1986), 183–84.

35. Cervantes, "The Two Damsels," in *The Exemplary Novels of Miguel de Cervantes Saavedra*, trans. Walter K. Kelly (London: Henry G. Bohn, 1855), 435.

36. W. W. Greg, ed., William Haughton, *Englishmen For My Money*, Malone Society Reprints 32 (London: Malone Society, 1912), vi–vii, establishes the date from references to the play by its subtitle, *A Woman Will Have Her Will*, in Henslowe's accounts for 1598. Subsequent references to this edition will appear in the text.

37. Andrew Gurr, lecture at the University of Illinois at Urbana-Champaign, March 10, 1990.

38. Woodbridge, *Women and the English Renaissance*, 157.

39. James Shirley, *The School of Compliment, or Love Tricks*, in *Dramatic Works and Poems*, ed. William Gifford and Alexander Dyce, 6 vols. (London: John Murray, 1833), 1:36. All subsequent references to Shirley's plays, by volume and page number, will appear in the text.

Chapter 6

1. Freeburg, *Disguise Plots*, 11–14, 80–83; Edward Berry, *Shakespeare's Comic Rites* (Cambridge: Cambridge University Press, 1984), 83, uses the term "disguise-within-disguise," which is misleading, for the second disguise is laid on top of, not inserted within, the first disguise.

2. Mary Ann Weber Gasior, ed., Thomas Heywood, *The Four Prentices of London* (New York: Garland, 1980), vii–xv. Gasior thinks the play may have been written as early as 1592. It was registered in 1594 but not published until 1615. A second edition appeared in 1632. I quote throughout from this edition.

3. The concept is developed by Bertrand Evans, *Shakespeare's Comedies* (Oxford: Oxford University Press, 1960).

4. Nevill Coghill, *Shakespeare's Professional Skills* (Cambridge: Cambridge University Press, 1964), 132.

5. On the date of *As You Like It*, see the play as edited by Agnes Latham (London: Methuen, 1975), xxvi–xxxiv.

6. For discussion of the theatrical aspects of Rosalind's voices, see Robert Hapgood, *Shakespeare the Theatre-Poet* (Oxford: Clarendon Press, 1988), 133–37; D. J. Palmer, *"As You Like It* and the Idea of Play," *CritQ* 13 (1971): 240–41; Robert B. Pierce, "The Moral Languages of *Rosalynde* and *As You Like It*," *SP* 68 (1971): 174–76; Hugh Richmond, *Shakespeare's Sexual Comedy* (Indianapolis: Bobbs-Merrill, 1971), 142; and Laurence Lerner, *Love and Marriage: Literature and Its Social Context* (New York: St. Martin's, 1979), 20–22.

7. Carol J. Carlisle, "Helen Faucit's Rosalind," *ShakS* 12 (1979): 65–94, argues that Faucit moved with particular liveliness from one layer of identity to another in the Ganymed scenes. Carol Rutter, *Clamorous Voices* (London: Routledge, 1989), 104, comments: "For Juliet [Stevenson] . . . Ganymede did not simply replace Rosalind in Arden; he ran parallel with her. The two would sometimes collude, sometimes collide and even sometimes betray each other."

8. Nancy K. Hayles, "Sexual Disguise in *As You Like It* and *Twelfth Night*," *ShS* 32 (1979): 63–72.

9. Kent van den Berg, *Playhouse and Cosmos: Shakespearean Theater as Metaphor* (Newark: University of Delaware Press, 1985), 91; and Novy, *Love's Argument*, 192–93.

10. Dusinberre, *Shakespeare and the Nature of Women*, 250; Hyland, "Shakespeare's Heroines," 33–34; Kimbrough, "Androgyny," 24.

11. Marco Mincoff, "What Shakespeare Did to *Rosalynde*," *ShJE* 96 (1960): 80; see also Edward I. Berry, "Rosalynde and Rosalind," *SQ* 31 (1980): 42–52; Walter R. Davis, "Masking in Arden: The Histrionics of Lodge's *Rosalynde*, *SEL* 5 (1965): 151–63; and Albert H. Tolman, "Shakespeare's Manipulation of His Source in *As You Like It*," *MLN* 37 (1922): 65–76.

12. Charles H. Frey, *Experiencing Shakespeare: Essays on Text, Classroom, and Performance* (Columbia: University of Missouri Press, 1988), 23–24.

13. W. Thomas MacCary, *Friends and Lovers: The Phenomenology of Desire in Shakespearean Comedy* (New York: Columbia University Press, 1985), 175–76, argues that Orlando sees Ganymed as an idealized image of himself. Cf. van den Berg, *Playhouse and Cosmos*, 96.

14. Smith, *Poetics of Homosexual Desire*, 145. Walter R. Davis, *Idea and Act in Elizabethan Fiction* (Princeton: Princeton University Press, 1969), 89–93, notes that Lodge switches from "he" to "she" to signal shifts between layers of gender, as required by the point of view at various moments in the narrative.

15. Elsewhere in this scene, Rosalind refers to such details of male attire as "doublet and hose" (III.ii.195–96 and 219–20) or to gender identity itself, as in "Do not you know I am a woman?" (l. 249) and "I thank God I am not a woman" (ll. 347–48).

16. For additional glosses on sexual innuendoes of this passage, see Peter F. Mullany, "Topographical Bawdy in Shakespeare," *AN&Q* 12 (December 1973): 51–53; and Robert H. Ray, "Addenda to Shakespeare's Bawdy: *As You Like It*, IV.i.201–18," *AN&Q* 13 (December 1974): 51–53.

17. Capell marks several of Rosalind's speeches as asides. Other speeches can be given as asides to Celia or the audience, as Janet Suzman did in the 1968 RSC production, according to Peter Ansorge, *Plays and Players,* July 1968, 51.

18. According to Latham, ed., *As You Like It,* app. B, 133–35, early modern audiences would have considered such a marriage valid under Elizabethan law and custom.

19. Peter W. Thomson, "A Shakespearean 'Method,'" *ShJE* 104 (1968): 198, argues—unpersuasively, in my view—that Oliver here "penetrates Rosalind's disguise."

20. Mary Hamer, "Shakespeare's Rosalind and Her Public Image," *ThR* 11 (1986): 109ff. See also Patty S. Derrick, "Rosalind and the Nineteenth-Century Woman: Four Stage Interpretations," *ThS* 26 (1985): 143–62. Clifford Williams directed an all-male production for the National Theatre in 1967, revived in 1974. He intended to create "an atmosphere of spiritual purity which transcends sexuality." Frank Marcus, "New Approaches," *London Magazine,* December 1967, 78, dismissed it as "simply sexless," while Irving Wardle, *The Times* [London], October 4, 1967, felt "real excitement in seeing this Rosalind and Jeremy Brett's very masculine Orlando being taken unawares by serious emotion in the midst of their game." The two Rosalinds also differed, at least according to Clive Barnes, *New York Times,* December 4, 1974, L 32, who noted that Ronald Pickup "made no attempt to feminize his acting," whereas Gregory Floy "plays her as a rather pretty girl being acted by a man." Philip Traci, *"As You Like It:* Homosexuality in Shakespeare's Play," *CLAJ* 25 (1981): 97–98, felt that the production differed from an Elizabethan production in its deliberate lack of physicality as well as in its use of men instead of boys for the female roles.

21. Whereas the line might seem to prove that Oliver has discovered Rosalind's gender, Latham, ed., *As You Like It* (115n), argues that "Oliver is joining in Orlando's make-believe, which he knows about already."

22. See Traci, *"As You Like It,"* 91–105. Leggatt, *Shakespeare's Comedy of Love,* 211, links the bawdy innuendo of "serve your turn" with the play's increasing stress on the biological sense of springtime renewal. But "Ganymed" denoted a young male prostitute in Elizabethan England and a young homosexual lover in medieval poetry and in Renaissance Italy. See chap. 2; John Boswell, *Christianity, Social Tolerance, and Homosexuality* (Chicago: University of Chicago Press, 1980), 251ff.; and James Saslow, *Ganymede in the Renaissance: Homosexuality in Art and Society* (New Haven: Yale University Press, 1986). Gordon Lell, "'Ganymede' on the Elizabethan Stage: Homosexual Implications of the Use of Boy-Actors," *Aegis* 1 (1973): 5–7, cites homosexual usages of the myth of Ganymede and points out that while Shakespeare found the name in Lodge's *Rosalind,* he added Rosalind's reference to "Jove's own page" (12).

23. Maura Slattery Kuhn, "Much Virtue in 'If,'" *SQ* 28 (1977): 40–50, believes that Rosalind is still in masculine attire. Her evidence is the first folio reading of Hymen's address to Duke Senior to "receive thy daughter . . . / That thou

mightst join *his* hand with his, / Whose heart within his bosome is" (V.iv.111–15; emphasis added). Most modern editors accept the third folio's emendation of the first "his" to "her."

24. Kuhn, "Much Virtue," 40, argues that the gap of seventy-eight lines would not have allowed enough time for the performer to change into woman's clothing in time for the wedding scene, although Touchstone's gratuitous disquisition on "the Lie" allows Rosalind time to change into theatrical costume, which was probably a radically simplified version of actual apparel. In the epilogue, Rosalind refers to herself as "the Lady," and notes that she is "not furnished like a beggar."

25. Adelman, "Male Bonding," 84–86; Peter Erickson, *Patriarchal Structures in Shakespeare's Drama* (Berkeley and Los Angeles: University of California Press, 1985), 34–35; Dusinberre, *Shakespeare and the Nature of Women*, 266; and Belsey, "Disrupting Sexual Difference," 181, 187–88. For "androgynist" readings, see Kimbrough, "Androgyny," 27; Margaret Boerner Beckman, "The Figure of Rosalind in *As You Like It*," *SQ* 29 (1978): 47; and Kay Stanton, "The Disguises of Shakespeare's *As You Like It*," *ISJR* 59 (1985): 304. Hayles, "Sexual Disguise in *As You Like It*," 67, argues that Rosalind appeals to men and women separately in the epilogue in order to reconcile them. Clara Claiborne Park, "As We Like It: How a Girl Can Be Smart and Still Popular," in *The Woman's Part: Feminist Criticism of Shakespeare*, ed. Carolyn Ruth Swift Lenz, Gayle Greene, and Carol Thomas Neely (Urbana: University of Illinois Press, 1980), 106–9, argues that Shakespeare sought to make Rosalind's assertiveness acceptable to male spectators. "Male dress," Park writes, "transforms . . . aggression into simple high spirits" (108).

26. Keir Elam, *Shakespeare's Universe of Discourse* (Cambridge: Cambridge University Press, 1984), 40.

27. Van den Berg, *Playhouse and Cosmos*, 100; and Albert Cirillo, "*As You Like It*: Pastoralism Gone Awry" *ELH* 38 (1971): 38.

28. Although the OED indicates that a "curtsy" was not at this time an exclusively feminine gesture, the citations suggest that it was appropriate only for boys and servants, which may explain why it shortly did become a feminine form of obeisance. Several plays use the term as an exclusively female gesture: see *Gallathea*, II.i.23–24, and quotations from *More Dissemblers Besides Women* in chapter 3 and *The Wise Woman of Hogsden* in this chapter.

29. Michael H. Leonard, ed., *The Wise Woman of Hogsden*, by Thomas Heywood (New York: Garland, 1980), 5–8. I have used this edition for all quotations from the play.

30. Gras, "All Is Semblative," 275, argues unpersuasively that "skattering" here means manually dispersing hair that was previously cut; see also 90–93. Removal of a wig, at once more economical and more spectacular, seems more likely. As Peter Stallybrass, "Transvestism and the 'Body Beneath,'" 66, observes, "the commonest technique for the revelation of the 'woman beneath' after the Restoration was the removal of a wig, whereupon the female actor's 'true' hair would be seen." But Stallybrass also suggests that such an effect would have been "perfectly possible on the Renaissance

stage . . . [for] the audience would have no means of knowing (any more than we do today) whether the hair beneath the wig was the hair of the actor or another wig."

31. Albert Tricomi, "The Dates of the Plays of George Chapman," *ELR* 12 (1982): 245–46, argues persuasively that *May Day* (pub. 1611) was written in 1601 or early 1602. This earlier dating is significant, for it locates this play much closer to *As You Like It* and well before the Jacobean explosion of disguised heroine plays. I quote throughout from George Chapman, *May Day*, ed. Robert F. Welsh, in *The Plays of George Chapman: The Comedies*, gen. ed. Allan Holaday (Urbana: University of Illinois Press, 1970), II.i.33–35.

32. Rita Belladonna, "A Jacobean's Source Revisited: George Chapman and Alessandro Piccolomini's *Alessandro*," *QI* 3 (1982): 67–70.

33. In context, "practis'd" can mean impersonated a woman on or off stage. It also had a sexual meaning in Shirley, *The Lady of Pleasure*, I.i.155–61, as pointed out by James T. Henke, *Courtesans and Cuckolds: A Glossary of Renaissance Dramatic Bawdy (Exclusive of Shakespeare)* (New York: Garland, 1979), 201. Lionell's reply of denial, "No, nor never meane sir," evokes a comment from Giovenelli, one of the play's true saucy lackeys: "Meane sir? No marry Captaine, there will never be meane in his practise I warrant him" (ll. 207–9). "Meane" can signify a pander or the money earned by or used for whoring, according to Henke, 167, and Rubinstein, *A Dictionary of Shakespeare's Sexual Puns*, 156–57.

34. Paula S. Berggren, "'A Prodigious Thing': The Jacobean Heroine in Male Disguise," *PQ* 62 (1983): 396.

35. Charlotte Spivack, *George Chapman* (New York: Twayne, 1967), 77–78; and Thomas Mark Grant, *The Comedies of George Chapman: A Study in Development*, Jacobean Drama Series (Salzburg: Institut für Englische Sprache und Literatur, 1972), 103–24.

36. On the date of the play, see David J. Lake, *The Canon of Thomas Middleton's Plays* (Cambridge: Cambridge University Press, 1975), 38–43; and Robert Levine, ed., *A Critical Edition of Thomas Middleton's "The Widow,"* (Salzburg: Institute für Englische Sprache und Literatur, 1975), xxi–xxvii. Citations refer to Levine's edition.

37. Woodbridge, *Women and the English Renaissance*, 244, 246–48, 257. In an unpublished paper, Heather M. McPhee, "Who's Got the Gun?: Performance, Gender, and Desire in Thomas Middleton's *The Widow*" (Sixteenth-Century Studies Conference, 1993), sees the appeal of the play in its subversiveness. It depicts a world in which the one-sex theory of human development has obliterated any meaningful differences between male and female so that sex and gender roles are performative.

38. Michael Hattaway, ed., *The New Inn* (Manchester: Manchester University Press, 1984), 7–8.

39. Harriett Hawkins, "The Idea of a Theater in Jonson's *The New Inn*," *RenD* 9 (1966): 214n.

40. Unlike spectators, readers of the 1631 printed edition were spared any uncertainty over Frank's gender: according to "The Persons of the Play," "*Franke*[,] suppos'd a boy and the *Hosts* sonne, . . . prooves to be *Laetitia*" (6:402).

41. Jon S. Lawry, "A Prospect of Jonson's *The New Inn*," *SEL* 23 (1983): 324.

42. Barton, *Ben Jonson*, 276–77; and George E. Rowe, *Distinguishing Jonson* (Lincoln: University of Nebraska Press, 1988), 167.

43. In his edition of 1860, William Gifford here added the stage direction, "Pulls off Frank's head-dress" (see Hattaway, ed., *The New Inn*, 196), probably recalling the end of *Epicoene*, when Morose's bride "removes her peruke" to establish male identity.

44. Lawry, "A Prospect," 327. Barton, *Ben Jonson*, 258–59, 281–84, sees the influence of Shakespearean romance as the result of the publication of the first folio. On the play's relation to romance and the problem of tone, see Alexander Leggatt, *Ben Jonson: His Vision and His Art* (London: Methuen, 1981), 35–44; and John Lemly, "'Make odde discoveries!' Disguises, Masques, and Jonsonian Romance," in *Shakespeare to Sheridan*, 137–41.

Chapter 7

1. For discussions of the date of *Twelfth Night*, see the introductions by Elizabeth Story Donno, ed. (Cambridge: Cambridge University Press, 1985), 1–3; and J. M. Lothian and T. W. Craik, eds. (London: Methuen, 1975), xxvi–xxxv.

2. Performers too feel anxiety when performing scenes that involve or suggest sexual intimacy. In an interview with Leslie Bennetts published in *New York Times*, November 17, 1987, C 11, both Kenneth Welsh and Kathy Bates describe anxieties they felt when performing in Terrence McNally's *Frankie and Johnny in the Clair de Lune*, "a two-character play which begins in Frankie's bed with the frenzied sounds of lovemaking, requiring some discreetly handled nudity." Mr. Welsh attributed his fear to the fact that "the play demands so much intimacy, not only physical but emotional," while Ms. Bates ascribed her initial reluctance to take the role to "fear of intimacy . . . a big one for me."

3. I quote from William Gager's letter to John Rainoldes, as quoted by Frederick S. Boas, *University Drama in the Tudor Age* (Oxford: Oxford University Press, 1914), 217–18. I discuss the Gager-Rainoldes controversy in chapter 2; see also Binns, "Women or Transvestites," 137–39. In the 1880s, by contrast, the vice-chancellor of Oxford, Benjamin Jowett, permitted the society to perform in public only on the condition that "the female parts . . . be taken by lady amateurs," as noted in Humphrey Carpenter, *O. U. D. S.: A Centenary History of the Oxford University Dramatic Society* (Oxford: Oxford University Press, 1985), 27. Smith, *Poetics of Homosexual Desire*, 81–86, describes schools, colleges, and inns of court as "the all-male social institutions that nurtured sixteenth- and seventeenth-century males from boyhood to manhood" (82).

4. Boas, *University Drama*, 235, 241.

5. John G. B. Streett, "Some Aspects of the Influence of the Boy-Actress Convention on the Plays of Shakespeare and Some of His Contemporary Dramatists" (Ph.D. diss., Oxford, 1973), chap. 3. Andrews, *Scripts and Scenarios*, 107–8, suggests commercial troupes were more willing than academic troupes to involve female characters in explicitly sexual stage business because the roles were played by "full time professional apprentices, not gentlemanly youths dragooned into acting just once or twice in their lives."

6. Thomas Kyd, *The Spanish Tragedy*, ed. Philip Edwards (London: Methuen, 1959), II.iv.23, 34–48. On the date of the play, see xxi–xxvii.

7. Prynne, *Histrio-Mastix*, 386, 166. The general problem of equipping male actors to display female breasts is discussed by June Schlueter, "'Stuffed, as they say, with honorable parts': Female Breasts on the English Renaissance Stage," *ShY* 3 (1992): 117–42. She also cites the ending of John Day's *Law Tricks* (Queen's Revels, c. 1604), ed. John Crow, Malone Society Reprints 89 (London: Malone Society, 1949 [1950]), V.ii, where a female character's "bosome bare" (l. 2168) is supposedly exposed to the view of another character, but not necessarily of the audience, to verify her female identity. (I am grateful to Alan Dessen for supplying both Schlueter and me with this example.) There are also examples of stage business involving "petting": in Fletcher's *Love's Pilgrimage*, a woman nursing the wounds of a lecherous man pretending to have been injured in battle, asks him, "What do you mean, why do you kisse my breasts?" (IV.iii.62); in Middleton's *Women Beware Women* (1613–22), ed. Roma Gill (London: Ernest Benn, 1968), the duke tells Bianca that he can "feel thy breast shake like a turtle panting / Under a loving hand that makes much on't" (II.ii.322–23); in Jonson's *The Devil Is an Ass*, the stage direction describes Wittipol's "playing with her [Mrs. Fitzdottrell's] paps" (II.vi.70).

8. James Paul Brawner, ed., *The Wars of Cyrus*, Illinois Studies in Language and Literature 28, nos. 3–4 (Urbana: University of Illinois Press, 1942), 10–20, 27–28. All references to the play are to this edition.

9. Sanders, ed., *James the Fourth*, xxv–xxix.

10. I quote from a translation of Chappuy's French translation (pub. 1583–84) of Cinthio's *Hecatommithi*, III.i by Sanders, ed., *James the Fourth*, 139. For a sensationalized, xenophobic treatment of the relationship between the lady and the female page, see Robert Daborne, *A Christian Turned Turk*, ed. A. E. H. Swaen, *Anglia* 20 (1898): 234 (l. 1530), where Alizia, disguised as her lover's brother, inflames the lust of a Turkish woman named Voada, who promises to help the lover escape on condition that "this night I shall enjoy thee."

11. Sanders, ed., *James the Fourth*, xliv; and Berry, *Shakespeare's Comic Rites*, 82.

12. Harold Jenkins, "Shakespeare's *Twelfth Night*," Rice Institute Pamphlets 45, reprinted in Stanley Wells, ed., *Twelfth Night: Critical Essays* (New York: Garland, 1986), 171–89.

13. Bullough, *Sources*, 2:351–52. All citations refer to this edition.

14. On the relationship of *Twelfth Night* to *Gl'Ingannati* and related plays of the *commedia erudita*, see Robert C. Melzi, "From Lelia to Viola," *RenD* 9 (1966): 67–81; Helen Andrews Kaufman, "Niccolo Secchi as a Source of *Twelfth Night*," *SQ* 5 (1954): 271–80; L. G. Salingar, "The Design of *Twelfth Night*," *SQ* 9 (1958): 120–22; Rene Pruvost, *"The Two Gentlemen of Verona, Twelfth Night, et Gl'Ingannati,"* *EA* 13 (1960): 4–9; and Muir, *Shakespeare's Sources*, 1:66–77. Quotations from *Gl'Ingannati* are from excerpts in Bullough. Shakespeare may have heard from John Hall or John Weaver of the Cambridge production of *Laelia*, a Latin version of the play produced at Cambridge in 1595; see Gras, "All Is Semblative," 179.

15. Clifford Leech, *"Twelfth Night" and Shakesperian Comedy* (Toronto: University of Toronto Press, 1965), 50, has stressed the affective implications of the audience's awareness of the performers' gender in the scenes between the two boy heroines: "we must remember that in a modern production the use of actresses for the women's parts materially lessens the disturbing quality." Some modern spectators of either gender might disagree. For example, Sue-Ellen Case, *Feminism and Theatre* (New York: Macmillan, 1988), 25–26, speculates on the detachment of women spectators from scenes of intimacy between female characters played by female impersonators. Matthew H. Wikander, "As Secret as Maidenhead: The Profession of the Boy-Actress in *Twelfth Night*," *CompD* 20 (1986–87): 352, suggests still another dimension: "What in the first exchanges between Olivia and Viola seems sexual rivalry might . . . also be construed as professional rivalry, for both 'ladies' enjoy the same marginal status in the company of which they are apprentice members."

16. A late chivalric narrative like *The Famous History of Parismus* (1598) by Emanuel Forde can titillate the reader by savoring erotic possibilities it never actually develops. See Bullough, *Sources*, 2:367.

17. Leggatt, *Shakespeare's Comedy of Love*, 235. See also Howard, "Crossdressing," 430–33.

18. J. Dennis Huston, "'When I Came to Man's Estate': *Twelfth Night* and Problems of Identity," *MLQ* 33 (1972): 275, notes that despite this line Cesario is always described as a page and never as a eunuch.

19. Gary Taylor, *To Analyze Delight: A Hedonist Criticism of Shakespeare* (Newark: University of Delaware Press, 1985), 86. See also Hyland, "Shakespeare's Heroines," 35; F. H. Mares, "Viola and Other Tranvestist Heroines in Shakespeare's Comedies," *Stratford Papers: 1965–67*, ed. B. A. W. Jackson (Hamilton, Ontario: McMaster University Library Press, 1969), 100; and Dale G. Priest, "Julia, Petruchio, Rosalind, Viola: Shakespeare's Subjunctive Leads," *MSE* 9 (1984): 45ff.

20. Leslie Hotson, *The First Night of "Twelfth Night"* (London: Rupert Hart-Davis, 1954), 63, identified one of the traveling companions of Don Virginio Orsino, Duke of Bracciano, as "a Spanish *youth*, Don Grazia de Montalvo" (emphases added).

21. E.g., Berry, *Shakespeare's Comic Rites*, 106.
22. Joseph Pequigney, *Such Is My Love* (Chicago: University of Chicago Press, 1985), 30–41, regards sonnet 20 as an attempt by the speaker to deny what he is also in the process of acknowledging as homoerotic attraction.
23. As Wikander observes, "As Secret as Maidenhead," 350, activating the audience's awareness of the gender of the boy actress threatens to make "Orsino's interest in Viola's mouth and throat . . . not merely bawdy but obscene." Jan Kott, "Shakespeare's Bitter Arcadia," in *Shakespeare Our Contemporary*, trans. Boleslaw Taborski, 2d ed. (London: Methuen, 1967), 202ff., reads Orsino's description of Cesario as that of an "ephebe"—what Jardine, *Still Harping*, 17, quoting the opening lines of Marlowe's and Nashe's *Dido* (Chapel Children, c. 1586), calls a "female wanton boy." In a more recent work, "Twins and Travesties: Gender, Dependency, and Sexual Availability in *Twelfth Night*," in *E.P.*, 27–38, Jardine modifies her views signficantly by stressing the real or presumed sexual availability of young household servants of either sex, but in my view she again somewhat overstates her case: "Eroticism, in the early modern period, is not gender-specific, is not grounded in the sex of the possibly 'submissive' partner, but is an expectation of that very submissiveness" (34).
24. Alexander Pope's insertion at this point of a stage direction, "Exit Curio," makes sense of "Enter Curio and others" two dozen lines later.
25. Priest, "Shakespeare's Subjunctive Leads," 38. See OED for the range of meanings of "favor," which also includes trinket, beauty, permission, and graciousness, as well as face.
26. Philip C. McGuire, *Speechless Dialect: Shakespeare's Open Silences* (Berkeley and Los Angeles: University of California Press, 1985), 19–37, discusses Antonio's attraction to Sebastian. See also Helene Moglen, "Disguise and Development: The Self and Society in *Twelfth Night*," *L&P* 23 (1973): 17–18.
27. Joseph Pequigney, "The Two Antonios and Same-Sex Love in *Twelfth Night* and *The Merchant of Venice*," *ELR* 22 (1992): 201–21. See also Nancy K. Hayles, "Sexual Disguise in *Cymbeline*," *MLQ* 41 (1980), 234, and "Sexual Disguise in *As You Like It* and *Twelfth Night*," 63–72.
28. Jean E. Howard, *Shakespeare's Art of Orchestration: Stage Technique and Audience Response* (Urbana: University of Illinois Press, 1984), 172–206.
29. Taylor, *To Analyze Delight*, 93, finds Orsino's agony deepened by allusions to Abraham's intended sacrifice of Isaac, as well as by the folio punctuation of two other passages.
30. John Russell Brown, *Shakespeare's Plays in Performance* (Baltimore: Penguin Books, 1969), 226.
31. Jörg Hasler, *Shakespeare's Theatrical Notation: The Comedies* (Berne: Cooper Monographs, 1974), reprinted in Stanley Wells, ed., *Twelfth Night: Critical Essays* (New York: Garland, 1986), 296–97, as "The Dramaturgy of the Ending of *Twelfth Night*."
32. Worthen, *The Idea of the Actor*, 52.
33. Adelman, "Male Bonding," 85–90, sees the addresses to Viola as if she were male as evidence of Orsino's wish for union with an androgynous figure,

either to legitimize his bisexuality or to integrate love and friendship. Dusin-berre, *Shakespeare and the Nature of Women*, 267, laments Viola's loss of the androgyne's freedom.

34. G. K. Hunter, *William Shakespeare: The Late Comedies* (London, Longmans Green, 1962), 45.

35. Philip Edwards, *Shakespeare and the Confines of Art* (London: Methuen, 1968), 65; see also William C. Carroll, "The Ending of *Twelfth Night* and the Tradition of Metamorphosis," in *Shakespearean Comedy*, ed. Maurice Char-ney (New York: New York Literary Forum, 1980), 59–60. For a discussion of similar strategies used in other plays, see Jacqueline Pearson, *Tragedy and Tragicomedy in the Plays of John Webster* (Manchester: Manchester University Press, 1980), 40–49.

36. Lording Barry, *Ram Alley*, ed. Peter Corbin and Douglas Sedge (Notting-ham: Nottingham Drama Texts, 1981), 5, ll. 1–6. All references to the play are to this edition and are cited in the text.

37. For the history of the Children of the King's Revels, see Harold N. Hille-brand, *The Child Actors* (Urbana: University of Illinois Press, 1926), 220–36.

38. The date is established by Johnson, ed., *No Wit, No Help Like a Woman's*, xi–xiii. All references to the play are to this edition and are cited in the text. On the source, see D. J. Gordon, "Middleton's *No Wit, No Help Like a Woman's* and Della Porta's *La Sorella*," *RES* 17 (1941): 413–14; and Rowe, *Thomas Middleton*, 114–30.

39. Richard Brome, *A Couple Well-Matched*, in *Six Caroline Plays*, ed. A. S. Knowland (London: Oxford University Press, 1962), II.i, p. 185. All refer-ences to the play are to this edition.

Chapter 8

1. J. S. Nosworthy, ed., *Cymbeline* (London: Methuen, 1955), xiv–xvii, argues for a date of 1608 or 1609, within a range of 1606–11.

2. John Lyly, *The Maid's Metamorphosis*, in *Complete Works*, ed. R. Warwick Bond, 3 vols. (Oxford: Clarendon Press, 1902), vol. 3, III.i.223. All refer-ences to the play are to this edition.

3. Shapiro, *Children of the Revels*, 180–84.

4. Peter Hyland, "Disguise and Renaissance Tragedy," *UTQ* 55 (1985–86): 165–68.

5. Howard C. Cole, *The "All's Well" Story from Boccaccio to Shakespeare* (Ur-bana: University of Illinois Press, 1981), 42–43.

6. The moment occurs in III.ii of Whetstone's play, which is reprinted in Bullough, *Sources*, 2:460. All quotations from Whetstone's work are from this reprint. Similarly, in adapting *Romeo and Juliet* from Arthur Brooke's poem, reprinted in Bullough, *Sources*, vol. 1, Shakespeare dropped (1) Ju-liet's eagerness to do as others had done and accompany Romeo into exile "in other weede . . . [as] thy hyred man" (ll. 1620–24), (2) Romeo's refusal to "cary thee . . . in mans weede disguised" (ll. 1680–81), and (3) Friar Law-

rence's proposal that Juliet return with Romeo to Mantua "disguisde in mans aray" (l. 2484).

7. See, for example, Carol Thomas Neely, *Broken Nuptials in Shakespeare's Plays* (New Haven: Yale University Press, 1985), 61–62. Howard Felperin, *Shakespearean Romance* (Princeton: Princeton University Press, 1972), 93, argues that the bed-trick in the two problem comedies differs from the "benign deception[s]" of earlier comedies and "reflects—and reflects upon—the moral ambivalence at the very core of these plays." Cf. Arthur Kirsch, *Shakespeare and the Experience of Love* (Cambridge: Cambridge University Press, 1981), 98.

8. Nosworthy, ed., *Cymbeline*, xx–xxv, argues that Shakespeare supplemented the wager story in Boccaccio, *Decameron* II.9 with details from the prose tale of *Fredryke of Jennen*. Herbert G. Wright, "How Did Shakespeare Come to Know the *Decameron*?" *MLR* 50 (1955): 45–48, suggests that Shakespeare may have used a well-known French translation by Antoine le Macon, first published in 1545. For other adaptations see L. Salingar, *Shakespeare and the Traditions of Comedy* (Cambridge: Cambridge University Press, 1974), 45–46; and F. D. Hoeniger, "Two Notes on *Cymbeline*," *SQ* 8 (1957): 132–33. Quotations from the *Decameron* are from the translation by Frances Winwar (New York: Random House, 1955); those from *Frederyke* are from the reprint in Bullough, *Sources*, vol. 8. For fuller discussion of Shakespeare's use of these two narrative tales, see Michael Shapiro, "Crossgender Disguise in *Cymbeline* and Its Sources," *ShY* 2 (1991): 132–48.

9. Arthur Kirsch, *Jacobean Dramatic Perspectives* (Charlottesville: University Press of Virginia, 1972), 73. In *Shakespeare and the Experience of Love*, Kirsch argues similarly that *Measure for Measure* "is deliberately designed to translate our awareness of theatrical artifice into a consciousness of transcendent forces in human life" (105). See also R. A. Foakes, "Tragicomedy and Comic Form," in *Shakespeare to Sheridan*, 81–82; F. D. Hoeniger, "Irony and Romance in *Cymbeline*," *SEL* 2 (1962): 219–28; and Joan Carr, "*Cymbeline* and the Validity of Myth," *SP* 75 (1978): 324.

10. Park, "As We Like It," 107; and Dusinberre, *Shakespeare and the Nature of Women*, 263. As Ruth Nevo, *Shakespeare's Other Language* (New York: Methuen, 1987), 64, writes: "Where Rosalind and Viola act out their maverick fantasies with a blithe insouciance, . . . Imogen is driven by desperate straits into hers. She wears . . . her cap and hose with a difference."

11. In a comment on this passage, Belsey, "Disrupting Sexual Difference," 182, points out that Imogen's ability to substitute masculine "waggish courage" for feminine "fear and niceness" implies the instability of such gender stereotypes and notes that the heroine concludes by casting herself in the role of "soldier" with "a prince's courage." However stirring this bravado may be when it is delivered, the effect quickly dissipates. As pointed out by Neely, *Broken Nuptials*, 179–82, Imogen is far more vulnerable than any of Shakespeare's other comic heroines.

12. Smith, *Poetics of Homosexual Desire*, 117ff.

13. Nevo, *Shakespeare's Other Language*, 84–85.

14. Susan Sontag, *Illness as Metaphor* (New York: Farrar, Straus and Giroux, 1977), 20–48. Sontag argues that consumption "acquired the associations of being romantic by the mid-eighteenth century" (26) and became "a metaphoric equivalent for delicacy, sensitivity, sadness, [and] powerlessness" (61). Consumptive heroines of the nineteenth century are sexually attractive because they are so "quintessentially vulnerable" (63–64), but the weakened state of Imogen and other Renaissance heroines in male disguise seems to me to have been calculated to make them (and consequently the play-boys cast in those roles) less sexually stimulating.

15. H. Granville-Barker, *Prefaces to Shakespeare,* 2 vols. (London: Batsford, 1930), 1:467. See also Barbara Mowat, *The Dramaturgy of Shakespeare's Romances* (Athens: University of Georgia Press, 1976), 35–69, 104–10.

16. Various critics count between twelve and twenty-four distinct revelations. See Nosworthy, ed., *Cymbeline,* 164n.

17. Righter [Barton], *Shakespeare and the Idea of the Play,* 175. See also John Scott Colley, "Disguise and New Guise in *Cymbeline,*" *ShakS* 7 (1974): 250–51.

18. Mares, "Viola and Other Transvestist Heroines," 101.

19. Norman Rabkin, *Shakespeare and the Common Understanding* (New York: Free Press, 1967), 209.

20. Mowat, *Dramaturgy,* 64ff., argues that the experience of the spectators of the romances often runs parallel to that of the characters. See also Roger Warren, "Theatrical Virtuosity and Poetic Complexity in *Cymbeline,*" *ShS* 29 (1976): 41–49.

21. James E. Savage, "The Date of Beaumont and Fletcher's *Cupid's Revenge,*" *ELH* 15 (1948): 286–94. I am not persuaded by David L. Frost, *The School of Shakespeare: The Influence of Shakespeare on English Drama,* 1600–42 (Cambridge: Cambridge University Press, 1968), 227n, that *Philaster* is the earlier of the two plays.

22. Squier, *John Fletcher,* 35 (emphasis added). Squier stresses the homoerotic overtones of the scene.

23. James E. Savage, "Beaumont and Fletcher's *Philaster* and Sidney's *Arcadia,*" *ELH* 14 (1947): 194–206. See also Lee Bliss, *Francis Beaumont* (Boston: Twayne, 1987), 57–61.

24. Freeburg, *Disguise Plots,* 86 n. 39. Ignoring prior experience of Jacobean playgoers with narrative and dramatic heroines in male disguise, several critics argue that the audience would have been surprised at the revelation of Bellario's true gender; see Joan Hartwig, *Shakespeare's Tragicomic Vision* (Baton Rouge: Louisiana State University Press, 1972), 28–29; Lee Bliss, "Three Plays in One: Shakespeare and *Philaster,*" *MaRDiE* 2 (1985): 163; Nicholas F. Radel, "'Then thus I turne my language to you': The Transformation of Theatrical Language in *Philaster,*" *MaRDiE* 3 (1986), 137; and John Greenwood, *Shifting Perspectives and the Stylish Style: Mannerism in Shakespeare and His Jacobean Contemporaries* (Toronto: University of Toronto Press, 1988), 111. Evoking the audience's suspicions about the page's gender creates the kind of ambiguity that Fletcher frequently exploited, as pointed out by Joseph W. Donohue, Jr., *Dramatic Character in the English Romantic*

Age (Princeton: Princeton University Press, 1970), 20–28. The opposite effect occurs at the end of *The Maid's Tragedy* (1610–11), where the audience knows what Amintor does not—that the brother of Aspatia, who provokes him to duel, is none other than Aspatia herself, as he will learn when she is slain.

25. Greenwood, *Shifting Perspectives*, 109.
26. Streett, "Influence of the Boy-Actress Convention," 81.
27. Bliss, "Three Plays in One," 161–62. As pointed out by Berggren, "A Prodigious Thing," 388, the account of Bellario weeping at the fountain realizes "the condition of sorrowful repose" that Viola describes in telling Orsino of her fictive sister who "pin'd in thought" (II.iv.112).
28. Gurr, ed., *Philaster*, lxiii–lxiv.
29. Bliss, *Francis Beaumont*, 153 n. 31.
30. Gurr, ed., *Philaster*, xxvi–xxix. Most scholars now agree that Shakespeare initiated the new mode of romantic tragicomedy with *Pericles* (King's, 1607) a Globe play, and that Beaumont and Fletcher imitated Shakespeare rather than vice versa. See also Frost, *School of Shakespeare*, 209–14, 226–32. Critics who dislike *Cymbeline* often argue, as does Robert Ornstein, *Shakespeare's Comedies: From Roman Farce to Romantic Mystery* (Newark: University of Delaware Press, 1986), that Shakespeare "mimics the new style of Fletcherian tragicomedy" (258 n. 4) and so "makes a joke of his own play" (212).
31. Harold S. Wilson, "*Philaster* and *Cymbeline*," *English Institute Essays* 1951 (New York: Columbia University Press, 1952), 162. See also Gurr, ed., *Philaster*, xlv–l; Hartwig, *Shakespeare's Tragicomic Vision*, 26–32; and Lee Bliss, "Tragicomic Romance for the King's Men, 1609–1611: Shakespeare, Beaumont, and Fletcher," in *Shakespeare to Sheridan*, 148–64. Verna Foster, "Ford's Experiments in Tragicomedy: Shakespearean and Fletcherian Dramaturgies," in *Renaissance Tragicomedy: Explorations in Genre and Politics*, ed. Nancy Klein Maguire (New York: AMS Press, 1987), 97–98, puts the difference succinctly: "Broadly speaking, Shakespearean tragicomedy has to do with the mystery of suffering, with man in his relation to the universe; Fletcherian tragicomedy, despite its extraordinary situations, comments on the vicissitudes of everyday social, especially sexual, relationships."
32. Bliss, "Three Plays in One," 161.
33. George R. Price, *Reading Shakespeare's Plays* (Great Neck NY: Barron's, 1962), 76.
34. Gurr, ed., *Philaster*, li–lviii. See also Philip J. Finkelpearl, "Beaumont, Fletcher, and 'Beaumont and Fletcher': Some Distinctions," *ELR* 1 (1971): 153–56.
35. Kirsch, *Jacobean Dramatic Perspectives*, 47. See also Kirsch's "Jacobean Theatrical Self-Consciousness," *RORD* 23 (1980 [1981]): 11–12. For Ornstein, *Shakespeare's Comedies*, 21, Fletcher's tragicomedies "teeter on the edge of calamity here and descend to farce there." For Foakes, "Tragicomedy and Comic Form," 82, Fletcher's plays generally depend on "artifice and theatricality . . . because a miracle, or the dramatic equivalent, is the normal way in such plays of resolving the apparently insoluble."

36. See, respectively, Radel, "The Transformation of Theatrical Language," 138; Bliss, "Three Plays in One," 166–67; and Gurr, ed., *Philaster,* lix–lxxi.

37. Robert Tailor, *The Hogge hath Lost his Pearl,* ed. D. F. McKenzie, Malone Society Reprints 121 (London: Malone Society, 1967 [1972]), vi. All references are to this edition.

38. Appleton, *Beaumont and Fletcher,* 72, suggests 1621.

39. Dorothy M. Farr, *John Ford and the Caroline Theatre* (London: Macmillan, 1979), 16–21. See also R. F. Hill, ed., *The Lover's Melancholy* (Manchester: Manchester University Press, 1985), 9. All references are to this edition.

40. For a discussion of this and other examples of the "theatrical cure" of madness, I am indebted to Alan Walworth's unpublished paper, "'To Laugh with Open Throate': Mad Lovers, Theatrical Cures, and Transference" (Shakespeare Association of America, 1993). In another unpublished paper, Nicholas F. Radel, "'He Is Like to Something I Remember': John Ford's *The Lover's Melancholy* and the 'Naturalness' of Heterosexuality" (Sixteenth-Century Studies Conference, 1993), argues that the play differs from most other disguised-heroine plays in that it treats the homosexual desire evoked by cross-gender disguise as a dangerous perversion rather than as a source of playful confusion.

Epilogue

1. Thomas Jordan, *A Royal Arbour of Loyal Poesie,* quoted in John Harold Wilson, *All the King's Ladies: Actresses of the Restoration* (Chicago: University of Chicago Press, 1958), 6.

2. Samuel Pepys, *The Diary of Samuel Pepys, 1633–1703,* ed. Robert Latham and William Matthews, 11 vols. (Berkeley and Los Angeles: University of California Press, 1970–83), 1:224. John Downes, *Roscius Anglicanus,* ed. Montague Summers (London: Fortune Press, 1928), 19, mentions some of Kynaston's female roles: Arthiope in *The Unfortunate Lovers,* the princess in *The Mad Lover,* Aglaura in the play of that name, and Ismenia in *The Maid of the Mill.*

3. Southerne, *Sir Antony Love, or, The Rambling Lady* (London, 1721). Katharine Eisaman Maus, "'Playhouse Flesh and Blood': Sexual Ideology and the Restoration Actress," *ELH* 46 (1979): 601, describes spectators' "obsessive . . . concern with the actresses' sexuality." See also Wilson, *All the King's Ladies,* 67–86; and Elizabeth Howe, *The First English Actresses* (Cambridge: Cambridge University Press, 1992), 59–61.

4. As Jean Peterson points out in "Male Disguising, Women's Parts: Reading the Restoration Actress," conference paper (Shakespeare Association of America, 1990), *Twelfth Night* was performed three times in the 1660s, *The Merchant of Venice* was not performed until 1701, *The Two Gentlemen* and *As You Like It* were assigned to the King's Company but never performed, and *Cymbeline* was not assigned to any troupe.

5. Jeanne Addison Roberts, "Shakespearean Comedy and Some Eighteenth-Century Actresses," in *Shakespeare, Man of the Theater,* ed. Kenneth Muir,

Jay L. Halio, and D. J. Palmer (Newark: University of Delaware Press, 1983), 219, 223.

6. Pat Rogers, "The Breeches Part," in *Sexuality in Eighteenth-Century Britain,* ed. Paul-Gabriel Bouce (Manchester: Manchester University Press, 1982), 244–58.

7. Russell Jackson, "'Perfect Types of Womanhood': Rosalind, Beatrice, and Viola in Victorian Criticism and Performance," *ShS* 32 (1979): 25.

8. Granville-Barker, *Shakespeare's Comedy of Twelfth Night, with a Producer's Preface by Granville-Barker,* quoted by Jackson, "Perfect Types," 23. Patty S. Derrick, "Rosalind and the Nineteenth-Century Woman: Four Stage Interpretations," *ThS* 26 (1985): 160, argues that American actresses of the Victorian period also tried to preserve Rosalind's "essential femininity."

9. Kathleen McLuskie, "The Act, the Role, and the Actor: Boy Actresses on the Elizabethan Stage," *New Theatre Quarterly* 3 (1987): 120–30.

10. William Wycherley, *The Country Wife,* ed. Thomas H. Fujimura (Lincoln: University of Nebraska Press, 1966), III.ii.376.

11. Dan Isaac, "Ronald Tavel: Ridiculous Playwright," *TDR* (1968): 109–11; and Anne Hermann, "Travesty and Transgression, Transvestism in Shakespeare, Brecht, and Churchill," *TJ* 41 (1989): 147–54.

Appendix A

1. John Anson, "The Female Transvestite in Early Monasticism: The Origin and Development of a Motif," *Viator* 5 (1974): 13.

2. Anson, "The Female Transvestite," 30. Marie Delcourt, *Hermaphrodite* (London: Studio Books, 1961), 101, reads these legends as deriving from "the gnostic image of an ideal androgyny." Even if the transvestite saint derives ultimately from earlier androgynous images, Anson suggests that her primary function in monastic tales was to represent the chaste exception to the rule of female sexuality, which was seen as the major problem for a male religious community dedicated to celibacy.

3. Giovanni Boccaccio, *Concerning Famous Women,* trans. Guido A. Guarino (New Brunswick: Rutgers University Press, 1963), 231–33. The opening tale of the *Decameron,* where the false confession of a dying rogue establishes his reputation for sanctity, parodies another type of saint's life, the one exalting a penitent sinner.

4. Megan McLaughlin, "The Woman Warrior: Gender, Warfare, and Society in Medieval Europe," *Women's Studies* 17 (1990): 201, 203. For later women warriors, see B. B. Ashcom, "Concerning 'La Mujer en Habito de Hombre' in the *Comedia,*" *Hispanic Review* 28 (1960): 59–62; and Estelle C. Jelinek, "Disguise Autobiographies: Women Masquerading as Men," *Women's Studies International Forum* 10 (1987): 53–62.

5. Gabriele Bernhard Jackson, "Topical Ideology: Witches, Amazons, and Shakespeare's Joan of Arc," *ELR* 18 (1988): 40–65. On Mary Ambree and Long Meg, see Jackson, "Topical Ideology," 57; and Shepherd, *Amazons and Warrior Women,* 70–74.

6. *Tristan de Nanteuil,* ed. K. V. Sinclair (Assen, Netherlands: Van Gorcum, 1971), 19, 31–33.

7. *The Boke of Duke Huon of Burdeux,* trans. Sir John Bourchier, Lord Berners, ed. S. L. Lee (London: Early English Text Society, 1882) nos. 40, 41, 43, 50, p. 729. The translation was published in English by Caxton about 1534.

8. Freeburg, *Disguise Plots,* 41.

9. Boccaccio, *Concerning Famous Women,* 170. Despite her devotion, her husband murders her in a jealous rage. Cf. Christine de Pizan, *The Book of the City of Ladies,* trans. Earl Jeffrey Richards (New York: Persea Books, 1982), 121. An English translation by Brian Anslay was published in 1521.

10. Lillian S. Robinson, *Monstrous Regiment: The Lady Knight in Sixteenth-Century Epic* (New York: Garland, 1985), 166–90, 314–55. Robinson sees the woman warrior of Renaissance works as an allegorical expression of the "new skills" needed for government in a postfeudal age—flexibility, humanity, and the ability to balance public and private lives. Robinson discusses Marfisa (179–88), whom Ariosto took over from Boiardo's *Orlando Innamorato* (see canto 18), and Radigund (314–55), as deliberate contrasts to the virtuous viragos, Bradmante and Britomart. See also Shepherd, *Amazons and Warrior Women,* 5–17. Jackson, "Topical Ideology," 49–52, argues that other writers of the period depict Amazons quite positively and do not distinguish them from other warrior women on moral grounds. Melveena McKendrick, *Woman and Society in the Spanish Drama of the Golden Age* (Cambridge: Cambridge University Press, 1974), 73–76, 292, argues that male disguise is a motif sometimes used in plays about such subtypes of the *mujer varonil,* or masculine woman, as the bandit, the amazon or virago, the scholar or career woman, and the beautiful huntress. She traces the motif of the female page to the Italian romantic epic but concludes that until the first decades of the seventeenth century classical influences are more important: "The references to Bradamante and Marfisa are far outnumbered by those to Penthesilea, Semiramis, and Diana" (308). Similarly, Freeburg, *Disguise Plots,* 52–53, briefly comments on French plays with heroines in male disguise and also stresses the Italian origins of such works.

11. Lodovico Ariosto, *Orlando Furioso,* trans. John Harington, ed. Robert McNulty (Oxford: Clarendon Press, 1972), 25:38 [25:44]. I quote throughout from this edition, supplying Ariosto's canto and stanza numbers in brackets. Harington's translation was published in 1591.

12. Marfisa too discloses her sex when she removes her beaver to reveal "Her golden haire trust up with carelesse art" (26:24 [26:28]).

13. Shepherd, *Amazons and Warrior Women,* 9. The motif of the virago's helmet derives from classical sources, such as Quintus Smyrnaeus's account of Achilles slaying Penthesilea, the queen of the Amazons, in *The Fall of Troy,* trans. Arthur S. Way (Cambridge: Harvard University Press, 1943):

Now from her head he plucked
The helmet splendour-flashing like the beams

Of the great sun, or Zeus' own glory-light.
(I.655ff.)

Propertius, *Elegies*, trans. H. E. Butler (London: William Heinemann, 1929), III.xi.15, also refers to same incident, "when the helm of gold laid bare her [Penthesilea's] brow." Christine de Pizan, *The City of Ladies*, following another tradition in which the Amazonian queen is slain not by Achilles but by his son Pyrrhus, adds the blond hair to the helmet:

although she defended herself boldly, they smashed through all her armor and struck off a large quarter of her helmet. Pyrrhus was there, and seeing her bare head with its blond hair, dealt her such a great blow that he split open her head and brain. (51)

For other Renaissance adaptations, see Jackson, "Topical Ideology," 59–60. In the cartoon strip *Prince Valiant* by John Cullen Murphy, *Champaign News-Gazette*, December 18, 1988, a young man prevents a slaver from kidnapping a boy and then looks amazed as he turns out to be a girl. The legend for the last frame reads: "What is it that causes Karen suddenly to remove her cap and toss her golden locks, and return the lad's gaze in a most alluring way? Is it a flash of premonition? The chronicles record only these words: 'You're not a boy.'"

14. Torquato Tasso, *Jerusalem Delivered*, trans. Edward Fairfax (New York: Capricorn Books, n.d.), 3:21. Fairfax's translation first appeared in print in 1600.
15. Edmund Spenser, *The Faerie Queene*, ed. J. C. Smith (Oxford: Clarendon Press, 1964), IV.i.10. I quote throughout from this edition.
16. Cf. Britomart's earlier revelation of her sex in Malbecco's castle, III.ix.20–21.
17. See *Hic Mulier*, 270–71, as quoted in chapter 1.
18. Philip Sidney, *The Arcadia* (Harmondsworth: Penguin Books, 1977), 528. I quote throughout from this edition. The story of Argalus and Parthenia was retold by Francis Quarles (1629) and dramatized by Henry Glapthorne (1639). It remained a popular tale through the latter half of the eighteenth century. Stories of forlorn women in male disguise are common in ballads; see G. Malcolm Laws, Jr., *American Balladry from British Broadsides* (Philadelphia: American Folklore Society, 1957), 201ff. In another ballad, "History of Two Dutch Lovers" (c. 1567), a fragment of which survives in the library of Jesus College, Oxford, a husband and his wife, who is disguised as a squire, share "one chamber and one bed":

He little thought it was his love,
which he has left behind. . . .
He tooke her for some gentleman,
in disguised array.

19. Jon S. Lawry, *Sidney's Two "Arcadias'* (Ithaca: Cornell University Press, 1972), 193.
20. Lawry, *Sidney's Two "Arcadias,"* 238.
21. Lady Mary Wroth, *The Countesse of Mountgomeries Urania*, Newberry MS, [book 2] fol. 25 A.
22. Lady Mary Wroath [*sic*], *The Countesse of Mountgomeries Urania*, 378–82.
23. Brawner, ed., *The Wars of Cyrus*, 64–66. Bevington, *From "Mankind" to Marlowe*, 66, classifies *Clyomon* as one of the plays performed by the popular troupes of professional adult actors. Casting requirements would have placed considerable strain on such a company, as the play calls for ten actors plus extras and requires that three female characters be onstage at one time. As in the case of *Horestes*, such casting requirements may indicate initial performance by one of the children's troupes; see Michael Shapiro, "John Pikeryng's *Horestes*: Auspices and Theatricality," in *Shakespeare and Dramatic Tradition: Essays in Honor of S. F. Johnson*, ed. William R. Elton and William B. Long (Newark: University of Delaware Press, 1988), 211–26.
24. Littleton, ed., *Clyomon and Clamydes*, 38–49.
25. Thomas Heywood, *The Fair Maid of the West*, part 1, II.iii.14–15.
26. Boccaccio, *Decameron*, 58. For other treatments of the heroine in male disguise in prose narratives, see D. P. Rotunda, *Motif-Index of the Italian Novella in Prose* (Bloomington: Indiana University Press, 1942), K 1837; and Freeburg, *Disguise Plots*, 42–44. Sanders, ed., *James the Fourth*, appends his own translation of Gabriel Chappuys's French translation of the tale from Cinthio's *Hecatommithi*, which Greene adapted. Other tales of heroines in male disguise in the collection are V.4, V.5, X.1, and X.6.
27. Giambattista Basile, *Il Pentamerone, Or, The Tale of Tales*, trans. Richard Burton (New York: Boni and Liveright, 1927), 335. I quote throughout from this edition.
28. Freeburg, *Disguise Plots*, 43–44.
29. Salingar, *Traditions of Comedy*, 194.
30. Salingar, *Traditions of Comedy*, 208–9.
31. Bullough, *Sources*, 2:344. In *Twelfth Night*, Cesario tells Orsino of his love for a woman "Of your complexion . . . / About your years, my lord" (II.iv.26–28). For discussion of *Gl'Ingannati*, see Andrews, *Scripts and Scenarios*, 92–101.
32. Bullough, *Sources*, 2:342. In *Twelfth Night*, Cesario tells Orsino that his father's daughter "lov'd a man / As it might be perhaps, were I a woman, / I should your lordship" (II.iv.107–09).
33. Freeburg, *Disguise Plots*, 51–52 n. 25; Melzi, "From Lelia to Viola," 67–81; and Kaufman, "Niccolo Secchi," 271–80.
34. Pruvost, "*The Two Gentlemen of Verona*," 1–9; Mary Augusta Scott, *Elizabethan Translations from the Italian* (Boston: Houghton Mifflin, 1916), 45, 217–19.

Appendix B

1. The list is adapted from appendix A of Doris Feil's "The Female Page in Renaissance Drama" (Ph.D. diss., Arizona State University, 1971), 104–5, supplemented by R. S. Forsythe, *Shirley's Plays and the Elizabethan Drama* (New York: Columbia University Press, 1914), 95–96; Freeburg, *Disguise Plots,* 61–99; *The Cambridge Companion to English Renaissance Drama,* ed. Braunmuller and Hattaway, chronological table, which is based on the 1989 edn. of Harbage's Annals; and Smith, "Making a Difference," 127–49. Scholarship on the dates of individual plays has already been noted. Freeburg also lists the following Latin plays: *Byrsa Basilica* (1569–70), *Laelia* (1590), *Labyrinthus* (1599), and *Zelotypus* (1600–1603). Alan Nelson has informed me in conversation that many more Latin disguised-heroine plays were produced at Oxford and Cambridge.

Index

Except for anonymous plays and those by Shakespeare, all plays are indexed under authors' names.